CYBERSPACE RESUME KIT

How to Make and Launch a Snazzy Online Resume

Online Research (Library)
Ministry of Education & Training
13th Floor, Mowat Block, Queen's Park
Toronto, Ontario M7A 1L2

Mary B. Nemnich

Fred E. Jandt

Send your comments to the authors via e-mail:
jobnet@aol.com.

jist

Indianapolis, IN

Cyberspace Resume Kit

How to Make and Launch a Snazzy Online Resume

© 1999 by Mary B. Nemnich and Fred E. Jandt

Published by JIST Works, Inc.
720 North Park Avenue
Indianapolis, IN 46202-3490
Phone: 317-264-3720   Fax: 317-264-3709   E-Mail: jistworks@aol.com
World Wide Web Address: http://www.jist.com

Also by Fred E. Jandt and Mary B. Nemnich
- *Using the Internet and the World Wide Web in Your Job Search*

Also by Fred E. Jandt
- *The Customer Is Usually Wrong!*

> *See the back of this book for additional JIST titles and ordering information. Quantity discounts are available.*

Development Editor: Barbara L. Potter
Editor: Susan Pines
Interior Design: Aleata Howard
Interior Layout: Carolyn J. Newland
Cover Design: Honeymoon Image & Design Incorporated
Indexer: Randl W. Ockey

Printed in the United States of America.

02 01 00 99   9 8 7 6 5 4 3 2 1

All rights reserved. No part of this book may be reproduced in any form or by any means, or stored in a database or retrieval system, without prior permission of the publisher except in case of brief quotations embodied in articles or reviews. Making copies of any part of this book for any purpose other than your own personal use is a violation of United States copyright laws.

We have been careful to provide accurate information throughout this book, but it is possible that errors and omissions have been introduced. Please consider this in making any career plans or other important decisions. Trust your own judgment above all else and in all things.

ISBN 1-56370-484-6

Table of Contents

Part I: Electronic Resumes 1

Chapter 1: Resumes on the World Wide Web 3
America's Job Bank 4

Chapter 2: What to Include in Your Electronic Resume 7
Evaluation 7
- *Take Inventory* 7
- *Target Your Employers* 12

Format 13
- *Chronological* 13
- *Functional* 17
- *Combination* 20
- *Curriculum Vitae* 25

Layout 26
- *White Space* 27
- *Bullets* 27

Contact Heading 28
Objective 33
Summary 33
Education 34
- *Vocational Certificate* 35
- *Undergraduate Degree* 36
- *Advanced Degree* 37
- *Significant Course Work* 37
- *Specialized Training* 39

Work History 39

Chapter 3: Preparing Your Scannable Resume 43

Scanners 44
OCR: Optical Character Recognition 44
Scanning Process 50
Skill Extraction 50
Resumix 52
Restrac 55

Chapter 4: Submitting Your Scannable Resume 59

E-Mail Resumes 59
Mailing Your Resume 68
Faxing Your Resume 69
Resume Templates 70
How Many Resumes? 71

Chapter 5: Your Own HTML Resume 75

Why Have an HTML Resume? 75
What to Avoid 76
What to Include 77
Using Forms 79
Writing Your Own HTML Code 88
Tags 88
Links 91
In-Line Media 91
The HTML File 92
Getting Help 92
Your URL Address 93
Adding Your HTML Resume to Resume Banks 93

Chapter 6: Specialty Resumes 113

Federal Government Resumes: The STAIRS Program 113
Military Resumes: Transition Assistance
Online (TAOnline) 129
TAS Software 131
College Graduates and Recent Alumni: BridgePath 142
How BridgePath Works 144

Chapter 7: Posting Your Resume to Usenet Resume Newsgroups 149

Newsgroups are Electronic Bulletin Boards 149
Preparing Your Resume for Newsgroups 151
The Subject Line 151
ASCII (or Plain) Text 152

    Resume Newsgroups 153
    Submitting Your Resume 154
    Special Considerations 155

Chapter 8: Overview of the Resume Banks 179

    Submitting Your Resume 179
    Passive Posting 180
    Interactive Data Banks 180
    Public or Confidential? 181
    Resume Mailing Services 183
    Evaluating Resume Banks 183
        Stability 184
        Major Corporate Sponsor 185
        Geographic Coverage Area 186
        Kinds of Resumes in the Data Bank 186
        Ratio of Resumes to Corporate Subscribers 187
        Ratio of Resumes to Daily Page Hits 188
        Fees 188
        Length of Time Online 189
        Online Help 190
        Special Features 190

Part II: Resume Banks 191

Appendix A: Resumix ResumeBuilder 301

Appendix B: HRSC Online Resume Writer 307

Appendix C: HRSC Civilian Job Kit 315

Index 321

Index of Resume Banks Organized by Career Field 327

Index of Resume Banks Organized by Geographic Area 331

Part I

Electronic Resumes

In this section of the book, we will show you how to craft an electronic resume that will help you in your online job search. You will learn about the following points:

- ✔ What to include to make your resume competitive

- ✔ What kind of resume to use and when to use it

- ✔ How to prepare a scannable resume

- ✔ What goes into an HTML resume

- ✔ How to use special sites that cater to certain specific job seekers

- ✔ How you can use newsgroups to post your resume

- ✔ How to use resume banks to get your resume to the right employer

Chapter 1

Resumes on the World Wide Web

There's no agreement as to what was the first modern computer. Some people think it was the ENIAC, which was built in 1944. It took up more space than an 18-wheeler's tractor trailer, weighed more than 17 Chevrolet Camaros, and consumed 140,000 watts of electricity! Today, most people wear more computing power on their wrists than existed in the entire world before 1961.

The Internet was born a little over 25 years ago out of the problem of interconnecting computer systems at research facilities and universities. By 1979, CompuServe, the first consumer online service, was launched independently of the Internet. In 1990, the first World Wide Web browser was developed, and by 1993, the Mosaic browser was developed.

Early in the 1990s, Fred Jandt, as a university professor, and Mary Nemnich, as a job-search specialist, began to track the development of job search on the Internet. In 1995, we published *Using the Internet in Your Job Search*. In this book, we wrote about the electronic resume and included only a few pages about the new World Wide Web.

By late 1996, the World Wide Web had grown to more than 70 million pages of content. By 1998, it had grown to 320 million pages. The growth of the World Wide Web happened so fast and Internet job search changed so much that by 1997 we published *Using the Internet and the World Wide Web in Your Job Search*.

Now two years later, so much change has again occurred that our third book focuses just on the resume. In the past two years, the places where job seekers can post resumes have mushroomed. Technology that company recruiters can use to search out and store resumes has also developed to such a level of sophistication that no one can any longer say that an electronic resume is simply a paper resume sent through e-mail.

After our first book, we were interviewed on the CNN program *Computer Connections*. The correspondent wanted to know how many resumes were on the Internet. We gave a tentative answer of "tens of thousands." After our second book was published, we were more prepared. After doing some counting, our best estimate at that time was more than one-half million. As this book is going to press, we're now estimating more than three million!

Three million resumes online. Should yours be one of them? A quick look at the changes in the job-search process may help you make that decision. One fundamental change is occurring right now, and computers and the World Wide Web have made that change possible. Job seekers can now post their resumes to job banks: they no longer have to search the classifieds and mail their resumes. Employers, in turn, search those job banks: they no longer deal with files of paper resumes that are discarded after a position is filled. And Human Resource departments also benefit: they now have desktop-recruiting software that searches resume banks for them.

America's Job Bank

Not only is this job-search change occurring in the private sector, but it is also being encouraged by labor departments in federal and state governments. Let's look at what the U.S. Department of Labor is doing, for example.

America's Job Bank (AJB) is a joint effort of the Department of Labor and the Employment Service offices of each state. More than 1,800 Employment Service offices are in operation nationwide. Employment Service offices have long been in the business of linking employers and job seekers. In 1979, the various offices began cooperating with each other to exchange information on job listings. Today, America's Job Bank is the computerized network that links these state offices electronically so that the public can have a more widespread and efficient method of sharing resources.

Originally, America's Job Bank was strictly a repository of job postings. Job seekers could search for job listings geographically. Then they could use certain job-related keywords to apply for a position by following the employer's stated procedures. Unfortunately, no other interactivity was available with this early system.

Beginning in late spring of 1998, however, America's Job Bank added a resume-posting service. When we last checked, we found more than 70,000 resumes and 700,000 jobs posted on America's Job Bank!

Most of the job opportunities listed on America's Job Bank come from the private sector and are for full-time positions. The openings are available nationwide and represent a broad cross section of qualifications, wages, and types of work. Because America's Job Bank is run by the Department of Labor in conjunction with the Employment Service offices, no fee is charged to the job seekers or the employers. All employers who register with America's Job Bank must be verified as legitimate employers.

You can conduct job searches with America's Job Bank simply by going to the following site and selecting various alternatives to conduct your search:

```
http://www.ajb.dni.us
```

For example, if you were looking for work as an accountant in Minnesota, you would enter the keyword *accountant* and select Minnesota from the drop-down list box. You are then presented with a list of accounting-related positions in Minnesota, arranged alphabetically by city.

To post a resume at America's Job Bank, you must first register with the service. This registration consists of a fill-in-the-blank online form where you provide such basic information as your name, address, and phone number. You then assign a user ID and password, which you will use in subsequent searches. Remember to make a note of these two items because you can't get into the resume area without them.

After you have completed your registration, you can begin entering your resume into AJB's Resume Builder form. When you submit it, your resume will be posted to America's Talent Bank, the sister service to America's Job Bank. You can modify your resume anytime. Resumes stay active for 60 days, but you also have the option of extending your active period at will. Only employers who have registered with America's Job Bank and have been issued a password can access your resume.

Besides resume posting, America's Job Bank also enables you to create cover letters to accompany your electronic resume. You can use AJB's online form, or you can incorporate your own cover letter into the form. With America's Job Bank, you can also create custom job searches. This feature enables you to save your specific search patterns so that you can call them up for subsequent searches. The site also contains helpful information for the job seeker.

If this description leaves you a bit overwhelmed, don't worry. America's Job Bank is just one of more than 80 resume banks we describe and rate in this book. Our objective is to help you write an effective electronic resume and post it to the resume bank that will most likely result in the job you want.

Part I: Electronic Resumes ....

One word of *caution:* You probably have a printed version of your resume. Don't assume that this printed resume is what you really need in today's world. In the following chapters, we'll tell you what you need to be successful in your electronic job search.

Three million resumes online. Should yours be one of them? You bet!

Chapter 2

What to Include in Your Electronic Resume

As with conventional resumes, certain elements must be present in your electronic resume, and these elements should be arranged in a certain order for the information to be effective. You will most likely be preparing two types of electronic resumes: scannable resumes and HTML resumes. In this chapter, you will examine the various elements that must be included when preparing either type of electronic resume. Because the rules for preparing the two resumes differ markedly, this chapter focuses on what to include in *any* electronic resume. The rules for preparing scannable resumes are covered in Chapters 3 and 4. HTML resume preparation is discussed in Chapter 5.

Evaluation

Before you begin to write a resume, you must first spend some time contemplating what, exactly, you want in a job and a career. You need to focus your objective, review your wish list of desirable goals, make decisions about where you want to work and the kind of work you want to do, determine your likes and dislikes, and decide about the tasks you would never consider doing. When asked what kind of work they are looking for, many applicants respond with "Anything!" In truth, there are many tasks they wouldn't want to do, so figuring out these choices in advance will avoid wasting their time and the employer's.

Part I: Electronic Resumes

Take Inventory

After you know what you want to do, you need to take a look at how equipped you are to get there. Review your entire work-related knowledge base. What are your skills? How much training have you had in your occupation, formal or informal? How much actual, hands-on experience have you had in doing the job you want? Honesty is key in answering this question. Did you actually perform the work, or did you merely observe others in the organization doing the work? How long have you performed the duties? Remember that six months is six months, not a year. Stretching your background is dishonest and doesn't serve either the employer or you.

Next, look honestly at your job-related strengths and weaknesses. Where do you really shine at work? Often, a correlation exists between the tasks you like to do and your greatest strengths on the job. Think about the times that you felt you really weren't giving your best. Or think about the situations when you felt you didn't quite meet standard. These points represent weaknesses, the areas where you need improvement. You want to concentrate on targeting jobs that have more opportunities to showcase your strengths, not your weaknesses.

Following an evaluation of your strengths and weaknesses, you should examine your accomplishments. Think about accomplishments at work and outside of the job because both places serve to point up your strengths. Ask yourself how and when your contributions made a positive difference to your organization. Quantify your achievements by putting dollar amounts and numbers on your efforts by answering these questions: *How much* money did my suggestion save the company? *How many* people did I manage? *How many* items did I produce? Think in terms of comparisons. For example, did your performance outshine others who did the same kind of work?

Remember, accomplishments make the individual applicant stand out from the others. They tell an employer how well you performed on a job, not just that you did that job.

Sample Resume 2–1 for Ronald A. Enomoto focuses strictly on the accomplishments of the applicant. This candidate wrote a resume targeted to a specific position. He was making a career change after having owned his own business for a long time. In this case, accomplishments are used to illustrate his experience with the target company and his strengths in areas outside his own company.

Sample Resume 2-1

Ronald A. Enomoto

Post Office Box 85 Half Moon Bay, CA 94019   Phone   (000) 000-0000
email ron@enomoto.com   Fax   (000) 000-0000

Objective

To obtain the management position of Interim Director of the U C Santa Cruz Arboretum that will utilize the broad based skills that have developed as a successful small businessman and through very significant involvement in the University and industry non-profit organizations.

Special Qualifications

A management professional with extensive experience in opportunity assessment, planning, and program execution. Proven ability to organize individuals, form consensus, motivate, coordinate participants, supervise staff, and work effectively with volunteers. Skilled in interpersonal relations, experienced in public speaking, public relations, media presentations, and fund development. Knowledgeable in shared leadership practice.

Selected Accomplishments

Served on University of California Board of Regents for 2 years. Chosen as vice-chair of Education Policy Committee, Chaired Student Regent Selection Committee.

Selected to a 3 year Kellogg Foundation Fellowship in leadership development that had state, national, and international study programs culminating in a 30 day international study trip.

As President of UC Davis Alumni Assn., initiated and led a $4.8MM Alumni Center project. Board was responsible for design, budgeting, and private fund raising. Center was completed on time and within budget. Center was largest private fund raising project on campus to date.

Developed and implemented innovative Internet marketing of roses in overnight delivery service nationwide in 1994. Increased profitability of company 30% in two years.

Grew commercial greenhouse roses completely pesticide free for 3 years. Reduced pest control costs 80%, improved quality, mitigated increased regulatory constraints, enhanced the environment, removed employees from pesticide contact.

Engineered and built greenhouse water recycling system saving 90% of former consumption. Local industry savings reduced community rationing in 7-year drought from 40% to 25%.

Developed computer control for greenhouse environment, 1986. Saved 20% of energy consumption, improved quality, increased production. System is now sold worldwide.

Employment History
Owner of Enomoto Roses, Inc., Half Moon Bay, for 32 years

Education
BA, University of California, Davis
Kellogg Foundation Fellowship-Agricultural Leadership Program

Sample Resume 2-1 continued

Ronald A. Enomoto -2-

SELECTED ACHIEVEMENTS

These selected accomplishments are presented to demonstrate ability in opportunity assessment, effective planning, shared leadership, consensus building, project supervision, successful plan execution, and team success.

Served on selection/review committee to select Vice Chancellor of University Relations, U. C. Davis; Director of Alumni Affairs, U. C. Davis.

Chaired U C Regents' Committee to select Student Regent. Brought consensus in selection process between Regents, Faculty and Students.

Spoke at inauguration ceremony of UCD Chancellor Theodore Hullar on behalf of Alumni Association before 4,000 attendees.

Conceived, planned, and supervised installation of Alumni Contact Service in U C Davis Alumni Association. Job referral and resource service is utilized by 2000 alumni a year.

Awarded Jerry Fielder Outstanding Alumni Award from U C Davis. Award is presented to alumna for Alumni and University service.

Serve as trainer at Forty Plus, Oakland, developing individuals in personal assessment, presentation, job search techniques, networking, personal development, and shared leadership.

Attended satellite transmitted "Lessons In Leadership" 2 day seminar sponsored by Fortune Magazine. Participated in presentation of information from seminar to Forty Plus members.

Conceived and guided formation of Kee Kitayama Research Foundation (privately funded) to serve California Cut Flower Industry. As first Chairman, Foundation generated $290,000 for endowment fund in first three years.

Led merger of California Ornamental Research Foundation into Kee Kitayama Research Foundation, consolidating effort and resources into a single effective foundation.

Engineered and built greenhouse water recycling system saving 90% of former consumption. Local industry savings reduced community rationing in 7-year drought from 40% to 25%.

Installed first co-generation unit in Northern California greenhouse, 1985. Saved 25% on heating energy costs. Installed first greenhouse heat curtains in Northern California, 1979, saving 25% in heating energy costs.

Developed computer control for greenhouse environment, 1986. Saved 20% of energy consumption, improved quality, increased production. System is now sold worldwide.

Organized and executed plan to sell roses that resulted in 6000 repeat customers at 3 Farmers' Markets in 3 years. Elected to Board of Directors, Ferry Plaza Farmers' Market, San Francisco.

Chaired Roses Inc. (national trade organization) Trade and Public Relations Committee for 6 years. Developed and executed program that increased per capita consumption of roses 65%.

Sample Resume 2-1 continued

Ronald A. Enomoto -3-

Serving on Ferry Plaza Farmers' Market Board of Directors. Currently planning for permanent market. Represent farmers' interest as well as business and community interests.

Served as Vice President and Board member of Shinoda Scholarship Foundation. Raised and granted $40,000 annually for college scholarships.

Served as Chair of Cabrillo Unified School District Advisory Committee. Advocated and initiated district survey of parents which had never been done previously.

Hosted 85 growers from throughout California and presented seminar and tour on biological/pesticide free control of greenhouse pests. First commercial rose grower in California to eliminate pesticides in greenhouse grown roses.

Led Cabrillo Unified School District Advisory Committee in effort that successfully prompted San Mateo County Board of Supervisors to fence local schools and provide funding for playground equipment.

Owned and operated Enomoto Roses Inc. for 32 years. Responsible for planning, budget, personnel, production, marketing, Internet sales, retail sales.

Have spoken on numerous radio and television interviews representing the cut flower industry; testified before legislative committees and have met with Congressional representatives.

Designed and presented a successful property subdivision within the California Coastal Commission jurisdiction that enhanced agricultural use of the property.

Served as President of the Sequoia Chapter of the Japanese American Citizens League. Members resided in San Mateo County and Santa Clara County.

Served on U C Davis Foundation Board. Involved in friend raising and fund raising to promote the University of California, Davis. Had fiduciary responsibility for fund raising activities.

Target Your Employers

After you know what you want to do and how you are qualified to do the job, you need to decide where you want to work. Begin by choosing the industry in which you want employment. You can be an office manager in a software company or an oil refinery. You can perform customer service in a department store or a utility company. Ask yourself which environment most appeals to you. Think about the kinds of industry where you have been employed in the past. Different industries call for different language and terminology choices on your resume. For example, a person who checks product quality can be known as a quality-control technician in a manufacturing environment, a quality-assurance evaluator in a service organization, or a production checker in a processing plant.

Next, make a list of specific companies—the A list, if you will—where you would most like to work. Before deciding whether a company should make your list, however, make sure to take the following points into consideration:

- ✔ **Geography:** Is the company within commuting distance or desirable enough that you would consider relocation?

- ✔ **Product/Service:** Are you familiar with the company product? Is it a product that you can support? (For example, if the company tests its products on animals and you are opposed to animal testing, you probably wouldn't be happy working there.) Have you experience with the product or service?

- ✔ **Size:** Are you looking for a large corporation, a small or medium business, a local or international company? Do you have more or fewer chances for advancement based on size? Are employment opportunities limited by the size of the company?

- ✔ **Pay Scale:** Obviously, you need to know that the wages at the company are in line with your desires; however, you must also take into consideration such company perks as a car, profit sharing, travel allowances, and so on. Consider, too, the chances for advancement.

- ✔ **Reputation:** Company esteem and character are important. Employees who work for disreputable companies often suffer low self-esteem and work-related stress. We tend to define ourselves by what we do. You want to feel good about the company you choose.

- ✔ **History:** Know about the company background before you decide to work there. How has the company progressed in the past? Has it been recently reorganized? Is it facing a merger? Are you catching it at the crest of its growth or on the downward slope of its decline?

- ✔ **Philosophy:** Does your target company prize individuality or teamwork? Are employees rewarded for suggestions or advised to stick to the status quo? Does the company encourage risk-taking or prefer that everyone play it safe? These questions go to understanding the philosophy of the company—its basic orientation toward its purpose. Decide whether that philosophy is in sync with your own.

- ✔ **Mission:** Why is this company in business? What does it hope to accomplish? Do you share the same sense of purpose?

Targeting specific companies helps you to write your resume by giving you an audience. Imagine a person preparing a speech on space exploration, for example. The preparation for the speech would be quite different for an audience of fourth-grade science students than for an audience of NASA scientists.

After you decide how you are qualified and whom you want to target, you are ready to build your resume. The following section focuses primarily on the content of traditional—or presentation—resumes and the HTML resume. Chapters 3 and 4 will address the scannable resume.

Format

You have three basic resume formats to choose from in laying out your resume: chronological, functional, and a combination of the two. In educational circles, you will also find the curriculum vitae. The following sections will take a look at these formats in detail.

Chronological

The chronological format puts the work history in a sequence that is based on the period of time that each position was held. This resume format enables you to emphasize your past work history. In a chronological resume, you generally arrange your work experience by date, starting with the most recent and working backward. This resume format works best when you have had continuous work experience in the field in which you are applying.

To construct this type of resume, you list the dates of employment in the left column of the resume, separated by several spaces from the body of the resume, or just above each job in the work history as shown in Sample Resume 2–2. Then you detail each job by listing the company, position title, and job description. Jobs are listed in reverse order, beginning with the most recent position and working backward to jobs held previously.

Employers prefer the chronological format because they can easily see where and when you attained the skills you say you possess. With this format, employers can also determine whether certain needed skills may be stale. For example, an employer who needs an employee for a word processing job doesn't need a candidate whose most recent experience in the field was attained five years ago. Word processing programs have changed dramatically over that period of time. An applicant that far removed from the labor market may have no knowledge of Windows 95 or Word 7.0, 6.0, or even 3.0. How could the employer consider that person to be competitive? Of course, if the same candidate showed recent course work in office information systems, this information would compensate somewhat for the lack of recent job experience.

Chronological resumes follow this basic pattern:

- ✔ **Contact Heading:** your name, address, phone number, and e-mail address

- ✔ **Objective:** a brief statement of your career objective

- ✔ **Summary:** a condensed list of your skills and qualifications in bulleted form

- ✔ **Work History:** arranged by date, last date first, in order

- ✔ **Education:** college degrees and/or relevant course work

- ✔ **Optional Information:** memberships, awards, military service, certificates, and activities

- ✔ **Personal Statement:** a short statement of your personal qualities that make you a fit candidate for the job

A possible problem with chronological resumes is that you must be careful not to leave a gap of time between jobs. If such a gap exists, you may want to consider the functional resume format.

Take a look at Sample Resume 2–2 for Andrew Simons. It contains several of the elements of a chronological resume.

Sample Resume 2-2

Andrew Simons
1900 Idea Avenue
Denver, CO 00000
555-555-5555

PROFILE

Results-Oriented Executive with 15 years' experience in Sales, Marketing, Product Management with expertise in many aspects of network based services: Internet/Intranet strategic planning and implementation and interactive voice response technology
Trouble Shooter who can recommend state of the art technology solutions and identify new market opportunities in the field of network communication and e-commerce

- Generate practical solutions applied to complex business communication problems based on a solid reputation for creative, innovative project management
- Effect a positive impact on the corporate bottom line by supporting companies through technical and strategic marketing changes
- Three years' sales and marketing experience in financial services industry addressing automated and interactive business applications: brokerage, investment banking and international banking

PROFESSIONAL EXPERIENCE

19XX-Present
    Computer Systems Company, Northern City, CA
    Senior Marketing Brand Manager for Internet Services:
- Standardize value added bundling of Internet/Intranet service
- Position company with industry analysts and customers through Extranets and Internet solutions
- Liaison with technical competency group to roll out training programs to sales teams

19XX-19XX
    Communications Company, Eastern City, NY
    Product/Marketing Manager:
- Create, develop and manage company's Internet Directory
- Market research and market sensing resulted in identification of 25 high end accounts with potential to host 4830 web sites
- Project Manager leading teams to develop and deliver multiweb bundled solution, responsible for growing 75% of forecast results in multiple sales channels.
- Strong team player, shared technical knowledge and Internet expertise with marketing team integral to research and assessment of competitive web pages, legacy systems and database integration
- Targeted Financial Services Community for Internet Directory links

19XX-19XX
    Another Communication Company in New York

Sample Resume 2-2 continued

Sales Account Executive:
- Managed Sales Territory as Account Executive driving sales of high end accounts in financial services:
brokerage, investment banking and mortgage companies and retail and professional service companies
- Earned branch recognition for 150% quota attainment
- Noted for retention management of client relationships, with highest base retention exceeding quota objectives month after month

EDUCATION

MBA   Western University. Graduate School of Business. Marketing, 19XX
MLS   Eastern University, Library and Information Science
BA   Eastern State College, Major in English and Education

Affiliations:

A National Marketing Association
A City Chamber of Commerce

Functional

The functional format enables you to focus on your skills and abilities without putting them into any time frame. This format is arranged by grouping your experiences and abilities under one or more broad skill categories, or functions. You place these categories in order of importance to your objective rather than by the dates when you attained them. For example, three basic functions to select on a business resume may include Management, Finance, and Accounting. You would use each of these functions as a heading and then detail all the skills, knowledge, and abilities you have for each major area. These broad functional paragraphs are followed by a brief employment history that shows places, titles, and dates. The functional resume is often used by applicants who have been out of the labor market for a while and need a way to showcase certain skills they possess without showing how long ago they developed them.

Functional resumes present two problems. First, an employer cannot gauge how long it has been since you had experience with each skill. Remember that recent experience is an important factor to employers. Second, writing an objective is difficult when you set up a functional resume. If you highlighted three different functions, you may need three objectives—not a good idea for clarity. You may be able to construct an objective that includes all the skill functions; however, such an objective may be extremely long.

The first part of a functional resume is similar to a chronological resume and includes the contact heading followed by a summary. The pattern then changes a bit to accommodate the different purpose of the resume. Look at the following functional resume pattern:

- **Contact Heading**
- **Summary**
- **Related Experience:** the functional part of the resume that includes several broad skill categories followed by a paragraph of function-related terms and accomplishments
- **Work History:** dates, places, titles, and so on
- **Education**
- **Optional Information**
- **Personal Statement**

Remember to target your resume to a specific audience so that you can choose the functions that are most pertinent to that job. Let's look at Sample Resume 2–3 for a functional resume.

Sample Resume 2-3

Stephanie Wood
0000 Some Street
Some City, Texas 00000
Phone: (555) 555-5555

OBJECTIVE

A challenging and creative senior position in the Sales Industry.

KEY QUALIFICATIONS

- Expert sales professional with over 12 years' hands-on experience.
- Demonstrated ability to work effectively with clients.
- Excellent communication skills, both written and verbal.
- Life, Health and Variable Annuity Insurance License.
- Life Underwriting Training Council.
- Computer literate - can quickly learn new software.
- Successful and proven ability to close sales.
- An experienced team player, bringing enthusiasm and energy into group efforts.
- Consistently make significant contributions to corporate goals for business growth and profit.

EDUCATION

Some University
Some City, Some State
Bachelor of Business Administration (19XX)
- Finance

BUSINESS EXPERIENCE

Sales and New Account Development
- Conceived, developed, produced and executed advertising campaigns and promotional activities that resulted in a significant increase in new accounts.
- Conducted financial planning seminars; located perspective clients by making formal presentations to groups and individuals.
- Provided continual follow-up to potential clients to insure future sales.
- Consistently successful in exceeding company quota.
- Ranked within the top 5 of a large national sales team.

Client Relations
- Utilized verbal communication and listening abilities to identify clients needs and/or problems.
- Ultimately responsible for customer satisfaction.

Sample Resume 2-3 continued

- Established contacts in the local Chamber of Commerce.
- Developed loyal client base and increased sales volume through personal attention and consultative selling approach to clients.
- Interacted daily with diverse clients on financial planning.
- Attained strong product knowledge and expanded client base while maintaining excellent client relations.

EMPLOYMENT HISTORY

Some Corporation (19XX - 19XX)
Any Town, TX
Financial Consultant

Another Company (19XX - 19XX)
Medium City, TX
Financial Consultant

A Large Corporation (19XX - 19XX)
Big City, TX
Financial Consultant

PROFESSIONAL AFFILIATIONS

- Well-Known Charitable Organization
- Speaker's Bureau
- Fraternal Organization

Combination

The combination resume combines elements of the chronological and functional resumes. The combination resume generally begins with a functional section, where the applicant details several areas in which he or she has expertise. In one type of combination resume, this section is followed by a brief chronological listing of places and dates where the applicant worked before. Sometimes this chronology contains brief job descriptions as well.

This format is attractive and fairly easy to read, but it has a problem. Although dates are provided, an employer may not be able to connect the skill in the functional section with the date that the applicant worked with that skill in the chronological section.

For example, if the applicant listed Sales Management as a function, but every job listed in the chronological section was in the field of sales, the employer would not be able to tell whether the management skill was attained at the most recent job or at the job held seven years prior to that. Look at Sample Resume 2–4 for Sarah Marx as an example of this type of combination resume.

In another type of combination resume, the applicant lists the functions within the chronology for each job held. Examine Sample Resume 2–5 for Alfred Newman to see how this combination resume looks.

Sample Resume 2-4

Sarah Marx
XXXX Summer Street
Bossier, LA 00000
(555) 555-5555

Objective: Sales/Marketing Position

Highlights of Qualifications

- Over 15 years' professional experience with the public.
- Personable and persuasive in communicating creatively with thousands of customers from all cultures and economic levels.
- Proven skill in persevering to solve customers problems.
- Self-motivated and confident in making independent decisions.
- Very well organized and able to meet deadlines.

Relevant Experience

Sales & Marketing

- Made direct presentations to retail store owners and buyers, marketing Christmas ornaments and gift items imported from the Philippines.
- Co-hosted sales seminars for potential real estate partnership investors.
- Oriented customers by answering questions regarding project details.
- Followed up by phone to verify their commitment to invest in the partnership.
- Canvassed by cold calling for contributions to a nonprofit organization.
- Consistently surpassed sales quotas in retail clothing and housewares departments.
- Persuaded 2500 citizens to sign a petition in support of placing a community improvement initiative on the ballot.

Organization & Customer Service

- Resolved wide range of customer problems, applying diplomacy and assertiveness to delivery delays, fee and budget problems, property management decisions, airline emergencies and in-flight problems, and culture/communication barriers.
- Organized the logistics of speaking engagements and investment seminars: location - catering - seating - literature - speakers - travel.
- Maintained extensive financial records regarding individual and corporate clients.
- Successfully collected thousands of dollars in overdue or unbilled fees by thoroughly auditing billing records and persevering in telephone collection follow-ups.

Sample Resume 2–4 continued

Employment History

19XX – Present
Office Manager/Bookkeeper Accounting Firm, Orlando, FL
Managed financial records; general ledger; handled collections; billing and receivables

19XX – XX
Office Manager/Bookkeeper Investment Company, Orlando, FL
Receivables, payables, payroll; made travel arrangements; budget planning

19XX - XX
Self-Employed, Nonprofit Organization Author/Lecturer
Made presentations, organized seminars; canvassed contributors by phone; marketed services area-wide to customers

Education
BA, Communication Studies – Excellent University, Miami, Florida

Sample Resume 2-5

Alfred Newman
1111 Loon Lake Rd.
Chicago, IL 00000
(555) 555-5555

Career Objective: An entry-level position in the human service field

EDUCATION

BA Sociology, Any University, Chicago, IL, 19XX

EXPERIENCES

19XX – 19XX: Adolescent Psychiatric Clinic, Springfield, IL

Staff Assistant

Teaching

- Taught academic and social skills
- Evaluated students growth potential and abilities
- Coordinated services with local school system
- Planned daily objectives and assignments

Counseling

- Counseled students, made recommendations/referrals to alternative services
- Reviewed case histories
- Monitored weekly support and supervision

Group Facilitating

- Led adolescent support groups and organized activities
- Coordinated weekly staff meetings
- Reviewed students physical, mental and emotional daily performance

19XX-19XX: Community Center, Springfield, IL

Assistant Manager

Management

- Supervised and trained new workers

Sample Resume 2-5 continued

- Handled staff relations
- Computerized and organized records

Community Relations

- Planned and organized center activities
- Facilitated meetings
- Led outreach efforts

Personal

A dedicated, sincere professional with excellent community relations abilities and a management perspective that has provided a healthy respect for the company bottom line.

Most employers prefer the straight chronological format because it is easy to read and easier still to match skills with the time period in which they were attained. Basically, the two resume formats that work best for electronic resumes are chronological and functional.

Curriculum Vitae

One other type of resume you should be aware of is the curriculum vitae. A curriculum vitae, also known as a CV or a vita, is the preferred format for those in education or science. In other countries around the world, resumes are commonly referred to as CVs, although these are not different in significant ways from standard resumes. In the United States, however, the CV is most often used for academic positions.

CVs typically are very lengthy because they chronicle not only the work history and educational background of the candidate but also all research projects, publications, academic awards, presentations and teaching history. If the candidate has served internships and residencies, these are included. Any post-doctoral studies are represented. Affiliation in professional societies are listed as well as memberships on boards.

At the Harvard School of Public Health Web site, you will find instructions for preparing a CV. You can access its Web site at the following address:

```
http://www.hsph.harvard.edu
```

Then you type **curriculum vitae** at its search engine.

It is not unusual for a CV to run to six, eight, or even more pages when printed. We have included a format for a CV so that you can see how it is laid out and what you need to include. A curriculum vitae follows this basic pattern:

- ✔ **Your Name and Title**

- ✔ **Office Address:** Include your department, office phone number, and e-mail address.

- ✔ **Education:** Follow the same pattern for listing your education as in a chronological resume.

- ✔ **Honors and/or Awards:** List by year, then award, in chronological order. Spell out the award—do not use acronyms.

- ✔ **Publications:** These should be listed under the following separate categories:

Papers	Works in Progress
Books	Journal Articles
Text Books	Book Chapters
Theses	Monographs

✔ **Conference Presentations:** List by date, in chronological order. List the title of the seminar or conference and give a one-sentence summation of what was presented.

✔ **Work Experience**

✔ **Teaching Experience**

✔ **Internships and Residencies** (if applicable)

✔ **Post-Doctoral Training** (if applicable)

✔ **Professional Affiliations**

✔ **References:** Unlike other resume formats, CVs contain the reference contact information on the resume itself.

Layout

One of the key differences between electronic and paper resumes is how they are arranged on the page. The unwritten rule of resume writing states that a paper resume should never be more than one or two pages long. Employers find it tiresome and inconvenient to shuffle through several pages of paper to get a profile of a candidate. However, on a computer screen, you are no longer held to the one-page rule. It is generally understood that a computer screen holds less information than a printed page. Thus, you have more freedom in editing your data. Employers simply scroll down your HTML or scannable resume until they are finished reading your information.

A word of caution, however: because you have a bit more latitude in using space, do not ramble on until the reader is forced to press the Stop button out of sheer annoyance. Be as concise as you can, while still including the most crucial information about your background and experience.

White Space

One way in which electronic and paper resumes are similar is the white-space rule. This rule refers to how the resume appears on the page, what we call the "lie" of your resume. Generally, the more white space, the more readable the resume. Of course, with electronic resumes, the white space becomes blue screen (or green or black or yellow or…), but the idea is the same. Employers appreciate a resume that is easy to read. The more uncluttered space they see, the easier the information is to process. The key is to choose only information that is germane to the position you seek and to use the most powerful and effective language to describe it. Also, use plenty of good spacing between headings and the body of the resume.

Bullets

One important factor that makes a resume readable is the use of bullets for arranging information. A bullet is a short sentence fragment rather than a full sentence. If you put all your information, including job descriptions, in paragraph form, employers have a difficult time finding the information that they need. Bullets make the job easy because employers can easily scan through the most important items to find the information they seek. Consider the following example in paragraph form of an accountant's resume:

> Responsible for all payroll and tax records. Did purchase orders and posted to general ledger. Did all accounts payable, accounts receivable, and trial balance. Kept inventory and prepared purchase orders. Prepared daily deposits and reconciled bank statements. Used Great Plains and Peachtree accounting software and Microsoft Excel spreadsheet software.

Contrast the preceding paragraph example with the same information presented in a bulleted list:

- Tax preparation
- Payroll for over 50 employees
- Inventory control and preparation of purchase orders
- Accounts payable and receivable
- General ledger and trial balance
- Daily bank deposits and statement reconciliation
- Proficient with Great Plains, Peachtree, and Microsoft Excel

The information presented is the same, but the bulleted list presents the information in a format that is easier to read, with lots of screen space. Furthermore, the information has been rearranged to give priority to the more highly prized skills. This job description is also more scanner friendly (see Chapter 3 for more information about scannable resumes).

Contact Heading

All resumes should begin by telling the employer who you are and where you can be found. Accordingly, start building your electronic resume by putting your name, address, phone number, and e-mail address at the top of the page. Include your URL and office phone number as well. Employers don't want to work very hard to find you, so give them as many options as possible to make the job easy.

> *Tip:* On an HTML resume, make your e-mail address a link so that a prospective employer can simply click on it to get to your pre-addressed e-mail screen.

With an HTML resume, you have several style options as to how you arrange your heading. The classic style places the name, address, and phone number centered, letter-style, at the top of the page, as follows:

Name
Address
City, State, Zip Code
Phone Number, E-mail Address

Another variation is the left-justified heading. This heading is the preferred choice when preparing a scannable resume. In this style, all the lines of the heading are aligned on the left side of the page, as follows:

Name
Address
City, State, Zip Code
Phone Number, E-mail Address

Another variation splits the address and phone information and puts them on opposite sides of the page, below the name, which is centered at the top:

Name

Address	Phone Number
City, State, Zip Code	E-mail Address

Yet another variation puts the name on one side and the balance of the information on the opposite side:

Name   Address
                                                                           City, State, Zip Code
                                                                           Phone Number
                                                                           E-mail Address

As you can see, you have many choices in arranging the contact information when you prepare an HTML resume.

Some resumes have a demarcation line that separates the header from the body of the resume. With an HTML resume, you have several style choices for your underline. You can also put a graphic as a break between your header and the body of the resume or as a decorative top border.

We saw a clever HTML resume for a pilot. The pilot had an animated airplane propeller spinning at the top of the page. Sample Resume 2–6 shows the first page of Kristofer M. Pierson's resume. On the next page, you can see what the graphic looks like—without the motion. The underscored elements are hyperlinks for the Web.

Part I: Electronic Resumes ....

Sample Resume 2-6

KRISTOFER M. PIERSON

XXXX Swell Avenue

Bloomington, MN 55437
email: xxx@xxx.com

CAREER OBJECTIVE	To gain employment in a flight operations position with a company possessing a dynamic concern for the aviation industry.
EDUCATION	• **Rocky Mountain College,** Billings, MT BS in Airway Science, Aircraft Systems Management, 1997 Minor in Music • **Thomas Jefferson Senior High School,** Bloomington, MN Graduated, June 1993
PILOT QUALIFICATIONS	• Commercial Pilot/Certified Flight Instructor - Instrument and Multi-Engine • Multi-Engine Land, Single-Engine Land, and Instrument Ratings • 600+ hrs. Total Time, 45 hrs. Multi, 220+ hrs. Dual Given • First Class FAA Medical
WORK EXPERIENCE	**June 1998-present** **Flight Operations Manager** **Academy Flight Operations, Inc.** **Crystal, MN** In this position, I administrate the flight training operations center for the Academy of Aviation, where I also flight instruct and serve as academic faculty (listed separately below). Duties include management of our aircraft fleet. **September 1997-present** **Academic Faculty and Flight Instructor** **Academy of Aviation** **Academy Education Center, Inc.** My position includes full-time flight instruction, as well as ground school for pilot certification and rating courses, and upper-level academic aviation courses at this private, two-year institution. I am also actively involved in curriculum management and development.

Sample Resume 2-6 continued

August 1997-December 1997

Lead Dispatcher
Thunderbird Aviation Inc.
Eden Prairie, MN
Duties entailed the smooth operation and coordination of all flights, schedules, office management, and customer services at this full-service FBO.

January 1996-June 1997

Student Assistant, Office of the Registrar: Rocky Mountain College
Billings, Montana
Duties included organizing and handling special research projects and reports as assigned by the College Registrar. Performed general office duties and information management, focusing on student academic data.

May 1996-August 1996 and
May 1995 to August 1995

Professional Line Service Technician
Elliot Aviation, Inc. Flying Cloud Airport
Eden Prairie, MN
Performed essential flight line and customer service duties at an executive-class FBO. Aircraft parking, fueling, servicing, cleaning, towing, fuel farm management, and aircraft storing comprised main duties. Also assisted customers with shuttle service to local hotels, other airports, and meeting sites.

May 1994-August 1994

Ground Ops Personnel, UPS/Corporate Air
Billings Logan International Airport
Billings, MT
Worked on the UPS Billings Gateway Operation. Handled air cargo and ground service equipment in close proximity to several aircraft.

May 1994-May 1995

Resident Assistant
Rocky Mountain College
Responsible as a role model, counselor, teacher, and administrator for 150 students in my residence hall. Assisted in coordinating the implementation and use of automated campus security systems.

INTERNSHIPS/
FIELD PRACTICUM

1994 Internship: Big Sky International Air Show
I served on the flight operations committee of this large air show, helping to coordinate show acts, flights, and operating as a roving liaison between officials and participants.

Sample Resume 2-6 continued

1995 Field Practicum: NIFA Region I SAFECON Flight Competition Director
In this practicum, I acted as the Director of this annual intercollegiate flight competition. A large part of my role was to coordinate flight operations with airport administrators and other operators.

AVIATION RELATED ACTIVITIES AND ORGANIZATIONS

Academy of Aviation Precision Flying Team
National Intercollegiate Flying Association (1998-present)
Coach and Advisor

Rocky Mountain College Precision Flying Team,
National Intercollegiate Flying Association (1994-present)
Assistant Coach, 1997
NIFA Council Student Representative, 1996-97
Team Captain, 1996
National Competition Participant, 1995, 1996

Rocky Mountain College Aviation Club (1993-1997)
Vice President, 1996

Alpha Eta Rho Aviation Fraternity, Rho Alpha Chapter (1996-present)
Charter Member and Vice President, 1996 to 1997

Active member of AOPA, NIFA, and NAFI.

SPECIAL AWARDS

- **Presidents Cup** Rocky Mountain College 1997
- **Outstanding Aviation Senior** Rocky Mountain College 1997
- **Eagle Scout Award** Boy Scouts of America 1993

References, curriculum vitae, and a complete listing of collegiate activities and awards are available on request.

Objective

Most classic resumes contain an objective. The objective—also known as a career goal, career focus, or target occupation—lets the employers know why you are contacting them. The objective also provides you with a blueprint to follow in constructing your resume. After you state an objective, everything following it should support it. Thus, if you are writing a resume with the stated objective of being an outside sales representative, including your experience as a janitor will not serve that particular resume. All the information that follows your objective in the resume should confirm the stated objective and reinforce your fitness for the job in question.

Objectives are a statement, not just a word or phrase. Many objectives contain a miniplan for moving forward with the company. For example, some objectives make mention of a desire for growth opportunity within the company, as in the following example:

> A position in food service, with career path leading to food service management

Some objectives discuss plans for continuing education, as in this example:

> Staff teaching position, where I can continue my doctoral studies in English literature.

Some objectives are merely a straightforward declaration of the job sought, as in the following examples:

> A position as a CAD drafter
>
> Sales/Marketing Director in the Retail Trade Industry

Others objectives are very specific, as follows:

> Staff Accountant/Audit Division, Public Accounting Firm

In any case, your objective should be broad enough that you merit consideration for related jobs, but specific enough to show the employer that you have a focused goal. An objective that is too specific is limiting. Lastly, your objective should be only one sentence long.

Summary

A summary is the hook that entices an employer to read the rest of your resume. The summary—also known as qualifications, profile, or overview—is a brief snapshot of your qualifications. The best summaries contain the most attractive highlights of your career and skills, in order of importance. You should also include some accomplishments—such as the percentage that sales increased after you became sales manager—in your summary.

> **Note:** The summary discussed in this section should not be confused with keyword summaries. Keyword summaries are used in scannable resumes and are discussed in Chapter 4.

In the interest of brevity and readability, summaries are best written in bulleted form. In the following summary for an advertising executive, bullets are used to briefly spotlight key skills. This summary begins by stating the number of years' experience attained in the desired position and goes on to provide information about what makes the applicant a professional in the targeted field:

- More than ten years in advertising
- Award-winning television and print campaigns
- Creative market and needs analysis
- Focus groups and customer surveys
- Sales force training

Remember that the summary paragraph is a brief commercial. It should highlight your best qualifications and present them in a way that raises the employer's interest. In the summary for the advertising executive, for example, the *award-winning* qualifier on the resume invites an employer to read on and to discover which award was won and for what purpose. The idea is to get the employer to click on that all-important down arrow and to read on.

As with other areas on your resume, you should use bullets to present the information in your summary for ease of reading. Let's look at another summary that successfully uses bullets:

- Over 15 years in professional sales management
- Designed and implemented competitive marketing strategies
- Boosted sales 102 percent
- Recruited and trained productive sales team
- Generated $1.5 million in new accounts

Again, the use of impressive figures is an incentive to an employer to read on. Putting the proof of the applicant up front assures a closer look.

Education

Following the summary, you will lead with either your education or experience, depending both on the position desired and your individual qualifications. For example, for a teaching position, where your educational background is of paramount importance, you should obviously start your resume with your education. Likewise, for positions that require an advanced degree in the field of science, you should put your educational background first. If the job in question requires certain vocational certificates, list them first. For recent college graduates, the advice is the same: put your newly acquired degree and relevant course work at the top of your resume.

However, if the most valuable asset you offer the employer is your work history, by all means, lead with that. And, of course, if you do not have a college degree, you should begin with your work experience. First, let's take a look at how to list your education.

Vocational Certificate

When listing vocational education, you should mention a few specifics contained within the certificate program. Often, the certificate itself is offered as proof of skills. If you have this kind of certificate, you should provide details of the relevant course work as much as possible. If you distinguished yourself academically, say so. List the name of the school and the city and state where it is located. Then give the name of the certificate program. If you received the certificate recently, add the year that you completed it. The idea in listing a date is to show the employer that your skills are fresh. Fresh skills are important in vocational education, where training is tied to current labor-market needs. The following examples provide you with different ways of setting up your vocational education information:

ITT Technical Institute, Los Angeles, CA
Medical Office Assistant Certificate, 1996

- 3.8 GPA
- Front and back office
- Medical terminology

Summit Career College, Colton, CA
Business Office Operations, 1997
Class Valedictorian

- Excel
- Basic Accounting and Bookkeeping
- Bookkeeping
- Keyboarding and Computer Operations

- Word Processing
- Electronic Spreadsheet
- Office Machines
- Business Communications

Undergraduate Degree

Regardless of occupation, employers value a college education, whether you completed your degree program or not. It is important, then, to list your education on your resume. Put your information in order, beginning with the name and location of the college or university. When you have attended a state school, and the name of the state is part of the name of the school, as in the University of Mississippi, you should list the city and state where the school is located:

University of Mississippi, Oxford, MS

It is also acceptable with state universities to list the city only, as in the following examples:

University of California, Los Angeles

State University of New York at Buffalo

Where the name of the college may not be readily recognizable, such as in Central University, or where the name does not contain the location, such as in Purdue University, you should definitely list both the city and state:

Central University, Central, AL

Purdue University, West Lafayette, IN

Following the name of the college, you should list the degree you attained. The preferable way to list the degree is to spell out the degree, such as Bachelor of Arts. Do not write *Bachelor's of Arts* or *Bachelor's degree.*

If you choose to use the acronym, you do not use periods, as you can see in the following examples:

BS Degree, Accounting

AA, Liberal Arts

The exception to this rule is Ph.D, where you do place a period after the *h.*

Next comes the field of study. Spell these words out, such as Liberal Arts, not L.A.; Physical Education, not P.E. or Phys. Ed.; Political Science, not Pol Sci. If you had a particular area of emphasis within your major, list the area. If you took a minor, be sure to indicate the field of study, with the *minor* designation, as in the following example:

Bachelor of Science, Economics
minor: International Business

The following examples show how you can list your undergraduate degree:

University of Minnesota, Duluth
Bachelor of Arts, Communication
emphasis: Public Relations
Highest Honors

Bronx Community College, New York, NY
Associate of Arts, Accounting, 1997

Advanced Degree

Advanced degrees appear first in the Education section of your resume. Then you list your other degrees, if applicable, in descending order: MA, BA, AA.

In general, the graduate degree is listed without further detail, except for honors designations, as in the following example:

Framingham State College, Framingham, MA
Master of Arts, Counseling
cum laude

> **Note:** The designation *cum laude* refers to the degree of educational excellence attained by the candidate. *Magna cum laude* refers to high honors; *summa cum laude* refers to highest honors (4.0, usually). These honors are written in lowercase. Applicants typically use only the *cum laude* designation, widely understood to mean that honors were bestowed.

Remember that you do not have to include a year of graduation on your resume because the year is a way of labeling the candidate's age. Realize, of course, that the year of graduation is no longer an accurate way of gauging the age of an applicant because people attend college at many different ages. However, if your degree is recent and constitutes the basis of your qualifications and the reason you are seeking work in your field, it is acceptable, and even wise, to put the year of your diploma on the resume.

Significant Course Work

In the Education area of your resume, you may want to list courses that detail the educational background that you have. This approach is usually used by a recent college graduate who is attempting to demonstrate pertinent knowledge of the desired field, although seasoned career professionals also use the approach. Consider the following Education entry on a resume for a photographer:

Brooks Institute of Photography, Santa Barbara, CA
Bachelor of Fine Arts, Photography, 1997
Relevant course work:

- Layout and Design
- Lighting Techniques
- Graphic Design
- Digital Images
- Portraiture
- Darkroom Techniques
- Large Format
- Adobe PhotoShop

Look at the following example for a business administration graduate:

University of California, Riverside
BS Degree, Business Administration
Departmental Honors
Significant course work:

- Business Law
- European Economics
- Human Resource Administration
- Organizational Development

To list college experiences that did not result in a degree, you can simply put the name and location of the school and the major course of study with no further explanation, as in the next two examples:

University of North Carolina, Charlotte
Sociology and Urban Studies

Pasadena City College, Pasadena, CA
Classes in Drug and Alcohol Counseling

Or you can detail any relevant course work that you completed, although you did not finish your degree program, as in the following example:

Hanover College, Hanover, IN
BA Degree Program, Business Administration
Courses in:

- Business Law
- Economics
- Accounting
- Finance

You can also project the graduation date if the work is currently in progress with completion likely in the near future, as follows:

State University of New York, Buffalo
Bachelor of Science, Biology
Projected Graduation: June 1999

If you have college course work to list on your resume, you do not have to list high school classes. In fact, if you have any work-related classes, whether college-level or not, it is preferable to list them, rather than your high school history. For students, of course, listing the high school data is obligatory. But in general, adults do not list their high school background in the education block unless the employer has specified a high school diploma as a prerequisite for the job.

Specialized Training

If you have had certain, work-related courses outside of college, vocational school, or high school, you should list them on your resume. These courses can include in-house training programs set up by former employers or extension courses that you took on your own to bolster your expertise on the job. You can list these courses under a subheading, such as Continuing Education Studies, within the Education block; or you can give them a separate heading altogether, such as Specialized Training.

Work History

The work history is really the heart of the resume. What you choose to include here will determine whether the employer decides to contact you. Remember that the work history you include must be relevant to the objective of the resume. Therefore, remove all data that does not support your stated objective, or realign job duties from other jobs so that they reflect relevant experience. Keep in mind that you should include accomplishments here, too. These accomplishments make the resume interesting to read and keep you from simply reciting job duties. The accomplishments also demonstrate your performance in relation to other candidates.

You can use several different headings to name this section, depending on what kind of information you want to impart to the employer. For example, Work History or Experience are descriptive but not too creative. Relevant Experience and Significant Experience, on the other hand, let the reader know that you will be concentrating only on that work history that is significant to the stated job objective. Career Highlights, Career History, and Professional Background are other options.

Bear in mind that a resume should not go back more than ten years. Job skills more than ten years old are considered stale by most employers. For high-tech fields, that number is shortened considerably. If, however, you have had sustained employment at the same company for more than ten years, your resume will necessarily break the ten-year rule. Concentrate on showing the skills and experiences you have had most recently with that company.

To write your work history in a chronological format, begin by putting the dates you were employed at the company (beginning with your most recent job) in the left margin of the resume. Use the month and year, writing out the month and using all four digits of the year: August 1991–August 1997. These dates must fit in a rather small column, so you will need to stack them such as in the following example:

August 1991–
August 1997

Then, after leaving a fair amount of spacing between the dates and the body of the resume, type the name of the company and the city and state where it was located, all on the same line. Following this information, type your position title.

You may want to put your position title first, followed by the company name and location. After you pick a style, however, make sure that you keep the order consistent throughout the resume. Look at the following examples to see how this information is set up.

SIGNIFICANT EXPERIENCE

June 1992–   Atlas Home Sales, Boulder, CO
June 1997   **General Sales Manager**

or

RELEVANT EXPERIENCE

June 1992–   **General Sales Manager**
June 1997   Atlas Home Sales, Boulder, CO

If you are writing an HTML resume, you may want to make your job title bold or put it in a different font. Some applicants type the company name all in caps, with the job title in bold. Or they put the company name in italics. All of these options are fine as long as you don't go crazy with different fonts, which junk up a resume. And as you will see in Chapter 3, you don't use special fonts at all on a scannable resume.

After you have indicated where and when you worked and what you did for the company, it is time to list your most significant job duties and achievements.

To write a job description for a resume, start by making notes for each job you held. Make a list of all the duties you handled during the course of a day. Think about the job you are applying for and decide which of your former duties best fit the new job. List these duties in order of importance.

Next, list any special achievements for which you were responsible. Consider their worth in painting you as a desirable candidate. Only include those achievements that have some relevance to the job and your fitness for it.

Then write a short summary of how your job fit the organization and helped meet its goals. This step is important in helping you to see yourself as part of the big picture in any company. When you understand your place, you can then communicate it to an employer.

Finally, take all the information that a prospective employer should know and that supports the objective at the top of your resume, and boil down this information into a few short sentences that you put in bullet form. When you add each job description to your resume, be sure that the duties are in order of importance.

Now, let's build a job description based on the following information about Jessica:

> "Jessica" is the Human Resource Manager for a medium-sized hotel, which is part of a large, international chain. She handles recruitment for all positions, from the room cleaners to the junior manager. She conducts new-hire orientation and supervises the training programs. She plans the advertising budget for recruitment and hotel events. She administers the employee benefits packages and keeps personnel records for over 100 employees. She directly supervises 8 managers and indirectly oversees 15 department supervisors. Whenever necessary, Jessica flies to other hotels and conducts training for new HR managers. She serves on the task force that plans the redesign of new facilities and the remodeling of existing ones. She was cited as HR Manager of the Year, Western Division, for her innovative ideas in conflict resolution.
>
> Jessica is applying for a position as regional HR manager for a large hotel chain. Her main responsibilities will be overseeing the HR operations of several hotels in her division. She will train management staff and hire new HR managers at various sites. She will conduct quality assurance checks to make sure that all branches are conducting HR operations according to hotel policy. Jessica's bulleted job description should look like the following example:
>
> - Trained and supervised new Human Resource managers at multiple sites
> - Planned recruitment for several hotels within Western Division
> - Designed training plan for desk managers, utilized throughout chain
> - Supervised 8 managers and 15 division supervisors
> - Hired staff at all levels
> - Developed advertising and marketing strategies for events and recruitment

- Designed and conducted Conflict Resolution training program, adopted throughout the chain
- Named Human Resource Manager of the Year, Western Division, for Conflict Resolution program

Notice that the job description starts with the most important duty of the new position: overseeing the HR staff at other hotels. She makes reference at different times to her experience with other sites. She also mentions the innovations she made that were adopted throughout the chain, a response to the part of the job that requires assurance of uniform operations. Hiring and training are prominently featured. Jessica has also highlighted her achievements—such as employee of the year and developer of innovative programs that were adopted company wide—not merely reciting her job duties.

> ***Caution:*** Resumes in these examples include bullets, formatted text, underlining, and graphics. These little enhancers will render your resume unreadable to some resume scanners. To facilitate scanning, a resume must be prepared by using 10- or 12-point Times New Roman, Courier, or Helvetica typefaces. You should avoid using any special fonts or formatting, such as bold text, underlines, italics, and bullets. Graphics are incomprehensible to a scanner. Think of the scannable resume as basic "vanilla." In the next chapter, you will explore the scannable resume and learn how to construct one.

Chapter 3

Preparing Your Scannable Resume

Whether you are searching for work by going online or by perusing newspaper ads, you will increasingly find employers who ask that you send them a *scannable* resume. You will still need a presentation resume for those companies that don't request a scannable resume, but you have to be aware of the problems that lie in wait for the paper resume. Many of the enhancements that make your paper resume attractive—such as special fonts, graphics, and even fancy paper—will not work with resume scanners. You will need to make some changes in your resume to make it scannable. In this chapter, you'll learn how resume scanners work and how you can write a resume that will make it past the scan and all the way to a job.

The process of electronic recruiting through the use of scanners and other software is known as automated staffing. The services that provide automated staffing assistance to businesses are generally referred to as applicant tracking or resume tracking services.

Some automated companies refer to the service they provide in other ways. Resumix™, for example calls the service "human asset management." Restrac refers to the service as "a client/server staffing system." Resumix and Restrac are the leaders in automated staffing. We'll look at both services in this chapter.

When you write a scannable resume, you are actually writing initially for a computer rather than a person. Resume tracking is made up of two parts: the scanner and the OCR (optical character recognition) software. An explanation of how these parts work will help you to understand what is needed to create a scanner-friendly resume.

Scanners

In the simplest terms, a scanner is the device that takes a "picture" of your resume so that it can be put into a computer. A scanner captures an image of your resume by using a moving beam of light. The scanner then digitizes the image so that it can be stored on a computer. Essentially, the scanner puts what you have written on paper into a form that is usable by a computer.

If you enlarge a photograph, page of text, or other image many times, you discover that it is made of thousands of tiny dots. These dots are known as pixels. Pixels are actually individual elements of varying shades that, taken altogether, make up a picture. As your resume passes through the scanner, light is bounced from the paper original to photosensitive cells within the scanner. These cells read the image by examining and analyzing each pixel. The cells then translate the light waves into impulses. These impulses are sent to the computer, where software takes the data and converts it into computer-friendly language. So what you end up with is an electronic representation of your resume.

OCR: Optical Character Recognition

After the image is scanned, the next step is for the image to be read by OCR software. OCR takes the data you have written—the printed text in the form of words—and converts it into usable computer language known as ASCII (American Standard Code for Information Interchange). Optical character recognition accomplishes this task by taking patterns of dots—again, the pixels—created by your scanner and converting them to characters that can be read by computers. After your resume is in ASCII format, the resume is in editable text that can be manipulated and revised in a word processor. In resume tracking systems, OCR software is usually included with the scanner.

Caere Corporation, with a well-established pedigree, is a market leader in OCR. Dr. Robert Noyce, the founder of Intel and the inventor of the integrated circuit, established Caere Corporation in 1976. The company counts its other successes in intelligent document management and image recognition technologies. Besides producing OCR software and hardware, Caere's main products are the OmniPage retail products, Developer Kits, and Automated Data Entry products. To get more information on OCR, we went directly to Caere.

Hans Roos is a marketing and sales representative for the Production OCR division of Caere. Mary talked to Mr. Roos about OCR and its application to resume tracking. He provided the following simplified definition of OCR directly from the Caere User's Guide:

OCR is the process of turning an image, such as a scanned paper document, into computer-editable text so you do not have to retype the text manually.

In order to convert the image, however, the OCR must first read the document that has been scanned. OCR utilizes a feature known as artificial intelligence to read printed text, such as your resume. Mr. Roos explained this extraordinary technology in this way:

> Artificial intelligence is the ability of the computer to "think" for itself. It can "reason," or make assumptions based on information that is available to it. It can be part of both the OCR software and the resume tracking software.

This capability to reason allows for some interpretation of what you have written. Thus, comparisons can be made between your skills as you have defined them and how the employer has specified those same skills. Applicant tracking software is programmed with hundreds of thousands of job-related terms so that there is the potential for recognition of synonyms.

What can confuse the OCR process is the condition of the document itself. When you prepare a traditional paper resume, you have lots of choices concerning fonts, color, graphics, formatting, and other features to make the resume look attractive. When you prepare a scannable resume, however, you must think in simplified terms. OCR responds best to the plain vanilla resume. As we discussed in Chapter 2, you need to keep font styles simple and avoid underlining and formatting. The use of these font-enhancing features can cause characters to become degraded; in other words, they become fuzzy, misshapen, or otherwise difficult to read. Hans explained the problem in this way:

> Fancy characters can confuse the OCR. If characters touch, or appear to touch, such as when underlining is used, the OCR software can have difficulties figuring out where one character stops and another starts. OCR also looks at the shape of the letters themselves to try and figure out what they are. If the shapes of the letters are too fancy, the OCR software can get confused.
>
> Any number of things can cause a character to be difficult to read. Poor printer quality, photocopying, putting in lots of italics, bolds, underlines on characters, making the type too small, tightly kerning (the spacing between characters) the characters—all of these can make the process difficult.

Roos also emphasizes that your copy must be very clean, with no smudges or specks, streaks or lines—elements often caused by poor quality photocopies or faxed images. If you do fax a resume, set the fax machine to the fine setting to ensure that your resume will be scannable when it arrives.

If you make a photocopy, clean the platen glass and inspect your copy for any extra marks or streaks. If it is a poor quality copy, it will not scan properly.

To prepare a resume that is most likely to be successfully read by OCR, Hans Roos offers these final suggestions:

> Keeping the layout and fonts simple will help the OCR. That doesn't mean your resume can't look good; just keep it clean. Always use good quality paper and send originals if possible. If not possible, use a high-quality photocopier when making reproductions.

Over the last few years, new OCR technology has mitigated to a great degree the problem of unusual fonts or degraded text. First came the use of trainable fonts, which led eventually to the concept of omnifont OCRs. To get a clear understanding of how these OCR programs have developed and how they affect you, Mary talked with Glenn Whitten, owner of Recruiters Online. Whitten has been involved with online recruiting since the earliest days of the World Wide Web. His company processes thousands of electronic resumes through the use of scanners and OCR.

Mary: Can you explain Omnifont technology?

Glenn: Omnifont technologies make it easier for OCR packages to deal with the variety of fonts and type sizes that are commonly found in today's printed business communications. As I understand it, Omnifont is a name that Caere Corporation gives to a set of pattern-recognition technologies that it implements in its OCR programs. Other companies may use other names for the same ideas. If you or someone you know is into photography, this technology is similar to the lens brand names of Rokkor (Minolta) or Nikkor (Nikon). The term *Omnifont* is meaningless outside of a Caere marketing context. However, some of the technologies it describes are germane and interesting.

A bit of historical context is probably useful here. The companies who began addressing OCR on the desktop during the 1980s started with rather primitive programs by today's standards. These programs attempted to compare discrete images of dots in a scan to a library of stored images (A,a, B,b, C,c, *and so on*). If the scanned image of dots was sufficiently close to the stored image—named H, for example—then the scanned image was duly recognized as such, and the scanner moved on to the next image. In an era where one's choices for typographic expression were limited to pica or elite, this method generated a reasonably accurate result set for the cost.

Mary: *So typewritten documents were generally limited in the style and size of fonts that were used. And this helped in the OCR process?*

Glenn: Several environmental limitations helped in this regard. Fixed width fonts, such as those used on most typewriters, were easy to parse (*space between letters*) accurately. The letters did not have the annoying habit of running into each other the way that proportionally spaced fonts did. Given an original document or a clean, first-generation copy, a program could—with a high degree of certainty—detect where one image (letter) ended and another began. Size was also restricted. Ten- or twelve-point fonts were standards. It was not hard to digitize and store images of every letter and number for these combinations of typestyles and sizes. This small number could be quickly compared to the scanned sample and recognized. For those situations where a strange or unknown type style was used in the original document, the makers of OCR software provided the capability for the user to "train" the program.

Mary: *How does the trainable font idea work?*

Glenn: This concept was (and still is) a generally laborious task, which consists of selecting the image from the scan onscreen that constitutes the capital letter A, for example, and then identifying it as such for the program. In essence, this process gives the customers the capability of adding their own sample images to the library of images that came with the program. These new images are used by the program during the recognition process when it compares scanned characters to its internal library of images.

Mary: *So this conversion must be accomplished for every letter individually?*

Glenn: If this sounds like drudgery, it is! I never sold an OCR package where someone used this feature more than once or twice. There were occasions where a client had used a special typewriter ball for years, and the time investment in a single training session could be amortized over hundreds or thousands of documents. It does not take much imagination to see that the people responsible for processing resumes would find this task rather unpleasant. In fact, I imagine that they do not waste time doing this process at all. If a candidate cannot supply a scannable profile, then it is discarded. Anyone can retype a complete resume in much less time than it takes to train an OCR package to deal with a strange font.

Unfortunately for the OCR companies, this period of time saw the rise of the personal laser printer. Laser printers—coupled with advances in computer interfaces (Mac/Windows)—brought those pesky proportionally spaced typefaces to the masses. Equally distressing was the lamentable manner in which people began using their newfound typographic freedoms. The ransom-note memo, in which a wide assortment of fonts were used in a single document, was born.

Mary: *This must have wreaked havoc on the whole OCR process.*

Glenn: The bottom line for the OCR companies was that their lives were triply complicated. First, their customers were using proportional fonts, which made it much more difficult to separate and read individual letters. Second, the variety of different typefaces increased by several orders of magnitude. Where once Courier, Pica, and Elite accounted for 90 percent of the target documents, now *Times, Palatino, Garamond, Helvetica,* and *Arial* were just the beginning. Thousands of other fonts were eventually available. Finally, these typefaces were scaleable. Instead of an 8-point to 14-point range, users became increasingly creative in reducing or enlarging the fonts at will. The combination of these trends—any one of which would have taxed the old system—rendered the old strategy of image comparison increasingly ineffective. The proliferation of new typefaces in business documents demanded a more flexible solution. What was needed was a new way to approach the problem.

Mary: *Which brings us to the present day and technology, such as Caere's Omnifont. How did Caere go about designing their Omnifont technology?*

Glenn: The question they tried to answer was "What makes a *W* a *W*?" How is it that humans can quickly and easily recognize that a Times Italic *W* is the same symbol as an Arial Extra-Bold **W**? These programs began looking at the patterns of letters. At an abstract level, a W is described as "a figure composed of four segments with two vertices at the bottom and one at the top in the middle"—or something like that. Anyway, this description applies to a *W* in *any* typestyle. Essentially, this type of analytical abstraction—taken to the *n*th degree for every letter, number and punctuation mark—is what Caere has named Omnifont. This explanation is vastly oversimplified but sufficient to cover the broad ideas.

Mary: Can this technology then be applied to other problems with the image, such as degraded text, as well as addressing the problem of unusual fonts?

Glenn: I expect that Caere would also include their procedures for dealing with poor quality originals (faxes, colors, bad photocopies, skewed documents, dot matrix printouts, *and so on*) under this umbrella. I suspect that there are still specific situations where some of the old-fashioned methods work better. The OCR program, therefore, has added new tools to complement old ones. Pattern analysis and recognition is still dependent on the capability to accurately parse, or separate, letters. This capability remains one of the most difficult and complicating problems for OCR software. Remember, too, that all the mature OCR programs have followed similar technology development lines. However, the objective, the time investment, and the cost constraints are generally the same.

Mary: So how does this vastly improved OCR technology impact job seekers who want to write a resume that will be successfully scanned?

Glenn: Several OCR packages advertise a 98 percent or better recognition accuracy rate. As with the federal mileage estimates for your car, the rate is seldom, if ever, so good. In the best case (let's suppose 95 percent accuracy), there will be 5 errors out of every 100 characters. If we assume an average word length of 5 characters, this means that the program will misread your resume at a rate of one word out of every twenty. I don't know about you, but that was enough to flunk me in any English class I ever took. Even worse, though, is the fact that the mistakes will not be randomly distributed. If the program misreads the characters *mi* as *ml* once, it is likely to do so throughout the document. If this happens to any of your keywords, your resume will not be found in searches for those words.

The objective is to get your resume into the Human Resources system of the target company. Anything that interferes with this goal—whether typos, OCR-induced inaccuracies, layout problems, and so on—is counterproductive. The *best* system cannot be expected to produce good results with poor quality resumes. GIGO (garbage in; garbage out).

Scanning Process

Now, let's follow a resume through the scanning process. First, you send your resume to company X via mail, e-mail, or fax. Your resume is then put through a scanner that makes a duplicate image of your resume and turns it into a computer file. In a sense, it's like a computerized picture of your resume. The resulting computer image is sent through the OCR (optical character recognition software). The OCR program reads the image of your resume by use of artificial intelligence and then converts it into language a computer can understand.

After the resume is in the applicant-tracking system, it can be edited by a technician to make sure that the computer version matches the paper version you originally sent to the company. Unfortunately, many changes can occur in the resume. Remember that many things can impact the way the OCR reads what you have written. Such processes as faxing and photocopying, as well as the use of font-enhancing features, such as formatting, can degrade your text and impede the OCR process. After a technician has cleaned up your resume, it is stored for future retrieval. Your resume is now in a database that can be searched for job openings.

Skill Extraction

The technology used by resume management systems to pull information from your resume is known as the extraction engine. The nucleus of the extraction engine is its knowledge base, the collection of career-related vocabulary, which enables the engine to recognize similar terms in your resume. This collection is known as *rules*. Rules specify and define the many factors that make up an applicant's career profile. These factors include education, work history, skills, job titles, and even personal traits. The knowledge base of an extraction engine comes from recruiters, technicians at automated staffing services, and the job seekers themselves. The knowledge base is comprised of millions of job-related terms and phrases, as well as a variety of contexts in which these factors occur. Resumix's knowledge base, for example, contains over 140,000 rules and more than ten million resume terms!

Ideally, the core grammar of an extraction engine should be a continually evolving collection. Employers are often able to customize the knowledge base to suit their needs by including in it their own in-house jargon, for example. Knowledge bases also need to keep pace with developing technology.

To begin the extraction process, your resume is first sectioned into such areas as Education, Work History, Skill, and so on. Then each of these sections is perused and the relevant data extracted. The extraction process is very thorough. It searches through every section and gleans all information that can be meaningfully categorized. The resulting data is then put into broad vocational categories, such as Finance, Sales, Marketing, Engineering, and so on. When your resume is scanned in an applicant search, these categories provide the first level of matching.

Following the initial categorization, your resume is next put through a skill extraction. Here the extraction engine seeks out specific skills, not just the broad vocational classification. So under the vocational category of Human Resources, for example, the organization may require the specific skills of Interviewing, Benefits Administration, EEOC, and Grievance Procedures. The knowledge base is key in making these selections. Remember that most extraction engines contain millions of terms within their knowledge base.

An interesting aspect of the extraction process is that some systems can recognize not only words, but also the context in which the words occur. This context can derive either from the placement of the term within the structure of the resume or from the sentence itself. Resumix provided this explanation to us:

> The resume structure context allows Resumix to differentiate among applicants with a first name of Ada, a person living in Ada, Michigan, and a person with the skill of ADA. The sentence context allows Resumix to further differentiate between a dentist with membership in ADA (American Dental Association), a programmer having experience with the language ADA, or a Human Resources professional who works with ADA (Americans with Disabilities Act).

Besides context, extraction systems are often capable of interpreting concepts, not just words or phrases. In concept-based searching, the extraction engine actually makes assumptions by assigning skills based on related terms it encounters. Consider these examples. If a resume stated "researched cases for precedent," the system would assign the skill of Paralegal. A resume listing "graded papers and tests for professor" as a responsibility would yield a skill assignment of Teacher Assistance. And the system would infer the skill of Programming from the notation "wrote in BASIC."

Experienced human resources and recruiting professionals routinely make these conceptual links. It is extraordinary to think that sophisticated extraction engines possess this same capacity. However, this remarkable capability of reasoning with concepts increases your chances for a match.

In addition, extraction engines have the capability to recognize key concepts and terms even when they are misspelled. The engines also look for synonyms and similarities. Consider the following: University of California at Berkeley, UC Berkeley, UCB, Berkeley, and even Cal are all ways of referring to the same school. A sophisticated system recognizes all of them! All these diverse ways of retrieving data decidedly work in your favor and increase your chance of getting a hit on your resume.

Some resume-processing systems extract a summary from the scanned resume. These summaries contain the key information about the applicant. They list your name, address, phone number, and other contact information; the pertinent data from your work history, such as companies, job titles, and dates; your educational background, including names of schools and degrees or certificates held; and all job-related skills, including the relevant keywords and phrases that describe your abilities. This summary is also stored in the company's database for searching.

To summarize: Your resume goes through a scanner. It is then looked at by OCR software and converted to usable computer language. It is read by artificial intelligence, from which a summary is extracted. It is cleaned up by a technician and is stored in the applicant tracking system where it is ready to be retrieved by employers. Sound simple? Okay, let's look at two automated staffing companies: Resumix and Restrac.

Resumix™

One of the best known automated staffing (resume tracking) companies—or, as it refers to itself, Human Skills Management Systems—is Resumix, headquartered in Sunnyvale, California (see Figure 3.1). The company is a wholly owned subsidiary of Ceridian Corporation, an information services and defense electronics company. Resumix has been around since 1988, when developers of artificial intelligence software from ESL/TRW Labs decided that the emerging technology could be used to manage the flood of resumes the company received every year. The developers initially marketed their product to two Bay Area companies, and their businesses grew from their original base of high-tech concerns to include a variety of other industries. Today, Resumix has over 400 customer installations and counts many clients among Fortune 1,000 corporations, as well as universities, health care organizations, and government entities.

Figure 3.1

The Resumix home page at http://www.resumix.com.

Resumix is *not* a resume-posting service, however. You cannot send your resume directly to Resumix, unless you are applying for a job with the company itself. Instead, Resumix provides an applicant-tracking system to companies that need help managing their staffing process. Simply put, Resumix takes over the cumbersome task of managing the crush of resumes that inundate most companies. It enables a company to identify top candidates—-both internal and external—-for positions within the company.

Lori Kameda, Marketing Manager of Resumix, summarizes the service that Resumix provides by saying:

> Resumix is a software company that provides advanced automated staffing and skills management solutions that enable organizations to source and identify the most qualified people to fill the open positions.

Carla Richards, Product Marketing Manager at Resumix, emphasizes that the corporation is not a service provider. Resumix furnishes the resume-management software that is used internally by a company. Richards also says:

> Companies first purchase the Resumix system software. Once purchased and installed, organizations can use the Resumix system to satisfy both internal and external hiring needs, monitor college recruiting efforts, fill temporary and part-time positions, and perform other Human Resource functions.

For the job seekers, their scannable resumes will be put into the Resumix database at the company itself. In addition, the company's Manager's Workbench integrates Resumix with the Internet. Manager's Workbench is available to employers through a no-cost download and enables them to access the resumes at online job boards, such as Career Mosaic. Manager's Workbench can also be implemented on a company's intranet, so the resumes can be distributed throughout the organization.

Richards goes on to say:

> Using desktop agents to do the work of presenting and routing information, Resumix becomes available to a much broader audience of Human Resource users, managers, and employees. Once candidates are entered into a company's Resumix system, they can be considered for any open position for which they are qualified. Candidate resumes can be tracked to open positions, and their progress through an organization's hiring process can be documented and monitored directly in the Resumix system.

So what happens when an applicant gets hired? Can a person request retention in the system for future hits? Richards responds by saying:

> If a candidate is hired through the Resumix system, the status of her resume becomes unavailable. Should a candidate be interested in other positions/opportunities with the same company in the future, her resume can be made re-available for consideration for other opportunities.
>
> Based on company policies and practices, applicants would not have to request retention of their resumes. Resumes are kept in the database for a minimum of six months to a maximum of two or more years. Applicants can update their resumes and resubmit them should they obtain new or additional skills, making them qualified for additional or other positions.

Of course, how long the resume is retained in general by the company varies by company policy and state regulation. Resumix also enables employers to utilize the Internet to find candidates online. The software that permits this capability is called ResLink. Carla Richards explains how ResLink connects the Resumix system with the Internet:

> ResLink is a plug-in software module for Resumix systems that lets companies automatically post jobs from a Resumix database to any of the ResLink partner Web sites and receive resumes from interested job seekers anywhere on the Internet.

One such partner site is The Monster Board. If you have a resume posted at The Monster Board, or several other online job sites, you may very likely be accessed from a company utilizing the Resumix system.

We asked the people at Resumix for their advice on how applicants can increase their opportunities for matching employer requirements—or, simply put, of getting hits. They offer the following tips for maximizing hits:

- ✔ Use enough keywords to define your skills, experience, education, professional affiliations, and so on.

- ✔ Describe your experience with concrete words, rather than vague descriptions. For example, it's better to use "managed a team of software engineers" than to use "responsible for managing and training."

- ✔ Be concise and truthful.

- ✔ Use more than one page if necessary. Additional pages permit you to provide more information than you would for a human reader.

- ✔ Use jargon and acronyms specific to your industry (spell out the acronyms for a human reader).

✔ Increase your list of keywords by including specifics. For example, list the names of software that you use, such as Microsoft Word and Lotus 1-2-3.

✔ Use common headings, such as Objective, Experience, Employment, Work History, Positions Held, Appointments, Skills, Summary, Summary of Qualifications, Accomplishments, Strengths, Education, Affiliations, Professional Affiliations, Publications, Papers, Licenses, Certifications, Examinations, Honors, Personal, Additional, Miscellaneous, References, and so on.

✔ If you have extra space, describe your interpersonal traits and attitude. Keywords can include skill in time management, dependable, high energy, leadership, sense of responsibility, and good memory.

Restrac

Restrac Inc., headquartered in Lexington, Massachusetts, was founded in 1982 (see Figure 3.2). Lars Perkins, cofounder of the company with Paul Costello, was an early pioneer of the automated staffing industry and is still the company's chief executive officer. The company grew out of the basic idea of using technology to handle the more labor-intensive aspects of the recruiting process: job order posting, applicant tracking, and resume processing. Over time, this idea evolved to encompass the capability of connecting workers and jobs by using the Internet.

Figure 3.2

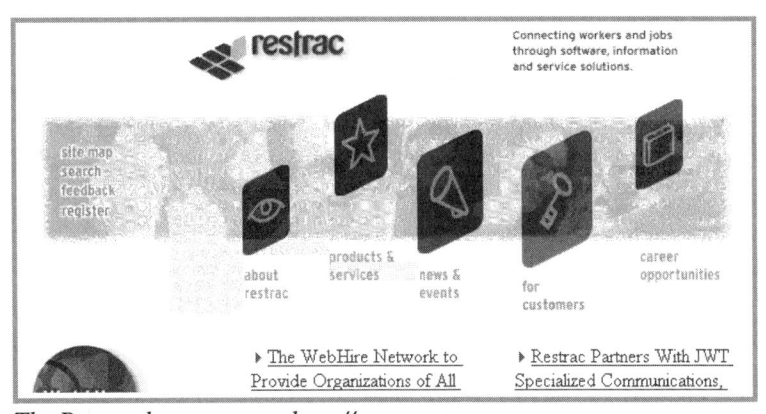

The Restrac home page at http://www.restrac.com.

In its own words, Restrac says the following about its company:

> Restrac's integrated recruiting solutions include the WebHire Network, an open network of Internet recruiting services. The WebHire Network uses the Internet to create a single connection between Restrac customers and an expanding network of more than 100 Internet-recruiting partners that provide job-posting services, searchable pools of candidate resumes, and other essential recruiting services.

Part I: Electronic Resumes

> Restrac's offerings combine software, services, and the Internet to create end-to-end recruitment solutions that streamline the way jobs and workers are connected. Restrac Hire for Intranet brings the most flexible, enterprise-wide solution on the market to corporate intranets and connects the corporate recruiting process to the Internet. Restrac WebHire is a browser-based solution designed to meet the unique needs of rapidly growing organizations by combining WebHire Network access with qualified candidate management and resume processing in a unique outsourced service delivered over the Internet.

Restrac's service assists companies in scanning resumes, identifying candidates, managing documents, and reporting results. The Restrac system also enables companies to keep track of affirmative action and EEO (Equal Employment Opportunity) records. A special reporting feature available to employers can even help with audits. But the main focus of the business is to help companies create and manage a resume pool.

Restrac boasts 90 clients among the Fortune 500 companies and has established partnerships with a host of technology companies, such as PeopleSoft. In a press release, Restrac states:

> More than 325 companies worldwide employ Restrac's client/server intranet- or Internet-based recruiting solutions. Restrac's clients represent a variety of industries including technology, communications, manufacturing, insurance, health care, and entertainment. Twenty-eight of the 50 most profitable US companies cited in *Fortune Magazine's* 1996 "Fortune 1,000" report use the company's software.

The company also offers a French Canadian version of its Restrac Resume Reader for PeopleSoft and a CV (curriculum vitae) version for the United Kingdom.

Mary talked with Greg Mancusi-Ungaro, Director of Marketing for Restrac. He summarized for us the way in which Restrac provides service to companies:

> Restrac software is used by companies to automate their recruiting process. Restrac does not supply its customers with resumes directly. Typically, Company A uses its Restrac recruiting solution to post a job requisition on its corporate home page or on any of a number of affiliated Internet job boards (The Monster Board, Online Career Center, Recruit USA, and so on). A candidate applies for that job online and forwards his resume information to Company A, where it is directly input into the Restrac candidate database that Company A maintains.
>
> Alternatively, a candidate sends her resume to Company A, and Company A scans the resume to place it in a searchable online database of resumes. (Company A also has the option to

outsource the scanning to the Restrac Resume Processing Center if it wants to avoid having to think about the scanning.)

Once the resume information has been received by Company A, the candidate is considered in every Restrac search that a recruiter at Company A might run. Whenever the qualifications of that candidate match the requirements of an open position at Company A, the candidate's resume will appear in the relevance ranked report of qualified candidates that the Restrac solution generates in every search.

A company has two ways to utilize the Restrac system. A company can purchase the system directly for in-house use, or it can turn over the management of the system to Restrac. In either case, the resume ends up in a searchable database. Restrac software also permits employers to recruit directly from Internet sites. Mancusi-Ungaro goes on to say:

Restrac has created an innovative new Internet service known as the Restrac PartnerPool. PartnerPools are created and maintained on the Internet by professional and affinity organizations and by recruiting-services providers. They contain collections of candidate resumes that are available for searching from Restrac WebHire (and eventually Restrac Hire for Intranet).

Restrac also uses Recruiting Workbench to connect the Human Resources manager's desktop to the Internet. With this feature, the employer can link to online job-posting sites and pull resumes directly from the Internet to its Restrac system.

Mancusi-Ungaro says that your resume is retained as long as the company wants to keep it, usually a minimum of six months. And while your resume is in the system, Restrac tracks its status. The Restrac system can keep track of the following statuses for each candidate: considered for a job, participating in interview(s), second interview, offer letters sent, accepted offers, and others. But the candidate does not control the resume after it is submitted to the company. Mancusi-Ungaro concludes by saying:

If an applicant wanted a company to no longer consider her for an opening, the applicant would have to contact the company directly.

Restrac offers many tips for preparing a scannable resume. Be sure that you DO the following on your resume:

✔ Use white paper.

✔ Provide a typed or laser-quality original document.

✔ Print on one side only.

✔ Use fonts that are 12 to 14 points in size.

- ✔ Use standard fonts, such as Arial, Futura, Optima, Universe, Times, Palatino, or Courier.
- ✔ Use a structured resume format because they scan very well.
- ✔ Use terms and jargon specific to your industry.
- ✔ Spell out any acronyms.
- ✔ Use words that describe your experience in a concise and accurate manner.
- ✔ List specific skills and increase your use of keywords.
- ✔ Use more than one page if necessary.
- ✔ Include

  Name, Address, Phone Number, Fax Number, and E-mail Address—each on a separate line
  Objective
  Experience
  Work History
  Positions Held
  Summary of Qualifications, Skills, Accomplishments
  Education
  Certifications

And be sure that you DON'T do the following on your resume:

- ✔ Use colored or dark paper.
- ✔ Send photocopies if you can avoid it.
- ✔ Fold or staple your materials.
- ✔ Use italics, underlining, shadows, or reverse type.
- ✔ Use bullets.
- ✔ Use lines (vertical or horizontal), borders, boxes, or graphics.
- ✔ Use vague or excessive descriptions of your experience.

A final word of *caution:* Remember that your scannable resume will still be read by a human reader at some point. Write a cohesive, organized resume that will succeed whether it is read by a computer or by a human being. After all, a computer will not be saying the words you want to hear: "You're hired!"

Chapter 4

Submitting Your Scannable Resume

After you have prepared your scanner-friendly resume, you have several different choices in how you send it to the company. Sometimes you will find the job online and then submit your resume online by pasting it into a resume template, where it will be scanned into a database—never having been seen by human eyes! Other times, you will simply respond to an online advertisement by sending your resume via e-mail. Some employers still prefer that you fax your resume. And other employers request that you mail your resume the old fashioned way. In this chapter, we will explain the finer points of each of these methods.

E-Mail Resumes

Many companies still ask applicants to e-mail resumes. To ensure that your resume arrives at the employer's screen in a usable and scannable form, it is best to prepare it in ASCII text. ASCII (American Standard Code for Information Interchange) is pure text, the simplest form that allows the exchange of information between computers. The beauty of ASCII is that it enables employers to view your resume, regardless of the computer platform they use.

Glenn Whitten, an expert in OCR with Recruiters Online, says that e-mail resumes are a smart idea. He goes on to say:

> I recommend sending e-mail whenever possible. It totally bypasses the errors, which *will* be introduced into your resume by OCR. The good news is that recruiters are increasingly seeing the value of this medium. In fact, there is a significant percentage of recruiters who no longer solicit paper resumes. Many no longer accept them at all.

Part I: Electronic Resumes

Your text resume prepared in ASCII is lean and mean, with no special fonts, formatting, graphics, or other pretty effects—exactly the way a scanner likes it! The resume is also completely left justified, even the heading. If you want to center a line or indent a sentence, you must perform this action by spacing everything as you type it. Remember, in ASCII you cannot use the centerline feature or tabs. You must use the spacebar.

Take a look at the following samples from Alexis Larson to see the differences between a standard resume and an ASCII resume. Sample Resume 4–1 is a conventional resume, also known as a presentation resume. This resume is prepared for a human reader. Note all the font enhancements.

Sample Resume 4–2 shows what happened when the presentation was saved as a text document. Note that the bullets in the bulleted lists (■) were turned into a parenthesis mark ((), but the asterisks (*) made the transition unchanged. The asterisk was preserved because it is a letter on the keyboard, not an imported symbol, which is really a picture. Also, notice that the indents were not saved and that words wrapped at unusual places at the ends of the lines.

Finally, after editing the text copy, Sample Resume 4–3 is the ASCII version that is suitable for sending to the employer via e-mail.

Sample Resume 4-1

Alexis Larson
75 Apollo Ct.
Halifax, NS
B3J 3G6
XXX-XXX-XXXX (W)
XXX-XXX-XXXX (H)
Email: aaa@aaaa.aaa

HIGHLIGHTS OF QUALIFICATIONS

* Over 10 years progressively responsible administrative/management experience
* Proven ability to manage effectively in complex environments
* Demonstrated ability to supervise in a team environment
* Completed MBA while working full time
* Effective communicator, motivated problem-solver

WORK EXPERIENCE

19XX-present   ADMINISTRATIVE OFFICER, Department of Medicine
                Prestigious University, Halifax, NS

The Department of Medicine at Prestigious encompasses an administrative office and 14 divisions, is situated in 5 locations, and employs over 225 faculty, 70 secretarial/support staff, and 45 grant paid/technical employees. This position coordinates the administrative management of the department including teaching and research programs and is responsible to:

- Participate in the development and monitoring of departmental goals and objectives;
- Manage and administer all aspects of financial management;
- Coordinate personnel management of 120 employees in two bargaining units; direct supervision of 15 staff;
- Assist in the screening, selection and orientation of residents and undergrad medical students;
- Manage the practice plan for a group of 60 physicians;
- Serve on Department and Faculty Committees;
- Liaison between the Director, Dean's Office, Committee Chairpersons, university and government officials;
- Manage a variety of special projects, conduct research, write reports, implement recommendations

Recent Accomplishments

- Developed and implemented personnel, financial and management guidelines which were accepted at the Faculty level;
- Computerized and streamlined financial management system resulting in more effective control and analysis;

Sample Resume 4-1 continued

ALEXIS LARSON
Page 2

- Implemented a comprehensive selection process for students and staff in consultation with faculty and human resource development;
- Implemented quality initiatives as a component of regular departmental meetings;
- Developed and monitored project teams within Department; drafted a comprehensive report for government on financial needs of the Department which was approved by the Department Head and Dean of the Faculty of Medicine.

19XX-19XX   ADMINISTRATIVE ASSISTANT, Faculty of Medicine
             Prestigious University, Halifax, Nova Scotia

- Monitored the finances of 30 departments within the faculty;
- Provided assistance to Departmental administrators;
- Managed accounts receivable/salary recovery data information system;
- Administered Dean's Office accounts payables;
- Monitored finances of restricted/endowment accounts for the Faculty;
- Processed payroll information at the Faculty level;
- Prepared detailed financial reports for government on monthly basis;
- Participated in budget projections and year-end financial operations

EDUCATION

19XX - Master of Business Administration, Prestigious University
19XX - Bachelor of Business Administration, Another University

CURRENT COMMITTEES

Finance Committee, Faculty of Medicine
Employee Relations Committee, Some General Hospital
Employment Equity Advisory Committee, Prestigious University Admin Group Representative

MEMBERSHIPS

National Board of Trade
Human Resource Association of Nova Scotia

REFERENCES
To be supplied upon request

Sample Resume 4-2

```
Alexis Larson
75 Apollo Ct.
Halifax, NS
B3J 3G6
XXX-XXX-XXXX (W)
XXX-XXX-XXXX (H)
Email: aaa@aaaa.aaa
```

HIGHLIGHTS OF QUALIFICATIONS

* Over 10 years progressively responsible administrative/management experience
* Proven ability to manage effectively in complex environments
* Demonstrated ability to supervise in a team environment
* Completed MBA while working full time
* Effective communicator, motivated problem-solver

WORK EXPERIENCE

19XX-present   ADMINISTRATIVE OFFICER, Department of Medicine
        Prestigious University, Halifax, NS

The Department of Medicine at Prestigious encompasses an administrative office and 14 divisions, is situated in 5 locations, and employs over 225 faculty, 70 secretarial/support staff, and 45 grant paid/technical employees. This position coordinates the administrative management of the department including teaching and research programs and is responsible to:

(Participate in the development and monitoring of departmental goals and objectives;
(Manage and administer all aspects of financial management;
(Coordinate personnel management of 120 employees in two bargaining units; direct
        supervision of 15 staff;
(Assist in the screening, selection and orientation of residents and undergrad medical
        students;
(Manage the practice plan for a group of 60 physicians;
(Serve on Department and Faculty Committees;
(Liaison between the Director, Dean's Office, Committee Chairpersons, university and
        government officials;
(Manage a variety of special projects, conduct research, write reports, implement
        recommendations

Recent Accomplishments

(Developed and implemented personnel, financial and management guidelines which
        were accepted at the Faculty level;
(Computerized and streamlined financial management system resulting in more effective
        control and analysis;

Sample Resume 4-2 continued

(Implemented a comprehensive selection process for students and staff in consultation
with faculty and human resource development;
(Implemented quality initiatives as a component of regular departmental meetings;
(Developed and monitored project teams within Department; drafted a comprehensive
report for government on financial needs of the Department which was approved by the
Department Head and Dean of the Faculty of Medicine.

19XX-19XX   ADMINISTRATIVE ASSISTANT, Faculty of Medicine
    Prestigious University, Halifax, Nova Scotia

(Monitored the finances of 30 departments within the faculty;
(Provided assistance to Departmental administrators;
(Managed accounts receivable/salary recovery data information system;
(Administered Dean's Office accounts payables;
(Monitored finances of restricted/endowment accounts for the Faculty;
(Processed payroll information at the Faculty level;
(Prepared detailed financial reports for government on monthly basis;
(Participated in budget projections and year-end financial operations

EDUCATION

19XX - Master of Business Administration, Prestigious University
19XX - Bachelor of Business Administration, Another University

CURRENT COMMITTEES

Finance Committee, Faculty of Medicine
Employee Relations Committee, Some General Hospital
Employment Equity Advisory Committee, Prestigious University Admin Group Representative

MEMBERSHIPS

National Board of Trade
Human Resource Association of Nova Scotia

REFERENCES
To be supplied upon request

Sample Resume 4-3

```
Alexis Larson
75 Apollo Ct.
Halifax, NS
B3J 3G6
XXX-XXX-XXXX (W)
XXX-XXX-XXXX (H)
Email: aaa@aaaa.aaa
```

HIGHLIGHTS OF QUALIFICATIONS

* Over 10 years progressively responsible administrative/ management experience
* Proven ability to manage effectively in complex environments
* Demonstrated ability to supervise in a team environment
* Completed MBA while working full time
* Effective communicator, motivated problem-solver

WORK EXPERIENCE

19XX-present ADMINISTRATIVE OFFICER, Department of Medicine
Prestigious University, Halifax, NS

The Department of Medicine at Prestigious encompasses an administrative office and 14 divisions, is situated in 5 locations, and employs over 225 faculty, 70 secretarial/support staff, and 45 grant paid/technical employees. This position coordinates the administrative management of the department including teaching and research programs and is responsible to:

Participate in the development and monitoring of departmental goals and objectives;

Manage and administer all aspects of financial management;

Coordinate personnel management of 120 employees in two bargaining units; direct supervision of 15 staff;

Assist in the screening, selection and orientation of residents and undergrad medical students;

Manage the practice plan for a group of 60 physicians;

Serve on Department and Faculty Committees;

Liaison between the Director, Dean's Office, Committee Chairpersons, university and government officials;

Manage a variety of special projects, conduct research, write reports, implement recommendations

Sample Resume 4-3 continued

Recent Accomplishments

Developed and implemented personnel, financial and management guidelines which were accepted at the Faculty level;

Computerized and streamlined financial management system resulting in more effective control and analysis;

Implemented a comprehensive selection process for students and staff in consultation with faculty and human resource development;

Implemented quality initiatives as a component of regular departmental meetings;

Developed and monitored project teams within Department; drafted a comprehensive report for government on financial needs of the Department which was approved by the Department Head and Dean of the Faculty of Medicine.

19XX-19XX ADMINISTRATIVE ASSISTANT, Faculty of Medicine
           Prestigious University, Halifax, Nova Scotia

Monitored the finances of 30 departments within the faculty;
Provided assistance to Departmental administrators;
Managed accounts receivable/salary recovery data information system;
Administered Dean's Office accounts payables;
Monitored finances of restricted/endowment accounts for the Faculty;
Processed payroll information at the Faculty level;
Prepared detailed financial reports for government on monthly basis;
Participated in budget projections and year-end financial operations

EDUCATION

19XX - Master of Business Administration, Prestigious University
19XX - Bachelor of Business Administration, Another University

Sample Resume 4-3 continued

CURRENT COMMITTEES

Finance Committee, Faculty of Medicine
Employee Relations Committee, Some General Hospital
Employment Equity Advisory Committee, Prestigious University
Admin Group Representative

MEMBERSHIPS

National Board of Trade
Human Resource Association of Nova Scotia

REFERENCES
To be supplied upon request

Prepare your resume (see Chapter 2) in your word processor. Make sure that you keep the lines to no more than 70 characters long. This spacing ensures that your resume will not come out looking haphazard on the receiving end. Then save the resume in ASCII. (*In your Windows program, choose File, Save As, Text.*) Be sure to spell check and examine your resume carefully for appropriate spacing. We recommend that you e-mail your resume to yourself first to make sure that the look is professional with even borders and line spacing. Open your e-mail program and address the message to yourself. Then, copy and paste your text resume directly from your word processing program into the body of your e-mail message and send it to yourself. Once you are completely satisfied that mailing your resume hasn't corrupted it, open your e-mail program and address your message to the company. Most online posting services and employers request that you put your name and the word *Resume* in the subject line. Copy your resume once again, paste it directly into the body of your e-mail message, and send it to the employer. The ASCII resume is also the preferred form for pasting into an online resume template.

> **Caution:** Nearly every resume site we visited and all the employers we interviewed cautioned job seekers *not* to submit their resume as an attachment to an e-mail message.

An attachment is a file that has to be downloaded separately from your e-mail into your computer. In the case of a resume, an attachment would be a document created in a word processing program. One problem with attachments is that the word processing program you use may not be recognizable by a program at the employer's site. Another problem with attachments is that they usually arrive in a compressed form and need to be expanded when they reach their destination in order to be readable. The employer's computer may not be compatible with that program; thus your resume is rendered useless.

Still another problem with sending attachments is Internet users believe—rightly or wrongly—that viruses often ride in on attachments. Many employers simply will not bother with an attachment, and they will skip it entirely.

Mailing Your Resume

Although many companies now refrain from accepting paper resumes altogether, some companies still accept resumes only by regular postal mail—that is, "snail mail" in Internet parlance. One advantage to mailing your resume is that you can send both a scannable type—one that is written to pass the OCR—and a presentation type—one that is attractive for a human reader. (We'll discuss the relative merits of sending two resumes in the section "How Many Resumes?")

Another advantage of mailing your resume is that you can send an original resume straight off your printer, or you can send a first-generation photocopy. Remember that scannable resumes must be clean and free of "noise" so that they can be scanned efficiently. Be sure that your photocopy is very clean, with no dark streaks or black flecks. Glenn Whitten, from Recruiters Online adds:

> If you copy your resume, make sure that the copy comes out straight. OCR programs have a hard enough time reading lines of text that go straight across the page—never mind those that trail off in one direction or another.

When you mail your resume, you should send it in a large envelope to avoid the wrinkles that can bedevil the scanner. Glenn Whitten agrees:

> If you have to mail the resume, buy a big envelope and mail it flat. I know it costs more, but scanners can choke on folded documents. Even if the scanner doesn't choke, folds could skew your resume just enough to introduce a significantly higher error rate into the OCR process.

Faxing Your Resume

Several companies prefer to accept their resumes via fax. Long before applicant-tracking systems existed, employers discovered that receiving resumes by fax was more efficient than taking them in person or receiving them by postal mail. Fax machines eliminated long lines in the Human Resources department and cut down on the labor-intensive task of sorting through, opening, and distributing mail. When applicant-tracking systems came along, some companies continued to accept scannable resumes by fax, but some problems developed.

Think about the faxes you have received. Often, they look dirty, with lots of streaks and lines. Sometimes one sheet has overlapped another, which wipes out several sections of the second sheet. Sometimes the sheet has a wrinkle, which causes the letters to look squashed and misshapen. And sometimes the resolution of the fax machine—based on its dpi (dots per inch)—doesn't match the dpi of the OCR. The faxed image is composed of millions of tiny dots at different shades: the greater the number of dots per inch, the better the detail in the image; the lower the dpi, the grainier or muddier the image appears to be. Such problems can cause havoc with the scanning process. Hans Roos is a marketing and sales representative for Caere Corporation, a company that makes OCR. He explains:

Faxing usually happens in low resolutions. Standard-mode faxes can have a dpi of 100 X 100. Even fine-mode faxes are only 100 X 200 or 200 X 200 dpi. While most OCRs can handle these lower resolutions, they are usually tuned at 300 dpi. Also, faxing can add a lot of noise—speckles, lines, and smudges—that makes faxes very difficult to read, even for humans. All of these things degrade OCR.

If you must fax your scannable resume, take steps to ensure that your faxed resume is still usable when it arrives at the other end. Set your fax machine to the fine setting by selecting it in the Control Panel. This adjustment increases the dpi and eliminates much of the noise on your faxed copy. Also, be sure to begin with a very clean and unwrinkled copy of your resume in the first place.

Resume Templates

Many companies now use resume templates to assist their applicants in writing scannable resumes. If you apply for a job at a company's Web site, you will often find a fill-in-the-blanks form at the end of the job posting. This easy-to-use template ensures that your resume is in a format that is easily read by the company's scanner. The template helps increase your chances of getting hit in a retrieval.

More companies are choosing to use resume templates as they increasingly opt for automated staffing. Through our research, we determined that templates are becoming the preferred means of obtaining resumes in usable form for a number of reasons. First, by designing their own forms, employers are able to specify and control the information they need from applicants. Second, employers can control the length of the resume. The templates we reviewed provided space for only three to six prior jobs in the Work History block, with three being the standard. Third, resumes that are pasted into a template are guaranteed to be scannable. They arrive in text and go directly into the company's applicant-tracking system. Finally, with an online template, employers are spared the task of wading through paper.

To submit your resume online, paste your ASCII resume directly into the template. You can also type your resume online, filling in the blanks as you go. Certain resume templates may ask for information that you did not include on your standard resume, so you would simply provide that information separately by typing it directly into the blanks. Remember, however, that your resume should be a text document and must fit the parameters of the employer's template.

Resumix™ makes its ResumeBuilder™ template available to its clients for posting at their Web sites or on their intranets. We have reproduced ResumeBuilder in Appendix A so that you can see how these forms are utilized.

These resume templates are also available at most of the large online job-posting sites, such as The Monster Board and Career Mosaic. The templates enable organizations to get more in-depth information on each candidate, and the templates take the uncertainty out of the scanning process. Remember, resumes built on templates are guaranteed to be scannable!

How Many Resumes?

Resume scanners are not especially particular about the style of resume you choose: chronological, functional, or a combination of the two. Skill extraction can be accomplished on any resume that is clean and of good quality. Formatting choices—graphics, lines, fancy fonts, custom papers—are what make the process difficult. However, at some point, human eyes will still read your resume, and these special enhancements make a resume more attractive for a human reader. So how do you accommodate both audiences?

There are two schools of thought here. Some companies recommend that applicants forward two different resumes, one for the scanner and another for the Human Resources representative. For the former, you follow all the rules for preparing a scannable resume: plain paper, simple fonts, and so on, as previously detailed. For the latter, you prepare an attractive resume that utilizes more creative choices in paper, graphics, style, formatting, and the like. You then send the scannable resume via fax or e-mail, and you mail the traditional resume under separate cover or take it with you when you are called in. (You can also fax the traditional resume, although the overall quality and your expensive paper will be sacrificed.)

To understand why some companies see a need for two different resumes, you need to think about how a printed scannable resume looks. Scannable resumes—with an abundance of facts and skills for the artificial intelligence to extract—tend to be more data-intensive than the traditional resume, and they often contain a keyword summary.

In the early days of resume scanners, people thought that a separate paragraph of nothing but job-related keywords could facilitate the scanning process. This reasoning was based on a notion of competition: If the scanner hit on you right away, you would have a better chance of getting called in for an interview. Consequently, many job seekers put a grouping of words that they hoped would be picked up in a scan at the beginning of their resumes. This grouping became known as a keyword summary.

When a human reader reads these resumes, the keyword summary stands apart from the rest of the resume and looks like a disembodied jumble of nouns. Scannable resumes may also be more than one or two pages in length, a major infraction of the rules governing traditional resumes. Traditional resumes do not contain keyword summaries and are, in general, only one page long.

Although you want to add as many keywords as possible to your resume, you don't want to end up with a disjointed jumble of words on a page. You should write comprehensive job descriptions that contain as many job-related terms as possible; therefore, a keyword summary is not necessary. Remember that a scanner passes the entire length of the document and that the OCR will read the resume in its entirety. The extraction engine will do its job whether the keyword is at the beginning, the end, or buried somewhere in the middle of your resume.

The aim of sending two resumes, then, is to look good in both formats. Glenn Whitten of Recruiters Online recommends preparing two versions of a resume:

> The presentation resume is designed to be viewed by a person. As such, we would all want it to *look* as good as possible. Prudence requires us, however, to acknowledge the possibility that the resume might be scanned for OCR at a later date. The OCR resume is designed from the outset to be scanned. Visual beauty is subordinate to OCR accuracy.
>
> Bring both types to an interview, if you can. Often the interviewer can review the "pretty" one while sending the OCR into the system. In this case, you gain the best of both worlds: you come across as understanding the interviewer's situation too.

Although Whitten prefers that you prepare two resumes, he also states that you can prepare one resume that accomplishes both objectives by choosing the type size, style, and font carefully:

> There are some broad guidelines you can follow to maximize OCR accuracy for a (presentation) document. Keep the type sizes between 10–14 points; 11–12 point looks and scans best. Times or Helvetica (or their common variants Dutch or Swiss/Ariel) type styles scan the most accurately for OCR, which lets you mix a serif font (Times) for body copy with a sans-serif font (Courier) for the headings. With these adjustments, you can benefit from the visual "warm fuzzies" that these styles and fonts produce without penalizing your resume unduly.

Whitten's advice for a dual-purpose resume corresponds to his general advice for all scannable resumes. He says to avoid boldface and underlined text because this formatting doesn't scan well. And he recommends using italics only when it is needed to represent publication titles and the like. Whitten also advises that job seekers resist using symbols (♦, ✓, →, *and so on*) for bullets when preparing a presentation resume because the OCR will not know how to scan the symbols. All in all, you should use plain text as much as possible to avoid errors in OCR scanning. He gives the following piece of advice:

> Use the keyboard test. If you don't see the symbol on the keyboard, don't put it in your resume. Just make it as easy on the dumb OCR program as possible.

Other companies recommend that you prepare only a scannable resume. We learned that many companies simply discard paper resumes that are not scannable. Although many other companies still don't use electronic applicant-tracking systems, eventually these systems will become the norm. As with other technology, the price for these systems will come down, making them available to a much wider public. Therefore, you need to learn how to prepare an attractive resume that will still pass a scanner by focusing on content and keeping your formatting choices simple.

What many companies are saying now is that you don't have to send several resumes that have different objectives to fit the various jobs you may be qualified for within the company. If you include all your skills in one resume, the scanner will select you for those various positions. After your resume is in the database, your skills will be extracted, regardless of which of them you have emphasized. Lori Kameda, Marketing Manager of Resumix, advises:

> Stress to your readers that they no longer need to send multiple resumes to companies that use automated systems. They should send one resume that highlights all their skills and experience, even if two or more pages are necessary.

We recommend, however, that you prepare two resumes: one traditional and one scannable. Send a scannable resume that has been written to maximize hits. But after you have received a hit, follow up with an attractive, well-planned presentation resume. Bring the resume with you to the personal interview. Put a notation in your scannable resume that you will be following up with a traditional resume. In this way, you accomplish both objectives.

Chapter 5

Your Own HTML Resume

An HTML (Hypertext Markup Language) resume enables you to take advantage of all kinds of creative possibilities that the World Wide Web offers. For example, you can add art, sound, links to other Web sites, and video to your resume.

Why Have an HTML Resume?

An HTML resume gives you more control of the content and form of your resume on the World Wide Web. One benefit of an HTML resume is the flexibility you have in the presentation of your resume. In the text itself, you can use bold, italic, underlining, and various font sizes. You can also include tables and graphics, and you can use shading and color.

A second benefit of an HTML resume is that it can potentially increase your exposure. If your resume is in only one resume data bank, potential employers have to be in that site to find you. With an HTML resume that is indexed in the major Internet search engines, anyone can find your resume by searching on your keywords.

With an HTML resume, you have your own unique Internet address, or URL, which you can include in correspondence and on your business card. The URL directs people to your presence on the Internet. This online presence with your own URL demonstrates to employers your awareness of technology and may be the little extra that puts you ahead of the competition.

What to Avoid

HTML enables you to use many creative, fun, and interesting items in your resumes; however, some of these items may not serve you well in the job search process. This section contains several warnings that we have developed.

First of all, don't use photographs. For many years, job seekers have been warned not to include a photo of themselves on a resume. The one exception to this rule has been for people in the arts, such as actors and singers. You should omit personal photographs because you don't want to include anything that may prejudice the employer *in any way*. Visual cues are powerful. Decisions may be made about you—rightly or wrongly—based on your facial expression, your mode of dress, and even your hairstyle in the picture. Before the advent of the Internet, conventional recruiting advisors never recommended the gamble of putting a photograph on a resume.

Then along comes the World Wide Web, and job seekers feel duty-bound to take advantage of all its capabilities, including photographs. Photographs of yourself are just not appropriate on a resume. Even in the electronic labor market of today, photographs can be risky. If the photograph is unprofessional or of poor quality, it can actually harm your chances. Some computer-generated images are so muddy that you can end up looking as if you suffer from chronic insomnia or you just got released from the penitentiary. Remember, this online resume is the very first look the employer has of you and your capabilities. You don't want to leave an employer with a bad impression because of a poor photograph.

Craig Bussey, formerly the head of Human Resources for Hüls America, Inc., a chemical manufacturing company in New Jersey, stated his feelings about photographs on a resume very bluntly:

> Putting your picture on a resume is stupid. It will tend to disqualify you because it sends the wrong message. I'm not looking for a "pretty face"; I'm looking for a skill. What you look like is not a skill.

Because Human Resource professionals don't want to view photographs of potential employees, many of them use a text-only WWW browser, which replaces slow-loading images with a graphics icon.

The second warning is don't overuse links to other sites because the links may not be in your best interest. Although you can add links to the university you attended and to your former employers, remember that links take the reader *away* from your resume. The employer may get sidetracked and never return! Or you may have included links that the employer may find offensive or that are not in line with the interests of the company. For example, if you are sending a resume to UPS (United Parcel Service) and you plug in a link to the home page of your former employer, which happens to be Federal Express, the link may not sit well with the UPS representative reading your resume.

Don't include a link to your personal home page, particularly if it includes photos of you at last year's New Year's Eve party, trivia about your dog, and your poetry. Your personal home page may not be the side of you that you want a potential employer to see. Most home pages are much more informal than what would be appropriate to show an employer.

The third caution is to use colors with care. When you create an HTML resume, you need to make several choices about headings, fonts, graphics, and background. Be especially careful in choosing a background color and pattern. A background that is too busy or dark may obscure parts of your text. For example, we had to squint to read a link on one resume we saw. The background was a variegated purple and black. The link—her e-mail address, a vital piece of information—was almost impossible to see.

Finally, if you choose to use a graphic on your resume, make sure that it is simple, tasteful, and appropriate. Remember that a graphic takes time to download, so it needs to be important to the resume. You don't want to "lock" an employer on your page, waiting and waiting for your page to finish downloading. Most employers use the Internet during normal business hours, and many use modems instead of a T1 line. If a resume takes longer than 10–15 seconds to load over a modem, the employer will stop and go on to the next one.

Keep graphics tasteful and appropriate. You want everything about your resume to reflect your professionalism. Remember, too, that not all artwork is in the public domain. You don't want to put a cartoon that is protected by copyright on your resume. Software packages for building Web pages usually include clip art that is available for public use.

What to Include

Now that we have warned you about items that should not be on your HTML resume, you need to know about the creative ideas you *can* use to catch an employer's attention and make your resume useful to you. This section offers several pointers for improving your resume.

You should include a counter. A counter simply records the number of times your resume has been viewed. Keep a record of the number of hits that are your own so that you know how many times potential employers have reviewed your resume.

Although we have already cautioned you about using too many links or using inappropriate links in a resume, putting one or two links in your resume can improve your employment chances. The key to remember is to keep the employer interested in your resume. The resume should be the destination, and the link should enhance that destination, not take the employer away from it. Keep the links to a minimum, and use the ideas we have listed here:

- **E-mail address:** This is one link we highly recommend because it is a fast, no-hassle way for the employer to get to you directly.

- **Publications:** If you've been mentioned favorably in a Web site, consider a link to that site. If you have been published, consider a link to a favorable review of that work. The same advice applies to designs, compositions, and art work.

- **Notable people and organizations:** If you have worked with someone who is a known public figure, link to an informational site about that person. However, be sure to consider carefully an employer's reactions to politically and religiously affiliated people.

- **Colleges and universities:** Boola-boola and all that network stuff. Remember, however, that some college and university sites may also have other graduates' resumes.

- **Scholastic societies:** Phi Beta Kappa, Phi Kappa Phi, and so on.

- **Awards:** If you mention an award you have received, an employer may be interested in learning more about it.

- **Multiple languages:** If you are seeking work in another country and you speak the language, prepare a separate resume in that language and then put a link to it within the English-language resume. We noted several resumes in other languages. One resume in German looked appealing. Although Fred has some facility with the language, we couldn't translate the resume fully. It would have been helpful to have found a link in English to a version in English.

Even though anyone can use sites on the Web to translate documents, you want to avoid having the *employer* make the extra effort to go to these sites. The *job seeker* should provide that link instead. In addition, by putting in a link yourself to a resume you have prepared in another language, you demonstrate your facility with that language. Remember that the WWW is international. Write for that audience.

You may want to consider including two more links in your HTML resume as well. At the top or bottom of your HTML resume, you should put a link to the other versions of your resume, including a scannable version (written in ASCII text) and a printable version (one that contains the attractive format choices missing from the scannable version). The printable version is always shorter than the HTML version, and you can use it as attractive hard copy to be handed around within the company. The scannable version can be printed and put in a scanner, or it can be cut and pasted into the Web form at the employer's site.

You may also want to put another link at the bottom of the page. This link will bring the reader back to the top of your resume and is a timesaving feature that employers will thank you for.

Using Forms

You don't need to know any HTML to create your own HTML resume. You can simply use existing forms on the World Wide Web to create your own HTML resume. In Chapter 4, you were introduced to the Resumix ResumeBuilder™. We'll use this product to show you how a form creates an HTML resume.

You start by filling out the form. At the following Resumix site, you'll find a sample form completed for Clark Kent (see Example 5–1):

`http://www.resumix.com/resume/resume-sample.html`

At the end of the form, you simply choose Format to create a resume for Clark Kent from the information in the form (see Example 5–2). You can view the resume at the following site:

`http://www.resumix.com/cgi-bin/resume.pl`

Now, let's go one more step so that you can see the HTML coding that created Clark Kent's HTML resume. If you can view Clark Kent's resume on Netscape, choose View and Document Source. You will now see this Web page in HTML coding, as shown in Example 5–3. What you see is all that you need to create the resume for Clark Kent. In the following section, we'll explain what the HTML codes mean so that you can write your own HTML code.

Part I: Electronic Resumes ....

Example 5–1

ResumeBuilder™
Sample Form

Form Instructions

Personal Information

Name (as you'd like it to appear on the resume): | Clark Kent |

Address 1: | Home ▼ |

| 1001 Main Stree |
| Apt 321 |
| |

City: | Metropolis | State: | MN | Zip: | 43211-0000 |

Address 2: | Work ▼ |

| The Daily Planet |
| Journalism Dept |
| 100 Planet Ave. |

City: | Metropolis | State: | MN | Zip: | 43200-0000 |

Phone Numbers

| Home ▼ | 612-555-3221 | (optional)

| Work ▼ | 612-555-3000 | (optional)

| Fax ▼ | 612-555-1000 | (optional)

E-Mail Address: | ckent@dplanet.c | (optional)

Example 5–1 continued

Objective

Give a brief one or two sentence description of the type of employment or position you desire.

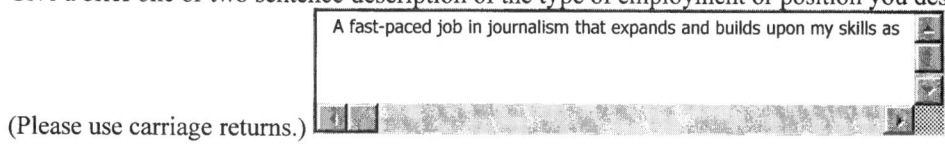

> A fast-paced job in journalism that expands and builds upon my skills as

(Please use carriage returns.)

Education

Please fill in your educational background. List at least one school you attended.

School: `Metropolis Unive` Major: `Journalism`
Degree: `B.A.` Year of Graduation: `1988` GPA: `3.75`

School: `Smallville High S` Major: `English`
Degree: `H.S.` Year of Graduation: `1984` GPA: `3.8`

School: `　` Major: `　`
Degree: `　` Year of Graduation: `　` GPA: `　`

School: `　` Major: `　`
Degree: `　` Year of Graduation: `　` GPA: `　`

Employment History

Please fill in the name of the employer, your job title, the dates you work (MM/YY format), and a brief description of your job responsibilities. Fill in at least one.

Employer: `The Daily Planet`
Job Title: `Reporter`
From: `Sept. 1990` To: `Present`
Description of Duties: (please use carriage returns)

Part I: Electronic Resumes

Example 5-1 continued

> Headline reporting for a major metropolitan newspaper. Responsibilities i

---

Employer: `Smallville Gazett`
Job Title: `Editor`
From: `Oct. 1989`   To: `Sept. 1990`
Description of Duties: (please use carriage returns)

> Head Editor and Chief for the Smallville Gazette. Managed a team of four

---

Employer: `Smallville Pizza`
Job Title: `Delivery Person`
From: `June 1988`   To: `Aug. 1989`
Description of Duties: (please use carriage returns)

> Delivery of hot, fresh, pizza to customers' doorstep. Never delivered a piz

---

Employer: `Smallville Red C`
Job Title:
From: `July 1982`   To: `June 1988`
Description of Duties: (please use carriage returns)

> First-aid and CPR instruction, swimming and water-safety instruction. Me

---

Employer:
Job Title:

Example 5-1 continued

From: [   ] To: [   ]
Description of Duties: (please use carriage returns)

[text area]

Employer: [   ]
Job Title: [   ]
From: [   ] To: [   ]
Description of Duties: (please use carriage returns)

[text area]

Additional Information

Use this area to write any additional information you may wish to include on your resume (e.g. - additional skills, strengths, abilities, etc.). (Please use carriage returns.)

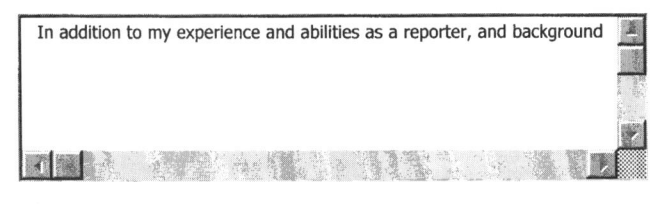

[text area: In addition to my experience and abilities as a reporter, and background]

To format your resume, press this button: [Format]

To clear this form, press this button: [Clear Form]

Part I: Electronic Resumes

Example 5–1 continued

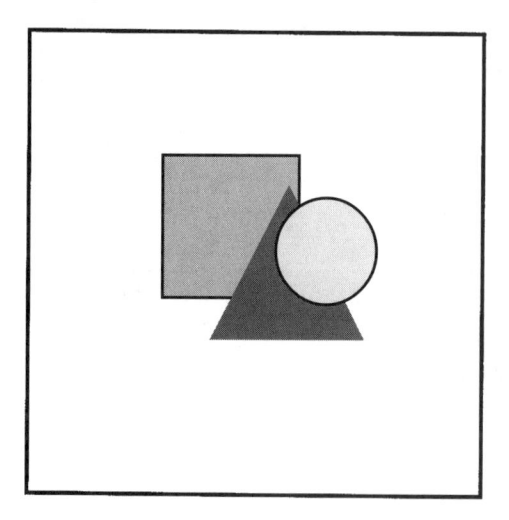

| Home | News and Information | Employment Opportunities | Products | Partners | Technical Support | Creating Your Resume | Table of Contents |

Example 5-2

Clark Kent

Home Address:
1001 Main Street
Apt 321
Metropolis MN 43211-0000

Work Address:
The Daily Planet
Journalism Dept.
100 Planet Ave.
Metropolis MN 43200-0000

Home: 612-555-3221
Work: 612-555-3000
Fax: 612-555-1000

E-mail: ckent@dplanet.com

OBJECTIVE:

A fast-paced job in journalism that expands and builds upon my skills as an experienced reporter.

EMPLOYMENT HISTORY:

Sept. 1990 - Present, Reporter at The Daily Planet

Headline reporting for a major metropolitan newspaper. Responsibilities include in-the-field reporting, writing and editing front page stories, and working closely with other reporters in covering the daily events of the world.

Oct. 1989 - Sept. 1990, Editor at Smallville Gazette

Head Editor and Chief for the Smallville Gazette. Managed a team of four reporters, plus oversight of typesetting and delivery of a newspaper with a subscription of over 600 loyal readers. Also managed fundraising and finances.

June 1988 - Aug. 1989, Delivery Person at Smallville Pizza Plaza

Delivery of hot, fresh, pizza to customers' doorstep. Never delivered a pizza late.

Example 5-2 continued

July 1982 - June 1988, Smallville Red Cross

First-aid and CPR instruction, swimming and water-safety instruction. Member of the Smallville National Disaster team.

EDUCATION:

B.A. in Journalism, Metropolis University, 1988, GPA: 3.75
H.S. in English, Smallville High School, 1984, GPA: 3.8

ADDITIONAL SKILLS:

In addition to my experience and abilities as a reporter, and background with the Red Cross, I can also leap tall buildings in a single bound, fly faster than a speeding bullet, stronger than a locomotive, have X-ray vision, and super-hearing.

Example 5-3

```
<HTML><HEAD>
<TITLE>Resume of Clark Kent</TITLE>
</HEAD>
<BODY BGCOLOR=#E4E4ff LINK=#0000ff VLINK=#0000ff>
<CENTER><H2>Clark Kent</H2><strong>Home Address:</strong><BR>1001 Main Street <BR>Apt 321 <BR>Metropolis MN 43211-0000<P><strong>Work Address:</strong><BR>The Daily Planet <BR>Journalism Dept. <BR>100 Planet Ave. <BR>Metropolis MN 43200-0000<P><strong>Home: </strong>612-555-3221 <BR><strong>Work: </strong>612-555-3000 <BR><strong>Fax: </strong>612-555-1000 <BR><P><strong>E-mail:</strong> ckent@dplanet.com<P></CENTER><H3>OBJECTIVE:</H3>A fast-paced job in journalism that expands and builds upon my skills as an experienced reporter.
<P><H3>EMPLOYMENT HISTORY:</H3><DL><DT><strong>Sept. 1990 - Present, Reporter at The Daily Planet</strong><DD> Headline reporting for a major metropolitan newspaper. Responsibilities include in-the-field reporting, writing and editing front page stories, and working closely with other reports in covering the daily events of the world.

</DL><DL><DT><strong>Oct. 1989 - Sept. 1990, Editor at Smallville Gazette</strong><DD> Head Editor and Chief for the Smallville Gazette. Managed a team of four reporters, plus oversight of typesetting and delivery of a newspaper with a subscription of over 600 loyal readers. Also managed fundraising and finances.
</DL><DL><DT><strong>June 1988 - Aug. 1989, Delivery Person at Smallville Pizza Plaza</strong><DD> Delivery of hot, fresh, pizza to customers' doorstep. Never delivered a pizza late.
</DL><DL><DT><strong>July 1982 - June 1988, Smallville Red Cross</strong><DD> First-aid and CPR instruction, swimming and water-safety instruction.

Member of the Smallville National Disaster team.

</DL><DL><DT><strong></strong></DL><DL><DT><strong></strong></DL><H3>EDUCATION:</H3>B.A. in Journalism, Metropolis University, 1988, GPA: 3.75<BR>H.S. in English, Smallville High School, 1984, GPA: 3.8<BR><H3>ADDITIONAL SKILLS:</H3>In addition to my experience and abilities as a reporter, and background with the Red Cross, I can also leap tall buildings in a single bound, fly faster than a speeding bullet, stronger than a locomotive, have X-ray vision, and super-hearing.
<P></BODY></HTML>
```

Other sites on the WWW provide forms to create HTML resumes. For example, visit the Tripod Resume Builder site at

`http://www.tripod.com/jobs_career/resume/`

At this site, you get a free membership and a free Web site that you can use to build your own HTML resume. At the Tripod site, you complete a short questionnaire about your education and work experience, the kinds of jobs you plan to apply for, the type of employer you're looking for, and so on. Tripod then suggests one of six formats, including chronological, functional, or a combination of each. After you use these forms to create your resume, you can then look at the HTML code and use it elsewhere.

Writing Your Own HTML Code

You can easily build your own HTML resume by learning a few facts about the process. Unlike most word processing programs, where what you see onscreen is what you see when you print out the document, HTML documents are different. They have the following four parts:

- ✔ **Content:** text that can be read on the Web page—your resume, for example.

- ✔ **Tags:** indicators that shape the way the content is displayed but are not seen by the reader.

- ✔ **Links:** connections from one document to another or from one part of a document to another part of the same document.

- ✔ **In-line media:** other media forms, most commonly graphics, that are displayed as part of the document.

Tags

Tags are set apart by angle brackets (< >) and typically occur in pairs—one at the beginning and one at the end of the content they affect. HTML tags are always the first and last tags in an HTML document. They identify where the document begins and ends, as illustrated in the following example:

Beginning of HTML document: `<HTML>`
End of HTML document: `</HTML>`

The head and body tags divide the document into two sections. The head contains the title of the document, which is displayed in the user's WWW browser display window. The title is critical. When a user makes a bookmark, the title becomes the name of the bookmark. More importantly,

World Wide Web search engines catalogue pages according to their title elements. The body contains all the content—the text, the links, and in-line media—that the browser displays.

So far, we have discussed the following tags:

`<HTML>`

`<HEAD>`

`<TITLE>`Fred Jandt's Resume**`</TITLE>`**

`</HEAD>`

`<BODY>`

`</BODY>`

`</HTML>`

Using a background color can enhance your resume's visual appeal if the color isn't overwhelming. To add color, you simply designate the color in the **`<BODY>`** tag. Background color is indicated by specifying a six-digit, hexadecimal (123456789ABCDEF) code. Each six-digit code has two characters for red, green, and blue. Green, blue, and turquoise are indicated as follows:

Green	00FF00
Blue	0000FF
Turquoise	3333FF

To choose a color, go to one of the following sites, pick a color you like, and record its code:

`http://www.lynda.com/hex.html`

or

`http://www.infi.net/wwwimages/colorindex.html`

Then change the **`<BODY>`** tag. For example, if I want my resume to have a turquoise background, I would indicate this color with the following code:

`<BODY BGCOLOR="3333FF">`

Section headings, such as Education on a resume, are created with **`<H>`** tags. There are six levels of headings with **`<H1>`** being the highest level. The actual size of the heading depends on the browser being used. You can make the Education heading on an HTML resume a level three heading by putting it as follows:

`<H3>`Education**`</H3>`**

Line breaks, which use the **`<BR>`** tag, indicate the start of a new line, as you can see in the following examples:

>BA, Texas Lutheran University **`<BR>`**
>
>MA, Stephen F. Austin State University **`<BR>`**
>
>Ph.D, Bowling Green State University **`<BR>`**

Paragraph marks, which use the **`<P>`** tags, indicate to the browser to skip a line.

The **`<HR>`** tag indicates a horizontal line, such as one that you can use to set apart your name and address from the rest of the resume.

Bulleted lists are typical in resumes and are easy to create in HTML. Bulleted lists are referred to as unordered lists, so they use the **`<UL>`** tag. Look at the list that follows:

- Increased sales 15 percent
- Reduced overhead 10 percent

To create this list in HTML, you would code it as follows:

>**`<UL>`**
>
>**`<LI>`**Increased sales 15 percent**`</LI>`**
>
>**`<LI>`**Reduced overhead 10 percent**`</LI>`**
>
>**`</UL>`**

To change from bullets to numbers, change the **`<LI>`** tags to **`<OL>`** tags for ordered list.

Style tags determine the appearance of the content when it is viewed with a browser. The effect of these logical style tags depends on the settings that individual users (the people who view the page) have selected in their browsers. The following list includes the most common visual effects:

Emphasis	`<EM> </EM>`	italics
Strong	`<STRONG> </STRONG>`	bold
Citation	`<CITE> </CITE>`	monospaced font, such as Courier

The person who views the page has little or no control over what are called forced style tags. Four forced style tags that are often used in resumes include the following:

Bold	`<B> </B>`
Italics	`<I> </I>`

Underline	`<U> </U>`
Typewriter text	`<TT> </TT>`

Links

You may want to include a limited number of links in your HTML resume. You can easily add the links by inserting an anchor tag. The general format for an anchor tag is as follows, where `<A` indicates an anchor:

`<A HREF="URL address">Content</A>`

HREF stands for **h**ypertext **ref**erence. This code indicates to the browser to highlight the words in the content area and make them a hot link. When the user clicks on the content word or words, the browser retrieves the document indicated by the URL address. **"URL address"** is the exact location for the page on the Internet. The **Content** is the word or words that will be seen as highlighted to indicate the link. And `</A>` closes the anchor.

To put a link to the publisher of this book in a Web page, the anchor tag would be as follows:

`<A HREF="http://jist.com/">Jist Works, Inc.</A>`

We recommend that you always make your e-mail address a hot link by using an address tag. To create a hot link to one of Fred's e-mail addresses, he would write the following address tag:

`<A HREF=mailto:fjandt@wiley.csusb.edu>fjandt@wiley.csusb.edu</A>`

In-Line Media

You can make video and sound media part of your HTML resume, but these media forms are beyond the scope of this brief introduction. Graphic images are the most common form of in-line media on the Web. An image refers to photos, drawings, and any other pictorial element. The most widely recognized format for in-line images on the Web is GIF, which stands for **G**raphic **I**nterchange **F**ormat. All graphical browsers recognize and are able to display images that are in GIF format. Generally, the GIF file is stored in the same file directory as your HTML document on the host server. When the page is read by a Web browser, the image is called up and displayed automatically. The basic in-line image tag is as follows:

`<IMG SRC="image.format">`

IMG SRC stands for image source. If your photo GIF file is labeled **photo1.gif**, for example, the in-line image tag would be the following:

`<IMG SRC="photo1.gif">`

When your Web page is called up and read by a browser, the photo would be automatically called up and displayed. By default, the text following a graphic is aligned to the bottom of the graphic. If you want text to appear to the side of a graphic, you make the following change to the tag:

```
<IMG SRC=10 ALIGN=LEFT SRC="photo1.gif">
```

The **10** indicates the space between the photo and the text. The **ALIGN=LEFT** indicates where the photo will be in relation to the text.

The HTML File

You can create a test HTML resume in your word processing program. Save the document as text if your word processor does not offer the option of saving it as an HTML document. The file name must have the extension .htm or .html. Then review the resume in a World Wide Web browser. In Netscape, for example, pull down the File menu and choose the Open File option. In the dialog box, indicate your resume file name.

You may want to purchase software for creating HTML documents. These HTML editors simplify the coding process and greatly reduce the HTML you need to know to create a page.

The next step is to upload your HTML resume to the server that will store it and make it available for viewing on the World Wide Web. Web sites have instructions and policies regarding the proper uploading and maintenance of Web pages. Contact the system administrator or the Help desk for specific information.

Getting Help

Remember, these directions are for creating a simple HTML resume. You don't need to be a computer genius to build an HTML resume, but we understand that some of these steps may be confusing. Therefore, you need to know about a site on the Web where you can learn about making an HTML document. Try the site by Bruce Simpson. It's a simple step-by-step online tutorial. You can access it at the following address:

```
http://www.voyager.co.nz/~bsimpson/html.htm
```

For a comprehensive list of helpful publications, go to the following address:

```
http://wwwiz.com/books/html.html
```

Your URL Address

Although you may relocate to a new residence, your HTML resume can remain your permanent address on the Internet so that employers can find you no matter where you have moved to. Basically, you can ensure that employers can find you in two ways: you can register your home page with search engines, and you can link your home page with other sites.

One way to register your home page with search engines is with The PostMaster submission service located at the following address:

```
http://www.netcreations.com/postmaster
```

PostMaster provides a free demo, which submits your site to two dozen top search engines including Alta Vista, Open Text, Webcrawler, and Yahoo.

A second way to keep your URL address is to link your home page with other sites. When a search engine robot—such as those used by Alta Vista—visits a site, it automatically indexes all linked pages at that site. Note that your HTML resume must be linked from somewhere else in the site; it is not enough to be located at a site that the robot visits. The search engine automatically indexes your resume so that it will come up in keyword searches.

Adding Your HTML Resume to Resume Banks

The following list contains the names of some resume banks that simply list your HTML resumes. These banks are fully described with their URL addresses in Part II of this book.

- ✔ **The Entry Level Job Seeker Assistant:** This resume bank is for people who have never held a full-time, permanent job in their field or who have less than a year of nonacademic experience. This bank does not accept resumes; instead, it contains links to your World Wide Web resume. There is no charge for being listed.

- ✔ **The Australian Resume Server:** This resume bank provides an optional free HTML resume home page.

- ✔ **A+ On-line Resumes, Lasting Impressions, Resume-Net, and Your Resume Online:** These resume banks provide resume Web page design, hosting, or promotion for a fee.

Let's check out some sample HTML resumes from the World Wide Web.

Part I: Electronic Resumes ....

HTML Resume 5-4

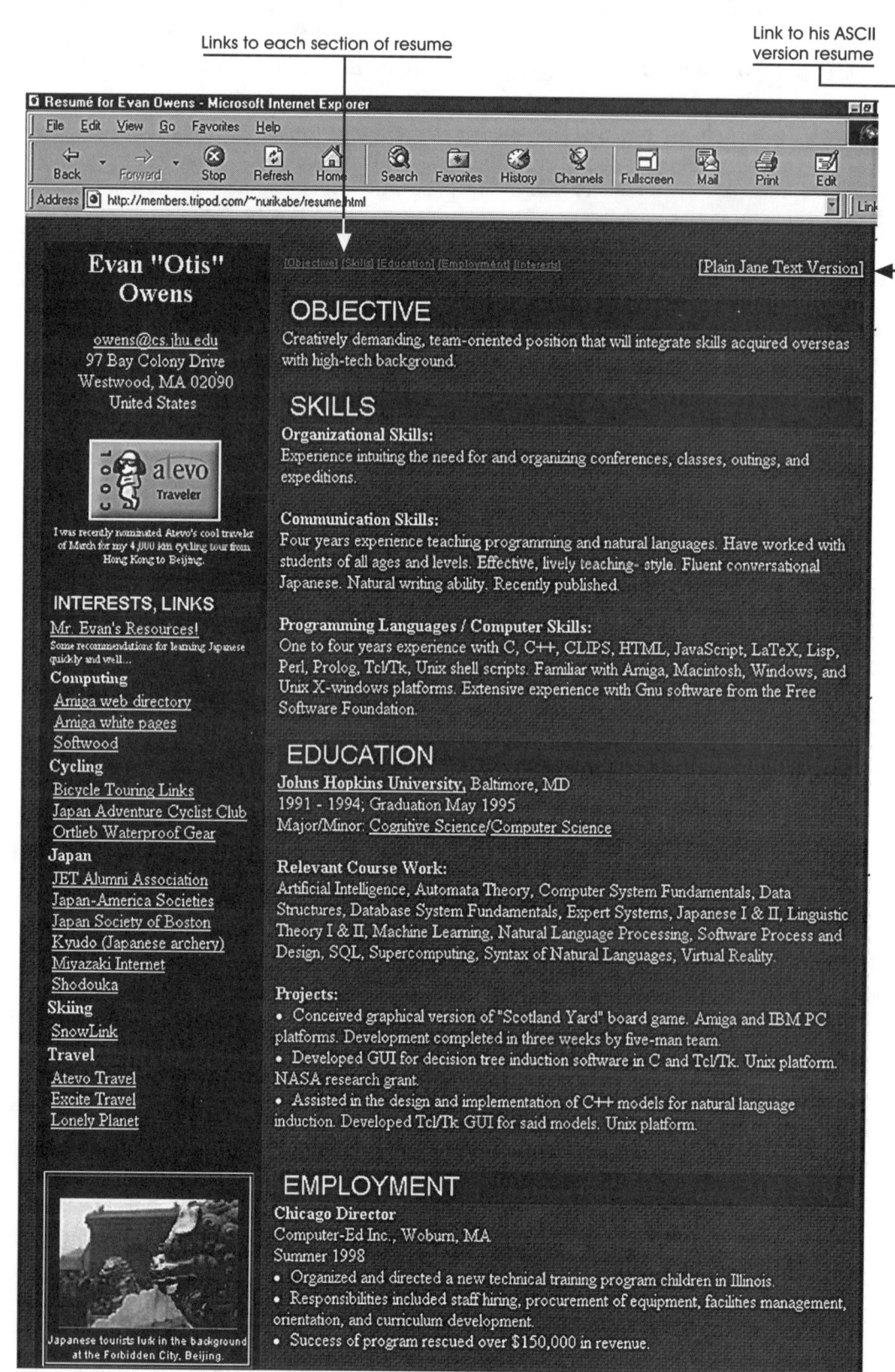

Links to each section of resume

Link to his ASCII version resume

Evan "Otis" Owens

owens@cs.jhu.edu
97 Bay Colony Drive
Westwood, MA 02090
United States

I was recently nominated Atevo's cool traveler of March for my 4,000 km cycling tour from Hong Kong to Beijing.

INTERESTS, LINKS
Mr. Evan's Resources!
Some recommendations for learning Japanese quickly and well...
Computing
Amiga web directory
Amiga white pages
Softwood
Cycling
Bicycle Touring Links
Japan Adventure Cyclist Club
Ortlieb Waterproof Gear
Japan
JET Alumni Association
Japan-America Societies
Japan Society of Boston
Kyudo (Japanese archery)
Miyazaki Internet
Shodouka
Skiing
SnowLink
Travel
Atevo Travel
Excite Travel
Lonely Planet

Japanese tourists lurk in the background at the Forbidden City, Beijing.

[Objective] [Skills] [Education] [Employment] [Interests]   [Plain Jane Text Version]

OBJECTIVE
Creatively demanding, team-oriented position that will integrate skills acquired overseas with high-tech background.

SKILLS

Organizational Skills:
Experience intuiting the need for and organizing conferences, classes, outings, and expeditions.

Communication Skills:
Four years experience teaching programming and natural languages. Have worked with students of all ages and levels. Effective, lively teaching- style. Fluent conversational Japanese. Natural writing ability. Recently published.

Programming Languages / Computer Skills:
One to four years experience with C, C++, CLIPS, HTML, JavaScript, LaTeX, Lisp, Perl, Prolog, Tcl/Tk, Unix shell scripts. Familiar with Amiga, Macintosh, Windows, and Unix X-windows platforms. Extensive experience with Gnu software from the Free Software Foundation.

EDUCATION

Johns Hopkins University, Baltimore, MD
1991 - 1994; Graduation May 1995
Major/Minor: Cognitive Science/Computer Science

Relevant Course Work:
Artificial Intelligence, Automata Theory, Computer System Fundamentals, Data Structures, Database System Fundamentals, Expert Systems, Japanese I & II, Linguistic Theory I & II, Machine Learning, Natural Language Processing, Software Process and Design, SQL, Supercomputing, Syntax of Natural Languages, Virtual Reality.

Projects:
• Conceived graphical version of "Scotland Yard" board game. Amiga and IBM PC platforms. Development completed in three weeks by five-man team.
• Developed GUI for decision tree induction software in C and Tcl/Tk. Unix platform. NASA research grant.
• Assisted in the design and implementation of C++ models for natural language induction. Developed Tcl/Tk GUI for said models. Unix platform.

EMPLOYMENT

Chicago Director
Computer-Ed Inc., Woburn, MA
Summer 1998
• Organized and directed a new technical training program children in Illinois.
• Responsibilities included staff hiring, procurement of equipment, facilities management, orientation, and curriculum development.
• Success of program rescued over $150,000 in revenue.

HTML Resume 5-4 continued

Counter

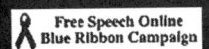

Free Speech Online
Blue Ribbon Campaign

This resumé has been visited 465 times since March 1, 1998.

Graphics Specialist
Colgate Pharmaceuticals, Canton, MA
Winter 1998
- Responsible for design and layout of customized logos using Adobe Illustrator and Photoshop.
- Maintained SAP customer database.
- Prioritized orders to adhere to tight production schedule.
- Coordinated efforts of sales, graphics, and production departments to ensure high quality and timely delivery of products.

Educator in Japan
Japan Exchange and Teaching Programme, Sadowara, Miyazaki, Japan
Summer, 1995 - Summer, 1997
- Hired by Japan's Ministry of Education to work with the Sadowara Board of Education.
- Developed course material.
- Conducted classes in elementary school, middle school, and adult education curricula.
- Periodically served as translator/interpreter.
- Editor of prefecture-wide English-language newsletter.
- Conceived of and organized weekly, prefecture-wide round-table discussions to improve the quality of English education in Miyazaki.

Score Report from the Japanese-Language Proficiency Test

NASA / HST Research Team Member
Medium Deep Survey, Johns Hopkins University, Baltimore, MD
Spring Semester, 1995
- Investigated methods for the classification of galactic morphology in Hubble Space Telescope data. Designed and customized software written in C with supporting Perl scripts.
- Results published as "Using Oblique Decision Trees for the Morphological Classification of Galaxies," Monthly Notices of the Royal Astronomical Society, 281, 153.

Teaching Assistant
Dept. of Computer Science, Johns Hopkins University, Baltimore, MD
Spring Semester, 1993; Spring Semester, 1993; Fall Semester, 1994 Prepared and graded material for multiple courses, including
- Intermediate Programming in C++.
- Organized and conducted additional lectures in all courses.

Educator
Computer-Ed, High-Tech Camp, Newton, MA
Summer, 1993; Summer 1994
- Taught a variety of classes, including Advanced Programming in C++ and Artificial Intelligence Programming in CLIPS.
- Organized extracurricular activities for groups of over 150.
- Director of Counselor Training, 1994.

References furnished upon request

This page written entirely in hand-coded HTML. No artificial preservatives, flavorings, or colors.

[Objective] [Skills] [Education] [Employment] [Interests]

Part I: Electronic Resumes

Plain Text Version of HTML Resume 5-4

Link to HTML version

It is a good idea to put all contact information in one place

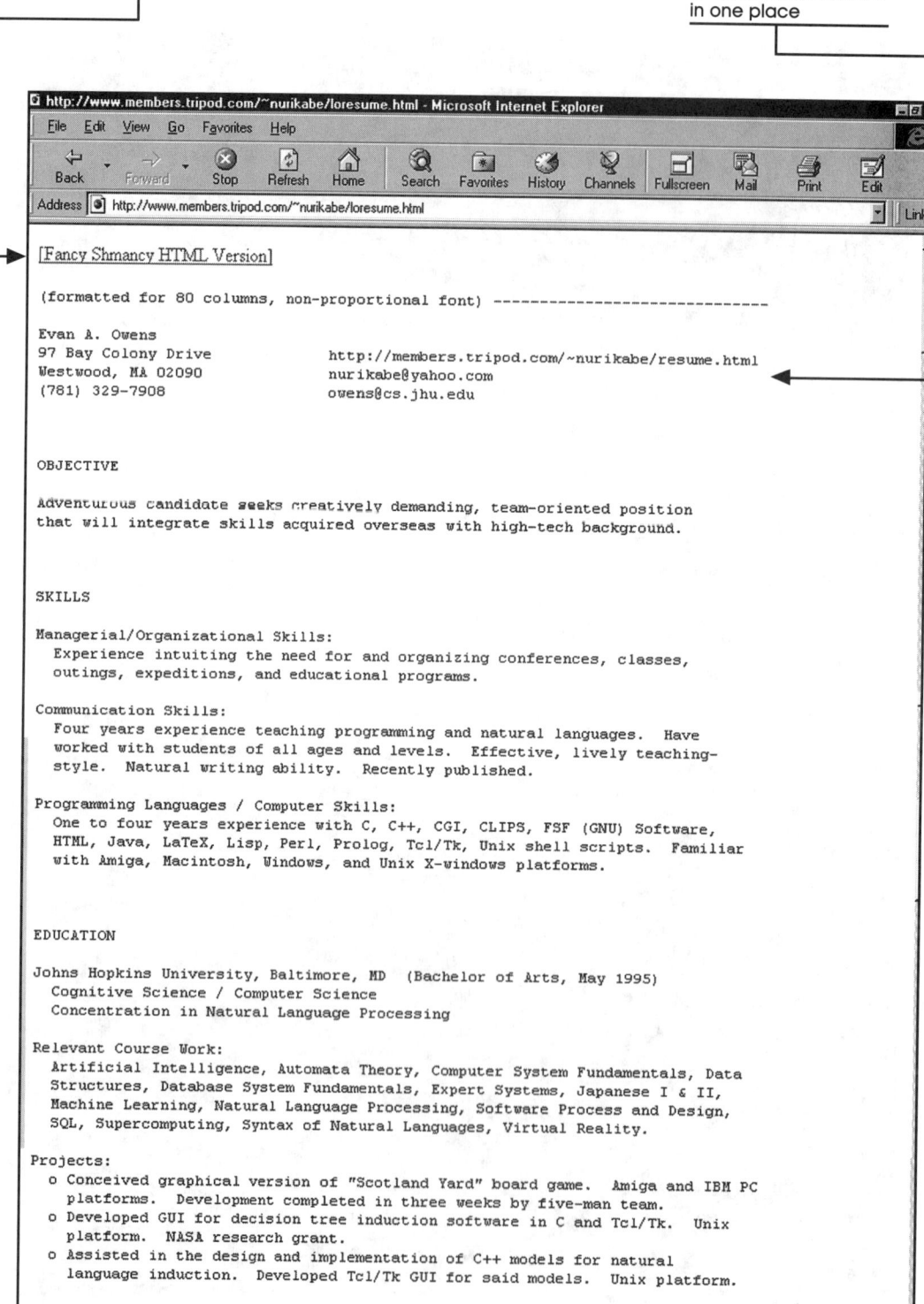

```
[Fancy Shmancy HTML Version]

(formatted for 80 columns, non-proportional font) -----------------------------

Evan A. Owens
97 Bay Colony Drive              http://members.tripod.com/~nurikabe/resume.html
Westwood, MA 02090               nurikabe@yahoo.com
(781) 329-7908                   owens@cs.jhu.edu



OBJECTIVE

Adventurous candidate seeks creatively demanding, team-oriented position
that will integrate skills acquired overseas with high-tech background.



SKILLS

Managerial/Organizational Skills:
  Experience intuiting the need for and organizing conferences, classes,
  outings, expeditions, and educational programs.

Communication Skills:
  Four years experience teaching programming and natural languages.  Have
  worked with students of all ages and levels.  Effective, lively teaching-
  style.  Natural writing ability.  Recently published.

Programming Languages / Computer Skills:
  One to four years experience with C, C++, CGI, CLIPS, FSF (GNU) Software,
  HTML, Java, LaTeX, Lisp, Perl, Prolog, Tcl/Tk, Unix shell scripts.  Familiar
  with Amiga, Macintosh, Windows, and Unix X-windows platforms.



EDUCATION

Johns Hopkins University, Baltimore, MD   (Bachelor of Arts, May 1995)
  Cognitive Science / Computer Science
  Concentration in Natural Language Processing

Relevant Course Work:
  Artificial Intelligence, Automata Theory, Computer System Fundamentals, Data
  Structures, Database System Fundamentals, Expert Systems, Japanese I & II,
  Machine Learning, Natural Language Processing, Software Process and Design,
  SQL, Supercomputing, Syntax of Natural Languages, Virtual Reality.

Projects:
  o Conceived graphical version of "Scotland Yard" board game.  Amiga and IBM PC
    platforms.  Development completed in three weeks by five-man team.
  o Developed GUI for decision tree induction software in C and Tcl/Tk.  Unix
    platform.  NASA research grant.
  o Assisted in the design and implementation of C++ models for natural
    language induction.  Developed Tcl/Tk GUI for said models.  Unix platform.
```

96

Plain Text Version of HTML Resume 5-4 continued

```
EXPERIENCE

Summer 1998       Director, Computer-Ed Lake Forest
                  Computer-Ed Inc., Woburn, MA
                      o Organized and directed a new technical training program for
                        children in Illinois.
                      o Responsibilities included staff hiring, procurement of
                        equipment, facilities management, orientation, and curric-
                        ulum development.
                      o Success of program rescued over $150,000 in revenue.

Winter 1998       Graphics Specialist, Brush Imprinting Plant
                  Colgate Pharmaceuticals, Canton, MA
                      o Responsible for design and layout of customized toothbrush
                        logos using Adobe Illustrator and Photoshop.
                      o Maintained SAP customer database.
                      o Prioritized orders to adhere to tight production schedule.
                      o Coordinated efforts of sales, graphics, and production dep-
                        artments to ensure high quality and timely delivery of
                        products.

1995 - 1997       Educator, Japan Exchange and Teaching Programme (JET)
                  Sadowara, Miyazaki, Japan
                      o Hired by Japan's Ministry of Education to work with the
                        Sadowara Board of Education.
                      o Developed course material.
                      o Conducted classes in elementary school, middle school, and
                        adult education curricula.
                      o Periodically served as translator/interpreter.
                      o Editor of prefecture-wide English-language newsletter.
                      o Conceived of and organized weekly, prefecture-wide round-
                        table discussions to improve the quality of English education
                        in Miyazaki.

Spring 1995       NASA / MDS Research Team Member, Department of Physics & Astronomy
                  Johns Hopkins University, Baltimore, MD
                      o Investigated methods for the classification of galactic morph-
                        ology in Hubble Space Telescope data.  Design and augmentation
                        of software written in C with supporting Perl scripts.
                      o Completed software used to aid in the automatic classification
                        of HST data thereby freeing researchers from this task.
                      o Results published in Monthly Notices of the Royal Astronomical
                        Society, 281, 153.

1992 - 1994       Teaching Assistant, Computer Science Department
                  Johns Hopkins University, Baltimore, MD
                      o Prepared and graded material for multiple courses, including
                        Intermediate Programming in C++.
                      o Organized and conducted additional lectures in all courses.

1993, 1994        Educator, Computer-Ed
                  Lasell College, Newton, MA
                      o Taught a variety of classes, including Advanced Programming
                        in C++ and Artificial Intelligence Programming in CLIPS.
                      o Organized extracurricular activities for groups of over 150.
                      o Director of Counselor Training, 1994.


INTERESTS

Cycling, downhill skiing/snowboarding, foreign film & subtitling, travel.
During the summer of 1997, organized and executed a solo cycling tour from Hong
Kong to Beijing.


References furnished upon request
```

Part I: Electronic Resumes

HTML Resume 5-5

Actress's resume includes photo...

...and personal information

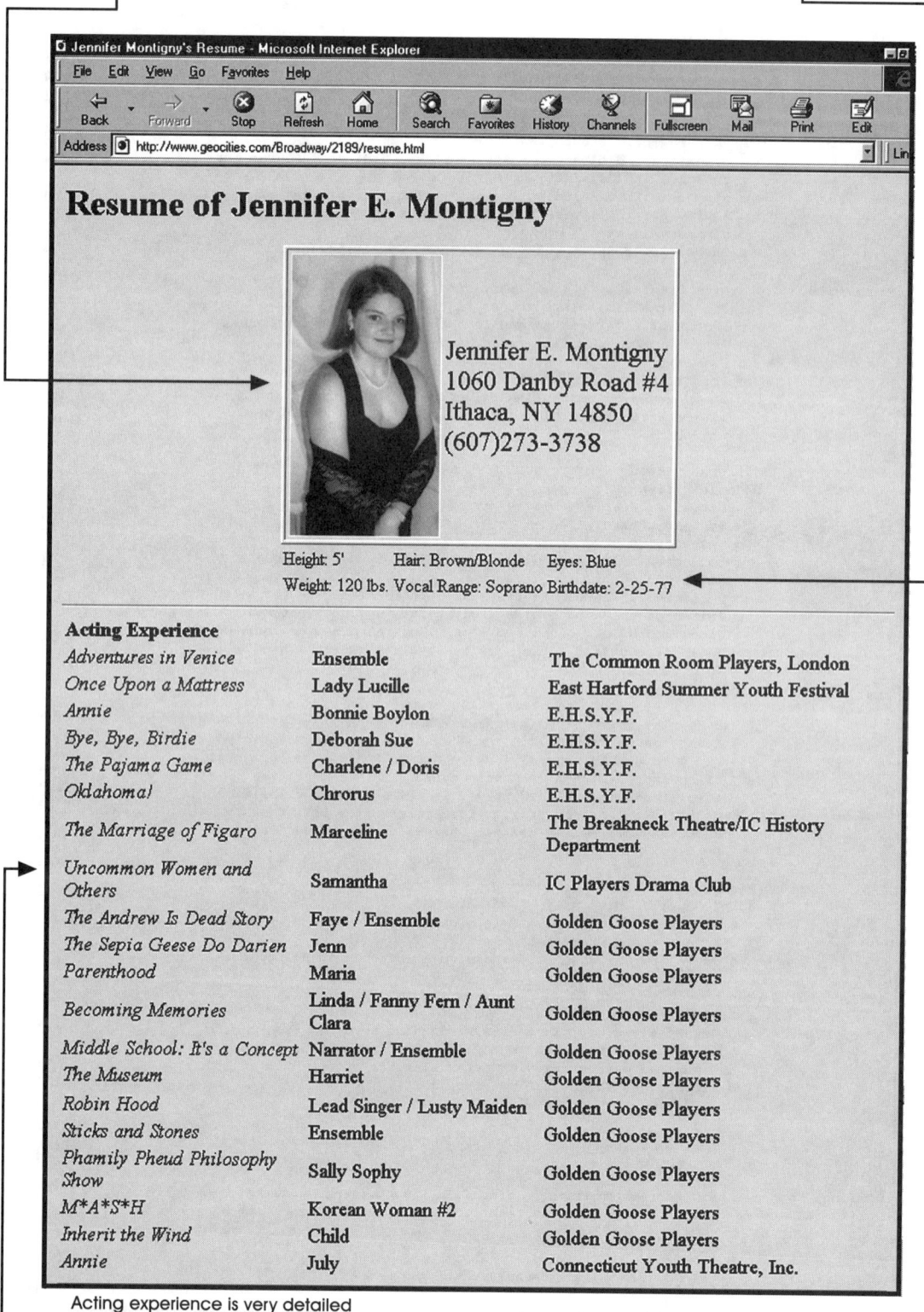

Resume of Jennifer E. Montigny

Jennifer E. Montigny
1060 Danby Road #4
Ithaca, NY 14850
(607)273-3738

Height: 5'   Hair: Brown/Blonde   Eyes: Blue
Weight: 120 lbs.   Vocal Range: Soprano   Birthdate: 2-25-77

Acting Experience

Adventures in Venice	Ensemble	The Common Room Players, London
Once Upon a Mattress	Lady Lucille	East Hartford Summer Youth Festival
Annie	Bonnie Boylon	E.H.S.Y.F.
Bye, Bye, Birdie	Deborah Sue	E.H.S.Y.F.
The Pajama Game	Charlene / Doris	E.H.S.Y.F.
Oklahoma!	Chorus	E.H.S.Y.F.
The Marriage of Figaro	Marceline	The Breakneck Theatre/IC History Department
Uncommon Women and Others	Samantha	IC Players Drama Club
The Andrew Is Dead Story	Faye / Ensemble	Golden Goose Players
The Sepia Geese Do Darien	Jenn	Golden Goose Players
Parenthood	Maria	Golden Goose Players
Becoming Memories	Linda / Fanny Fern / Aunt Clara	Golden Goose Players
Middle School: It's a Concept	Narrator / Ensemble	Golden Goose Players
The Museum	Harriet	Golden Goose Players
Robin Hood	Lead Singer / Lusty Maiden	Golden Goose Players
Sticks and Stones	Ensemble	Golden Goose Players
Phamily Pheud Philosophy Show	Sally Sophy	Golden Goose Players
M*A*S*H	Korean Woman #2	Golden Goose Players
Inherit the Wind	Child	Golden Goose Players
Annie	July	Connecticut Youth Theatre, Inc.

Acting experience is very detailed

98

HTML Resume 5-5 continued

Shows different types of experience, besides acting

Scenes

The Thickness of Skin	Laura	with Susannah Berryman, 1997
The Glass Menagerie	Laura	with Judy Levitt, 1996
Ambrosio	Antonia	with Barbara Anger, 1996
From *Win, Lose, Draw Little Miss Fresno*	Doris	with Barbara Anger, 1995

Technical Experience

Stage Manager	*Adventures in Venice*	The Common Room Players, London
Stage Manager, Tech Director, Lighting Designer, Set Designer	*Anne of Green Gables*	Lake Bryn Mawr Camp
Stage Manager, Tech Director, Lighting Designer, Set Designer	*Rogers and Hammerstein Revue*	Lake Bryn Mawr Camp
Stage Manager, Tech Director, Lighting Designer, Set Designer	*Joseph and the Amazing Technicolor Dreamcoat*	Lake Bryn Mawr Camp
Sound Crew	*The Bartered Bride*	Ithaca College Theatre
Electrics Crew, Spotlight Operator	*1776*	Ithaca College Theatre
Spotlight Supervisor and Operator	*The 6th Annual RHS Talent Show*	The RHS Service Club
Spotlight Supervisor and Operator	*The Mr. RHS Pagent*	The RHS Senior Class
Spotlight Operator	*Trixie the Teen Detective*	The Golden Goose Players

Directing Experience

The Marriage of Figaro by Beaumarchais; A staged reading produced in association with the IC History Department, April, 1997
Parenthood an original One-Act produced at the Golden Goose Players' Evening of One-Acts 1995
Sistertales an original One-Act produced at the Golden Goose Players' Evening of One-Acts 1994

Playwriting Experience

With a Little Help an original One-Act in progress, 1998
Water an original, absurd One-Act with Jonah VanSpreecken, 1998
The Lighter Side of the Trojan War an original One-Act, 1998
Music Is My Life an original Monologue featured in the Golden Goose Players' collection *It Could Happen To You*, 1995
Parenthood an original One-Act produced at the Golden Goose Players' Evening of One-Acts 1995
Sistertales an original One-Act produced at the Golden Goose Players' Evening of One-Acts 1994
Clytemnestra's Way an original Video Script awarded First Place in English Prose at the Connecticut State Latin Day 1994

HTML Resume 5–5 continued

Use of humor is okay for a theatrical resume

Training

Playwrighting with J. Fred Pritt (1998)
Aesthetics and Criticism with J. Fred Pritt (1998)
British Styles of Acting with Mel Churcher (1997)
Acting II with Susannah Berryman (1997)
Acting I with Judith Levitt (1996)
Intro to Acting II with Barbara Anger (1996)
Intro to Acting I with Barbara Anger (1995)
Advanced Acting with Margaret Kline (1994-5); including multiple public performances culminating with an appearance at the Connecticut Drama Association Festival 1995
Intro to Theatre II with Margaret Kline (1994); concentration on Acting
Intro to Theatre I with Margaret Kline (1993); concentration on Technical Theatre
Catholic Choir at Ithaca College's Muller Chapel 9PM services, including holidays (1995-)
Women's Choir with Eileen Sullivan (1991-5); performing a variety of pieces including Madrigals, Classical, Jazz, and Showtunes
Mixed Choir with Eileen Sullivan (1991-5), Thomas Faris (1988-91), and Anne Baldwin (1986-88); performing a variety of pieces including Classical, Madrigals, Jazz, and Showtunes
Private Voice Lessons with Salvadore Cicciarella (1994-5) and Marion Hanson (1995); studying Classical, Operatic, and Showtunes
Intro to Design with Craig Clipper (1996)
*Availaible upon request: Ithaca College Transcript including related courses and grades

Special Skills

Recent Spokesmodel for *Drippo Orphan Gruel*, Played Guest Kazoo with the Massachusetts Institute of Technology Marching Band, Can twirl a flag (Member of the RHS Marching "Ram" Band Color Guard 1993-5), Has experience in elementary Jazz and Ballet, Learns rapidly, Currently holding a 3.6 GPA, Multiple appearance on Dean's List and member of Oracle Society, Works well with others, and runs with scissors.

Return to Jenn's Homepage

Like me? E-mail at Ifferjenn@aol.com

Includes a link to the home page...

...and e-mail

HTML Resume 5-6

Animated fishtail and bubbles. Nice artwork because resume is for design

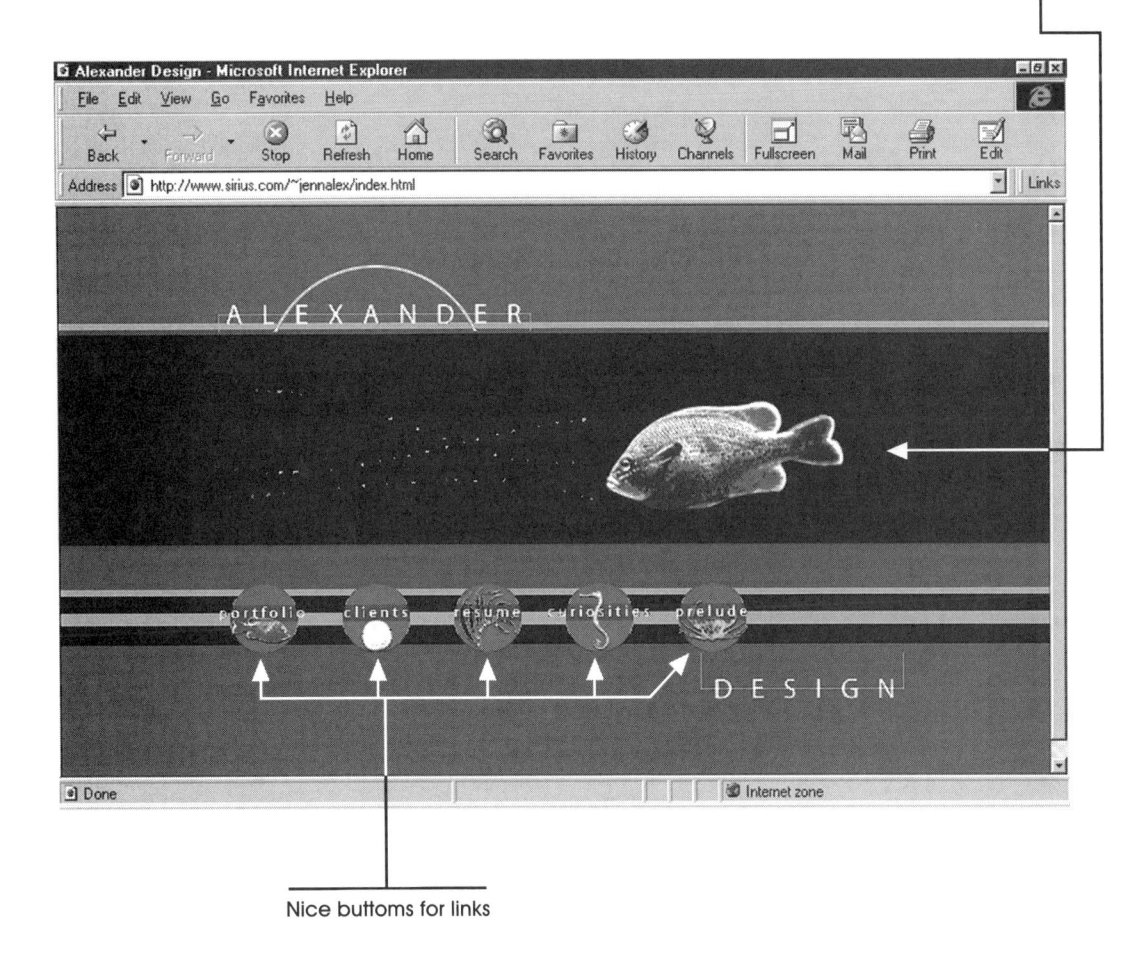

Nice buttoms for links

Part I: Electronic Resumes

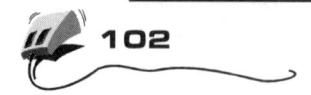

HTML Resume 5-6 continued

Phone number is prominently displayed

JENNIFER ALEXANDER
designer

4 1 5 . 3 3 3 . 1 5 7 9   jennalex@sirius.com

education

B.F.A. Scene Design - The North Carolina School of the Arts

experience

portfolio
clients
curiosities
prelude
entrance
exit

Alexander Design

Freelance Web Design: All aspects of site concept and production. (4/96-Current)

Projects include:

- Organic Online **-Designer**
  Developed concepts, created and implemented designs for proposals, banners, and active websites. (8/97-12/97)

  Clients include:
  Feld Entertainment (aka. Ringling Bros and Barnum and Bailey)* - Proposal
  Hyundai* - Proposal
  eBay* - Banners
  Palm Pilot* - Proposal
  Netgrocer - Production

  *Contact for visuals

- eMergingmedia **-Designer**
  Created template designs, as well as new elements for pre-existing designs (11/97-2/98).

  Clients include:
  Intershop - Designed templates
  the goodguys - Created elements for pre-existing designs
  Brightware - Proposal

- Symantec **-Designer**
  Designed logo and web presence for the Authorized Training Center division of the company. (6/97-8/97)
  URL: http://www-cu.symantec.com/javacentral/atc/intro.html

- Sage Interactive/Bay Networks **-Designer**
  Worked in conjunction with these two companies to create a web environment to be used as an online sales tool. (6/96-9/96)

HTML Resume 5-6 continued

Links to examples of work

- Numenet/Oracle -**Designer**
  Developed a look and feel for a business resource in collaboration with these two companies. Illustrated graphics for Numenet's Home site. (5/96-7/96)
  URL: http://www.sirius.com/~jennalex/numenet/brr-bl2.html
  URL: http://www.numenet.com

Cybernautics

Lead Designer/Project Director : Project direction, graphic design, interface design, site architecture, animation, and HTML. (9/96-4/97)

Projects include:

- Turner Interactive -**Project Director**- *Space Ghost*
  Directed project from concept through completion. Guided the overall artistic vision, managed a team of artists, designers, and writers, and created most of the design work.
  URL: http://www.sirius.com/~jennalex/sgfinals
- Netiva -**Project Director**
  Developed overall design concept, led a team of designers, supervised the web commerce area of the site as well as the BBS implementation.
  URL: http://www.netiva.com
- NetChannel -**Interface Designer**
- Microprose -**Production Graphics and HTML**
- Diamond Multimedia -**Production Graphics and HTML**

Mt. Lake Software

Designer: Created original content and design for a young web-savvy crowd. (7/95-5/96)

Projects include:

- Cyberteens -**Designer**
  Created several award winning Shockwave animations and developed the design interface for the main body of this website geared for teenagers.
  URL: http://www.cyberteens.com/ctmain.html
  URL: http://www.cyberteens.com/multimedia/shockwave/index.html
- Cyberkids Launchpad -**Designer and Content Developer**
  Compiled links for this vast kid safe resource, wrote commentary and designed banners.
  URL: http://www.cyberkids.com/Launchpad/Launchpad.html

Part I: Electronic Resumes

HTML Resume 5–6 continued

CMP Media/Woodwind Internet Services

Designer and Illustrator: Basic Web development for a wide range of clients (7/95-3/96)

Projects include:

- NetGuide -**Designer**
  Designed prototypes for an online web service
- Bank of America -**Designer**
  Basic HTML and graphics manipulation
- Ketchum Kitchen -**Designer**
  Basic HTML and graphics manipulation
- Weblust -**Designer**
  Created a few graphics, but wrote commentary for much of the site.
  URL: http://www.weblust.com/links/women.html
- Woodwind Internet Services -**Designer**
- George Coates Performance Works -**Designer**

notices

Shocked Site of the Day
4 Star Magellan Site
C|Net's Best of the Web
Nominated for the Global Information Infrastructure Awards

"...One very imaginative and fantasia-like Shockwave movie runs on a page created by Cyberteens...."-The New York Times

skills

Computer Skills: Photoshop 4.0, Illustrator 6.0.1, Painter 4.0, Director 5.0, HTML 3.2, Autocad 13, Strata Studio Pro

Related Skills: Drawing, Painting, Sculpting, Model Building, Drafting, Carpentry, Basic Electronics, Lighting Design, Sound Design, Public Speaking, Directing, Writing

References available upon request

Good idea to include a positive review of work

Chapter 5: Your Own HTML Resume

HTML Resume 5-7

Street and Web page addresses

Contains illustration samples

Angie Mason

36 Manner Avenue Garfield, New Jersey 07026-1410
www.angiemason.com

http://www.angiemason.com/res_ill.htm

Education
- Parsons School Of Design B.F.A. Illustration
- New School for Social Research course work
- Ridgewood Art Institute studio classes
- Summer Arts Institute of NJ intensive five week painting program
- Center for Book Arts book binding workshop

Exhibits
- N.J. Arts Council Exhibition Tour includes exhibits @ Johnsons' & Johnsons' and Mutual Life Benefit Corp.
- Parsons B.F.A. Exhibit + Represented in Private Collections

Awards
- Deans' List @ Parsons School Of Design
- Parsons 98 Catalog Chosen to represent Illustration Dept.
- Parsons Tuition Scholarship
- Mutual Life Benefit Award for excellence in the arts

Employment
- UN Productions Creative Producer — print, net + media production + design, original character design
- Snailworks Publishing Production Designer — original character + font design, scanning, color corrections
- The Puppet Company Assistant Internship — restoration of puppets + general office duties
- The Childrens' Museum of Manhattan — volunteered to assist with childrens' activities
- Pearl Paint displays, customer relations, general retail duties

Media Watercolor, color pencil, acrylic, computer, gouache, collage, pen + ink, marker, printmaking, oil, clay, wood and fabric

Software Photoshop, Illustrator, Quark Express, Freehand, Painter
BBEdit, Hot Dog Pro, Fontographer, Pagemaker + Acrobat

Hardware Skilled with both Macintosh and Windows operating systems. Presently own a Mac, a PC + a color scanner.

Portfolio Available Upon Request

973*253*1244

All images & NOOKS font © Angie Mason 1997

All images + writings © 1995-98 Angie Mason

Note copyright, due to artwork

Prominent phone number

105

Part I: Electronic Resumes ....

HTML Resume 5–7 continued

Two versions of resume highlighting different skills

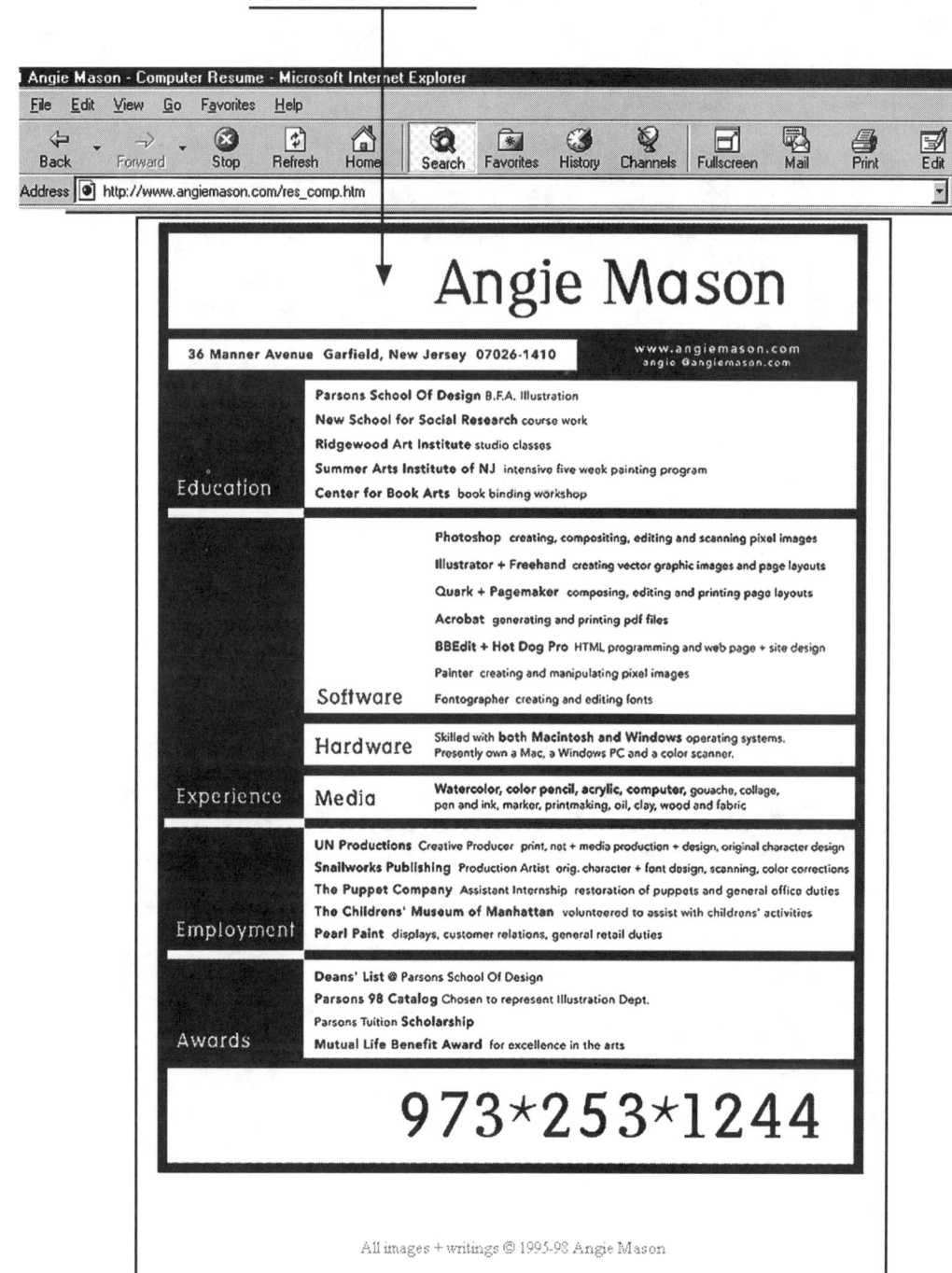

Angie Mason - Computer Resume - Microsoft Internet Explorer

Address: http://www.angiemason.com/res_comp.htm

Angie Mason

36 Manner Avenue Garfield, New Jersey 07026-1410
www.angiemason.com
angie@angiemason.com

Education
Parsons School Of Design B.F.A. Illustration
New School for Social Research course work
Ridgewood Art Institute studio classes
Summer Arts Institute of NJ intensive five week painting program
Center for Book Arts book binding workshop

Experience

Software
- **Photoshop** creating, compositing, editing and scanning pixel images
- **Illustrator + Freehand** creating vector graphic images and page layouts
- **Quark + Pagemaker** composing, editing and printing page layouts
- **Acrobat** generating and printing pdf files
- **BBEdit + Hot Dog Pro** HTML programming and web page + site design
- **Painter** creating and manipulating pixel images
- **Fontographer** creating and editing fonts

Hardware Skilled with **both Macintosh and Windows** operating systems. Presently own a Mac, a Windows PC and a color scanner.

Media Watercolor, color pencil, acrylic, computer, gouache, collage, pen and ink, marker, printmaking, oil, clay, wood and fabric

Employment
UN Productions Creative Producer print, net + media production + design, original character design
Snailworks Publishing Production Artist orig. character + font design, scanning, color corrections
The Puppet Company Assistant Internship restoration of puppets and general office duties
The Childrens' Museum of Manhattan volunteered to assist with childrens' activities
Pearl Paint displays, customer relations, general retail duties

Awards
Deans' List @ Parsons School Of Design
Parsons 98 Catalog Chosen to represent Illustration Dept.
Parsons Tuition Scholarship
Mutual Life Benefit Award for excellence in the arts

973*253*1244

All images + writings © 1995-98 Angie Mason

106

Chapter 5: Your Own HTML Resume

HTML Resume 5-8

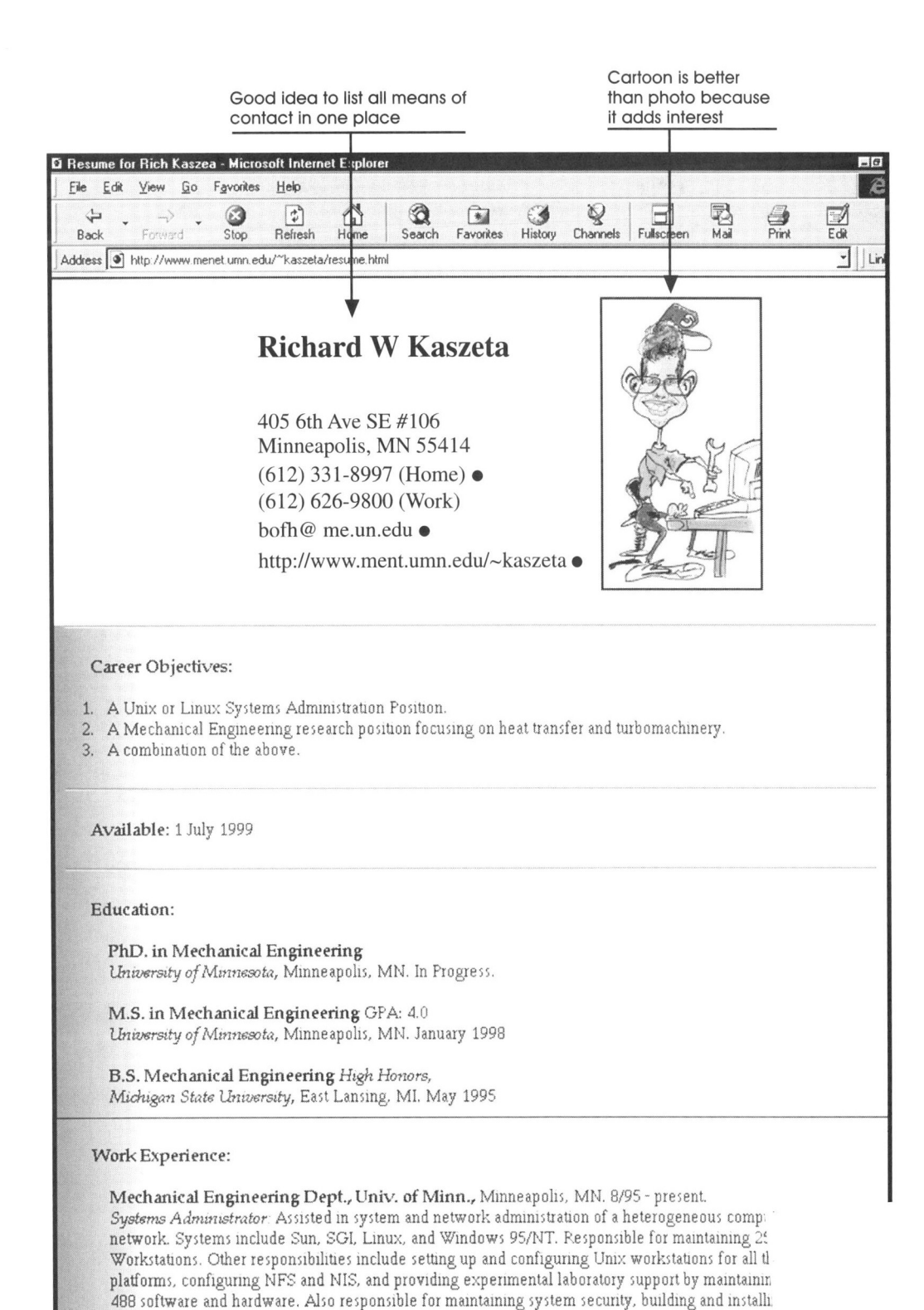

Good idea to list all means of contact in one place

Cartoon is better than photo because it adds interest

Resume for Rich Kaszea - Microsoft Internet Explorer

File Edit View Go Favorites Help

Back Forward Stop Refresh Home Search Favorites History Channels Fullscreen Mail Print Edit

Address: http://www.menet.umn.edu/~kaszeta/resume.html

Richard W Kaszeta

405 6th Ave SE #106
Minneapolis, MN 55414
(612) 331-8997 (Home) •
(612) 626-9800 (Work)
bofh@ me.un.edu •
http://www.ment.umn.edu/~kaszeta •

Career Objectives:

1. A Unix or Linux Systems Administration Position.
2. A Mechanical Engineering research position focusing on heat transfer and turbomachinery.
3. A combination of the above.

Available: 1 July 1999

Education:

PhD. in Mechanical Engineering
University of Minnesota, Minneapolis, MN. In Progress.

M.S. in Mechanical Engineering GPA: 4.0
University of Minnesota, Minneapolis, MN. January 1998

B.S. Mechanical Engineering *High Honors,*
Michigan State University, East Lansing, MI. May 1995

Work Experience:

Mechanical Engineering Dept., Univ. of Minn., Minneapolis, MN. 8/95 - present.
Systems Administrator: Assisted in system and network administration of a heterogeneous comp network. Systems include Sun, SGI, Linux, and Windows 95/NT. Responsible for maintaining 25 Workstations. Other responsibilities include setting up and configuring Unix workstations for all t platforms, configuring NFS and NIS, and providing experimental laboratory support by maintainin 488 software and hardware. Also responsible for maintaining system security, building and installi software, and providing software and hardware support.

HTML Resume 5–8 continued

Mechanical Engineering Dept., Univ. of Minn., Minneapolis, MN. 7/96 - Present.
National Science Foundation (NSF) Fellowship: Conducting research on turbulent fluid flow and heat transfer in gas turbine flows (Wake-Induced Turbulent Boundary Layer Transition in Low-Pressure Turbine Blades).

Mechanical Engineering Dept., Univ. of Minn., Minneapolis, MN. 3/96 - 6/96.
Teaching Assistant: Assisted in the teaching of the graduate level course ME 8332: Radiation

Mechanical Engineering Dept., Univ. of Minn., Minneapolis, MN. 8/95 - 7/96.
Graduate Research Assistant: Conducting research on turbulent fluid flow and heat transfer in gas turbine flows (film cooling).

Oak Ridge National Laboratory, High Flux Isotope Reactor, Oak Ridge, TN. 5-8/95, and 5-8/94.
Assistant Systems Administrator and Engineering Intern: Responsibilities included Unix systems administration for Linux and AIX machines, engineering software development, and conducting mechanical analyses of spent fuel storage arrays.

Oak Ridge National Laboratory, High Flux Isotope Reactor, Oak Ridge, TN. 9-12/93.
Engineering Intern: Developed and implemented a x-ray based technique for verifying the thickness of cadmium sheeting in spent-fuel storage shrouds.

Michigan State University, Thermal Engineering Research Laboratory, East Lansing, MI. 9/91-5/95.
Research Assistant: Assisted primary researchers in a variety of thermal engineering projects, including thermal property measurements of live tree tissue, electro-rheological (ER) fluids, R134a refrigerant, and silver-tin solder. Also developed software for interpretation of Mach-Zender interferometry images.

Computer Related Experience:

Operating Systems: Various flavors of Unix including Solaris, SunOS, IRIX, and Linux; and MS-DOS/Windows;

Computer Hardware: Sun, SGI, IBM PC, IEEE-448 devices.

Networks: Ethernet, ATM, TCP/IP, Internet, and Appletalk.

Computer Languages: Perl, C, C++, FORTRAN, [c]sh, HTML, Java, and Pascal.

Personal: Own and administrate a private Unix system in my home. Also a software developer for the Debian Linux Project.

Miscellaneous: TeX/LaTeX, Internet News, Anonymous ftp, WWW, GPIB, Process Control, ssh, PGP/GPG, and other assorted topics.

Heat Transfer Related Experience:

Experimental Methods: Hot Wire Anemometry, Various Flow Visualization Techniques, Thermocouples, and Computer Controlled Data Acquistion.

Graduate Course Work: Courses have focused on heat transfer (conduction, convection, and radation), thermal design, experimental methods, turbulence, fluid dynamics, and computational modelling of fluid flow and heat transfer.

HTML Resume 5–8 continued

Notable Web Publications and Tools:

X Window System Terminals: A New Use for Old and Outdated PCs, published in the April 1998 Linux Gazette.

The Crappy Divesite Home Page, a guide to inexpensive diving in lakes, quarries, and rivers. Listed as one of the top 50 scuba-related web sites by Rodale's Scuba Diving Magazine, and featured in the Aqua magazine's series "Diving Across America" (April/May 1998).

VR Chia Head, a Java applet which allows you to interactively "spin" our department's Chia Head. Selected for inclusion on Bonus.Com, the web site for kids.

CoffeeCam, a web page showing the real-time status of our office's coffee maker. Winner of the Editors' Choice Award from Goto.Com.

The ME/AEM Pressure Server, a page which shows both the real-time atmospheric pressure and the last week's pressure history, which is used to support departmental research activities, with interfaces via C, http, telnet, and the unix command line.

Recent Technical Publications:

Kaszeta, R.W., Oke, R.A., Burd, S.W., and Simon, T.W., "Flow Measurements in Film Cooling Flows with Lateral Injection(draft)." ASME Paper 98-GT-54, presented at the 1998 Turbo Expo, Stockholm, Sweden. (also available as postscript).

Burd, S.W., Kaszeta, R.W., and Simon, T.W. "Measurements in Film Cooling Flows: Hole L/D and Turbulence Intensity Effects." ASME Paper 96-WA/HT-7, presented at the 1996 IMECE.

References: Available upon request.

Richard Kaszeta kaszeta@me.umn.edu

E-mail link at bottom of resume is a good idea

Part I: Electronic Resumes

HTML Resume 5-9

E-mail address only; this should include a phone number

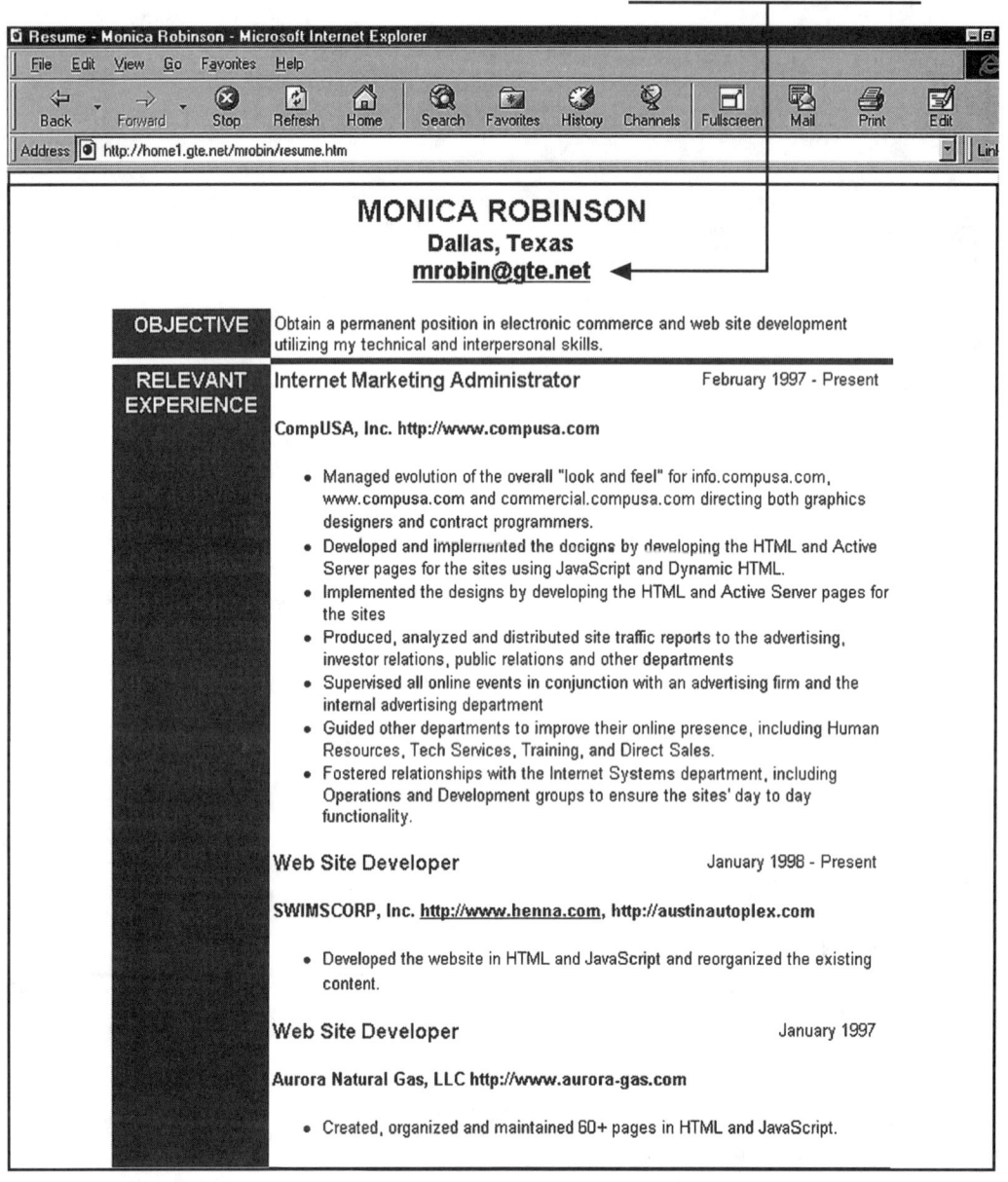

MONICA ROBINSON
Dallas, Texas
mrobin@gte.net

OBJECTIVE

Obtain a permanent position in electronic commerce and web site development utilizing my technical and interpersonal skills.

RELEVANT EXPERIENCE

Internet Marketing Administrator February 1997 - Present

CompUSA, Inc. http://www.compusa.com

- Managed evolution of the overall "look and feel" for info.compusa.com, www.compusa.com and commercial.compusa.com directing both graphics designers and contract programmers.
- Developed and implemented the designs by developing the HTML and Active Server pages for the sites using JavaScript and Dynamic HTML.
- Implemented the designs by developing the HTML and Active Server pages for the sites
- Produced, analyzed and distributed site traffic reports to the advertising, investor relations, public relations and other departments
- Supervised all online events in conjunction with an advertising firm and the internal advertising department
- Guided other departments to improve their online presence, including Human Resources, Tech Services, Training, and Direct Sales.
- Fostered relationships with the Internet Systems department, including Operations and Development groups to ensure the sites' day to day functionality.

Web Site Developer January 1998 - Present

SWIMSCORP, Inc. http://www.henna.com, http://austinautoplex.com

- Developed the website in HTML and JavaScript and reorganized the existing content.

Web Site Developer January 1997

Aurora Natural Gas, LLC http://www.aurora-gas.com

- Created, organized and maintained 60+ pages in HTML and JavaScript.

110

HTML Resume 5–9 continued

Frames give a professional, attractive appearance ↓

TECHNICAL SKILLS	**Languages** • HTML 3.2 • JavaScript • Dynamic HTML **Software** • Macintosh OS 7.0+ • Microsoft Internet platform • Windows 95, NT • MS Internet Information Server 3.0 • Netscape Browsers • MS Commerce Server • MS Internet Explorer • MS SQL Server • Numerous Helper Applications • MS Index Server • Numerous Plug-Ins • MS Active Server Pages • Adobe PhotoShop • MS FrontPage • Paint Shop Pro • HomeSite • MS Office applications • Lotus Notes • WebTrends **Hardware** • Apple Macintosh PowerMacs • PCs and Compatibles
STRENGTHS	• Computer/internet enthusiast and quick learner • Responsive to customer demands and feedback as it relates to the functionality of the website • Conscientious planner and organizer • Project-oriented self-starter • Exceptionally versatile, analytic and congenial
EDUCATION	**Master of Arts Degree in Biochemistry** May 1997 The University of Texas at Austin, Austin, Texas Cumulative GPA: 3.05/4.00 **Bachelor of Science Degree in Chemistry** June 1994 Washington and Lee University, Lexington, Virginia Cumulative GPA: 3.18/4.00 Dean's List 4 years
ACTIVITIES & INTERESTS	Fitness, charity fun runs, community service, horseback riding, and creative cooking

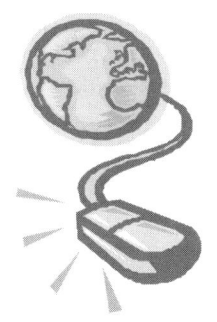

Chapter 6

Specialty Resumes

As electronic resumes have increasingly become the norm for business and industry, so has the government begun to utilize this new approach. When you consider the numbers of applicants for government jobs and the thousands of military personnel who separate or retire from the service and enter the labor market every year, you can see the need to automate some of the process. The same is true for the large numbers of college students who join the workforce annually. In this chapter, we will profile the procedure for filing a resume with the federal government and introduce you to very successful online job services for separating and retiring military personnel and college students.

Federal Government Resumes: The STAIRS Program

In response to the drove of federal applications they receive every year, the Federal Department of Defense (DoD) decided to try to automate the applicant-tracking procedure. The DoD went to Resumix™, the software company that designs resume-tracking software for private industry. The people at Resumix developed Resumix Federal™, a customized version of its image-processing software, just for federal applicants. The DoD integrated the Resumix Federal program into its application procedures, and the result was STAIRS, the Standard Automated Inventory and Referral System now used by DoD.

Working with Resumix, DoD developed a system in which applicants could file for jobs online via e-mail, conventional mail, or a Web site resume template that utilizes a scannable-resume format. However, given the reporting responsibilities of the federal government, the system also needed to track other governmental information. Resumix complied and developed a sophisticated system that was responsive to federal agency needs.

In 1995, the first Resumix system was installed at Bangor Naval Submarine Base. The pilot program was so successful that STAIRS has now become the standard throughout the DoD.

Resumix Federal incorporated a program called FormReader™ that "reads" federal forms, including OF-612, the federal job-application form that was in use at the time STAIRS was developed. The same patented artificial intelligence feature that Resumix uses for skills extraction on its commercial software is utilized to pull information from federal forms. A summary containing skills and qualifications is then prepared and put into a database that is searchable whenever job openings occur in the Department of Defense. Then a list of qualified candidates—consisting of applicants for new hire, promotion, or reassignment—is compiled.

FormReader can also generate reports and handle information that is typically needed by federal agencies. Government applications require certain applicant information not usually requested on private industry applications, such as veteran preference eligibility, US citizenship status, and the highest civil-service grade held. Applications also include the job announcement number. FormReader can capture all this information.

Because STAIRS has come into wide use throughout the DoD, the old OF-612 and SF-171 forms have been discontinued. What the DoD now uses is a scannable resume. You prepare these resumes by using the same rules as we have discussed in previous chapters: typed, with black ink on white paper; no special fonts or enhancements, such as bolding, underlining, column formatting; clean copies or original laser prints; and so on. The skills extraction is accomplished in the same way, with a summary in a searchable database from which qualified candidates may be selected in response to a job requisition.

When the federal government generates a job announcement, Resumix Federal enables the government to build a requisition that contains all the needed requirements. The requisition provides for the position description as well as the knowledge, skill, and ability—KSAs in federal parlance—that are needed for the job. When the requisition is entered into the Resumix Federal system, a list of qualified applicants is generated. These applicants match the criteria as specified by the requisition.

Resumix Federal also contains the folder concept. This service enables users to attach to the resume certain other documents that often accompany a federal job application. For example, veterans are required to furnish a copy of their DD-214, the document that defines their veteran status. Some other appended documents include college transcripts and personnel action forms, which document a federal employee's career progress. With the folder concept, a case record can be built without a bulging paper file.

The Washington Headquarters Services (WHS) National Capital Region (NCR) Human Resource Services Center (HRSC) is the federal agency that accepts scannable resumes under the STAIRS program (see Figure 6.1). HRSC advises that under this new system, a major difference for federal job applicants is that only one resume is now required for positions at several different locations. Prior to STAIRS, applicants had to file separately for *every* new position in which they were interested. The old SF-171 was a bulky, complicated application form that, when unfolded, was almost three feet long! The automated process is a major time-saver for federal employees and applicants. Another positive outcome of converting to STAIRS is that the process of applicant selection has greater objectivity because the method of skills extraction is uniform and consistent.

Figure 6.1

The Human Resource Services Center home page at http://www.hrsc.osd.mil.

Part I: Electronic Resumes

HRSC enables applicants to update their resumes when necessary. When STAIRS first became available, this capability was not usable unless candidates had a change in education or skills. Now HRSC permits changes to be made but will process them only on the first working day of each month. HRSC further requires that you submit a cover memorandum explaining your desire to *replace* your current resume on file in STAIRS with your revised resume. Timing is important here. For example, if you filed for a job that closes in the middle of the month and you revised your resume to qualify for the position, the updated resume would not display until the first of the following month; therefore, the new resume would not be used.

Just as with other automated staffing programs, STAIRS is skills based. The scanner reads from top to bottom and extracts up to 80 different skills. HRSC recommends that you list your most important skills first and that you be as specific and relevant as possible.

For entering your work experience in STAIRS, HRSC suggests that you list only those jobs that pertain to your career goals. However, with recent governmental downsizing, current federal employees may want to enter previous KSAs, too, as space allows. Remember, the old SF-171 is gone and your old work history with it. Office of Personnel Management (OPM) won't be able to refer to your old SF-171 to determine your prior skills. Entering your prior skills on the new resume may keep you in the mix for reassignment to other jobs in the event of a reduction in force. Remember, however, that you get only 80 skills, so make every one of them count!

For each job listed, you must include dates, hours, titles, pay (series and grade, if federal employment), full name and address of employer, and supervisor's name and phone number. Besides duties and KSAs, HRSC recommends that you list your accomplishments and specify the programs in which you worked. HRSC also advises that you list the tools and equipment you may have used, if relevant.

In STAIRS, you should use nouns and verbs to excerpt the most relevant information. When training current federal employees in scannable resume preparation, HRSC suggests that they go over the federal position description (PD) and line out all words *except* nouns and verbs to get the flavor of what to include in their scannable resumes.

The STAIRS resume is limited to a three-page maximum. In fact, resumes that are more than three pages long will have only the first three pages scanned.

On a federal resume, you are required to include your social security number at the top of the first page along with your contact information. This information ensures that you will be distinguishable from other applicants who may share your same name and birth date. The federal government has been using the social security number to order records since 1943, under Executive Order 9397. Although providing your social security number (SSN) is voluntary, the NCR HRSC cautions that it cannot process your application without the SSN. You should also put your name at the top of each subsequent page of your resume.

If you are not currently employed by a defense agency served by the HSRC, you are required to submit a supplemental sheet with your resume. On this sheet, you include the vacancy announcement number, your name and SSN, any specialized training and licenses, and awards and other information pertaining to your career goals (language skills, professional affiliations, and so on). If you are a current or former Civil Service employee, you must also include your highest grade held and length of service for each position and your employment status. This information is to be submitted on a separate 8 ½-x-11-inch sheet of paper. For veterans, you include your preference-points standing and also provide a photocopy of your DD-214.

You can submit your federal resume in any of the following three ways:

✔ E-mail to:

    `resume@hrsc.osd.mil`

> *Note:* The word **resume** must be in the subject line; include a string of ten @ symbols immediately before the start of your text; type your resume in the body of your e-mail message or paste in an ASCII version; do *not* send the resume as an attachment.

✔ Upload at the Web site:

    `http://www.hrsc.osd.mil/`

✔ Mail to:

    Resume
    Washington Headquarters Services
    NCR Human Resource Services Center
    5001 Eisenhower Avenue, Room 2E22
    Alexandria, VA 22333-0001

Part I: Electronic Resumes

As of April 1998, HRSC no longer accepts faxed resumes because they are often of poor quality. Before this change in policy, applicants had to be notified individually to resubmit their resumes via conventional mail if the faxed version was of poor quality. In addition, a tremendous volume of traffic was on the fax number with some applicants faxing multiple copies of their resumes, so the fax number is no longer viable. (See Chapter 4 for a discussion about faxing your scannable resumes.)

To simplify the process of preparing a scannable resume, HRSC provides an Online Resume Writer at its Web site. You can see this form in Appendix B. The Online Resume Writer looks similar to other online forms, but it contains some notable exceptions, such as a place for your social security number, federal grade, military service information, and merit promotion procedures—all information limited to the federal job-application process. The work history area contains room for six former jobs, and the education area contains blocks for six former schools, more room than you generally find on private-sector resume templates.

The HRSC also provides detailed instructions for applying for federal civilian jobs. Besides resume preparation instructions, the HRSC Civilian Job Kit also contains a list of do's and don'ts and explains who can apply, how they can apply, and when they can apply. You can see the Civilian Job Kit in Appendix C.

Let's look at a suggested resume format from the HRSC (see the Sample HRSC Format on the next page). It shows all the information you need to include in a federal resume.

Now we'll examine some sample resumes from the HRSC site (see HRSC Resumes 6–1, 6–2, 6–3, and 6–4). You will notice some key differences between these resumes and resumes for private sector jobs. Each of the federal resumes contains a social security number at the top, per HRSC instructions. The job titles contain the pay plan, series, and grade of the positions held. Former supervisors' names and phone numbers are listed. The resumes also specify the lowest grade acceptable to the applicant and the highest grade attained and career status in the federal civil service. Military preference is listed as well. None of this information would ever appear on a resume for a private sector job. Notice that the federal resumes are text-intensive, containing many keywords and KSAs.

Sample HRSC Format

RESUME FORMAT

NAME: FIRST MIDDLE INITIAL LAST
SSN: XXX-XX-XXXX

MAILING ADDRESS:
STREET, APT NO.:
CITY, STATE ZIP CODE:
HOME TELEPHONE NUMBER:
WORK TELEPHONE NUMBER:
E-MAIL ADDRESS:
VACANCY ANNOUNCEMENT NUMBER:

SUMMARY OF YOUR SKILLS: Include in this portion of your resume a summary of the skills you possess. Describe these skills in one or two words. It is not necessary to list all of your skills. Be sure to emphasize those skills in occupations where you are most interested in employment and those that are relevant to your career.

EXPERIENCE (When Describing Duties Be Sure To Include):
Start and end dates (month and year).
Hours worked per week.
Position Title.
Pay Plan, Series, Grade (if Federal civilian position). List highest grade held and number of months held at that grade level. If experience describes Federal civilian positions at different grade levels, include month and year promoted.
Employer's name (agency or company name) and mailing address.
Supervisor's name and telephone number.
All major tasks. Be sure to include any systems which you have worked on; software programs or special tools and equipment you have used; and any special programs you have managed. **Any other job related information** you wish to include, e.g., licenses/certificates (including date(s) certified and state), awards, language proficiencies, professional associations, etc.

TRAINING/EDUCATION: Give your highest level of education. If degree completed (e.g., AA, BA, MA), list your major field of study, name of college or university, and year degree awarded. If your highest level of education was high school, list either the highest grade you completed; year you graduated; or the date you were awarded your GED. List specialized training pertinent to your career goals.

Part I: Electronic Resumes ....

LIMIT THE ABOVE RESUME INFORMATION TO THREE (3) PAGES
USE 8.5" x 11" WHITE BOND PAPER, PRINTED ON ONE SIDE
****

<u>**NOTE**</u>: Submit the following information on a separate sheet of 8.5" x 11" white bond paper, printed on one side. If the information does not apply to you, please respond with "N/A". At the top of the page, repeat your <u>Name</u> and <u>Social Security Number</u> for identification purposes.

1. LOWEST ACCEPTABLE GRADE: _____

2. CURRENT/FORMER FEDERAL CIVILIAN EMPLOYEES:

(A) List highest grade held and number of months held at that grade level.

(B) Provide employment status (i.e., career, career-conditional, temporary, excepted).

3. MILITARY SERVICE AND VETERANS' PREFERENCE:

Provide photocopies of DD-214(s) (Member–4 Copy). In addition, if claiming a compensable disability or other 10 point veteran's preference you must provide an "Application for 10 point Veterans' Preference (SF-15)" and supporting documentation listed on the reverse of the SF-15.

(A) Discharged from the military service under honorable conditions: No _____ Yes _____ (List dates and branch for all active duty military service.)

(B) If all your active military duty was after October 14, 1976, list the full names and dates of all campaign badges or expeditionary medals you received or were entitled to receive.

(C) Retired Military: No _____ Yes _____, Rank at which Retired _____, Date of Retirement _____

(D) If claiming Veterans' Preference, indicate eligibility: 5 Point; 10 Point/Compensable; 10 Point/Other; 10 Point/Disability; or 10 Point/Compensably Disabled, 30% or more.

You will be required to provide documentation to verify eligibility/status. If you are sending your resume or self nomination via electronic means, you must mail in the documentation and annotate the vacancy announcement number you are applying for. Remember to mail in copies – not originals

HRSC Resume 6-1 (Engineer)

JANE E. SMITH
SSN: XXX-XX-XXXX

11712 Main Street
Anytown, VA 88888
Home Telephone No.: (703) 111-1111
Work Telephone No.: (703) 123-4567
E-mail Address: xxxx@xxxx.xxx.xx
Vacancy Announcement Number: XXXX

Lowest Acceptable Grade: GS-14

SUMMARY OF SKILLS:

Mechanical Engineering; aerospace engineering; Spacecraft; AHIP Helicopter; Symbolic Manipulation Program; IBM 3090; VAX; FORTRAN; NASTRAN; UNIX; DOS; Department of Defense Top Secret clearance.

Extensive experience in the disciplines of structural and simulation dynamics, structures, aerospace engineering, mechanical engineering, and software application and development. Demonstrated ability to apply these methodologies to analyze, evaluate, and incorporate design changes to fixed and mobile structures, vehicles, and other environments.

EXPERIENCE

May 1991 to present; 40 hours per week; Staff Engineer, GS-0801-14; promoted to GS-14 July 1994; Imaginary Agency, 123 West Image Dr., Arlington, VA 88888; Supervisor: John Doe, (703) 123-4567.

Developed detailed comprehensive element structural models for dynamic and stress analysis with particular expertise to model and evaluate integrated spacecraft and mechanical systems. Designed theoretical model and software for dynamic and aeroelastic response of coupled, rotor-airframe helicopters in high speed forward flight. Participated in vibration test requirements and data reduction for AHIP and YAH-64 helicopters.

September 1989 to April 1991; 40 hours per week; Staff Engineer; $XX,XXX per year; Any Aircraft Corporation, Anytown, MD 22222; Supervisor: Amy Jones, (410) 111-2222.

HRSC Resume 6-1 (Engineer) continued

Project leader for major projects under the Symbolic Manipulation Program (SMP). Conducted time simulation studies of complex multibody systems. Applied SMP for developing dynamic equations of motion of multibody systems. Programming and computer experience includes developing software on IBM 3090 mainframe, VAX, and PC computers using FORTRAN, NASTRAN DMAP, BASIC, and C languages under DOS and UNIX operating systems. Membership in the Society of Women Engineers: Chair, Annual Meeting, 1994. American Society of Mechanical Engineers: Chair, membership Committee, 1991-92.

EDUCATION

Doctorate in Aeronautical Engineering, University of California at Los Angeles, 1989.

Master of Science in Mechanical Engineering, University of Virginia, 1986.

Bachelor of Science in Mechanical Engineering, Summa Cum Laude, University of Maryland, 1984.

SUPPLEMENTAL DATA

1.Lowest Acceptable Grade: GS-14 2.High Grade Held: GS-14, 3 years

Federal Employment Status: Career 3.Military Service/Veterans' Preference: N/A

HRSC Resume 6–2 (Clerical)

JOHN Q. DOE
SSN: XXX-XX-XXXX

555 West Capital Street
Washington, DC 99999
Home Telephone No.: (111) 111-1111
Work Telephone No.: (111) 111-1112
E-Mail Address: xxxx@xxxx.xxx.xx
Vacancy Announcement Number: XXXX

SUMMARY OF SKILLS:

Secretary, receptionist, typing (40 WPM), stenography (80 WPM), word processing, file management, records management, editing, proofreading, office management, PowerPoint software, customer service.

EXPERIENCE

Three years, progressively responsible work in office management.

January 1995 to present; 40 hours per week; Secretary (OA), GS-0318-07, promoted to GS-07 August 1995; Imaginary Agency, 123 West Image Dr., Arlington, VA 88888; Supervisor: Fred Smith, (703) 123-4567.

Perform various secretarial duties to manage the administrative functions of the office. Type correspondence, take and transcribe dictation, answer telephone calls and greet visitors, create and maintain office filing system, coordinate conferences and meetings, make travel arrangements. Read all incoming correspondence, determine proper action, and occasionally prepare response before referring to supervisor. Explain non-technical policies and procedures promulgated by the supervisor. Make recommendations on administrative matters. Use suite of business software (OfficePRO, WordPRO, and PointPRO) to prepare briefing charts, graphs, and text documents. Maintain supervisor's calendar and schedule meetings.

February 1993 to December 1994; 40 hours per week; Receptionist; $22,000 per year; Jay's Lumber Company, 123 East Tree Dr., Bethesda, MD 77777; Jay Smith, (301) 123-4567.

Answered the telephone and greeted customers at the receptionist desk. Directed customers to the appropriate office. Heard, resolved, or referred customer complaints. Received all incoming and outgoing mail and routed items directly to the appropriate office for actions. Made travel arrangements for supervisor and staff.

HRSC Resume 6-2 (Clerical) continued

Provided advice to clerical personnel in subordinate branches concerning such matters as time and leave procedures, travel vouchers, and reporting and correspondence procedures. Organized and maintained files and records, manuals, handbooks, and other related materials. Typed correspondence and other items.

EDUCATION

AA, Business Management, Texas State University, 1993, Austin, Texas; GPA 3.2

SUPPLEMENTAL DATA

JOHN Q. DOE
SSN: XXX-XX-XXXX

1.Lowest Grade Acceptable: GS-08 2.GS-07; 2 years, 11 months Excepted Service 3.Military Service/Veterans' Preference: N/A

HRSC Resume 6–3 (Police)

SHERRI M. LEVAN
SSN: XXX-XX-XXXX

7890 Lawful Ave. Apt. 123
Washington, DC 99999
Home Telephone No: (202) 111-1111
Work Telephone No: (202) 222-2222
E-Mail address: levans@personal.access.com
Vacancy Announcement Number: XXXX

SUMMARY OF SKILLS:

US Air Force and Defense Protective Services; keep law and order; arrest and interviewing techniques; experience in high crime areas; foot and vehicular control; weapons and munitions qualified; SWAT qualified; undercover experience; report writing; training officer; weapons supply officer; access control; Excel, Word Perfect and DBASE proficiency.

EXPERIENCE:

May 1993 to present; 50 hours per week; Police Officer, GS-083-6; Defense Protective Services, Washington Headquarters Services, 1234 Defense, Washington DC, 11119; Supervisor: Joan Doe, (703) 111-2222

Preserved law and order by enforcing laws and regulations on a daily basis. Maintained security by foot and vehicular patrol. Controlled potentially violent and disruptive situations with tact and professionalism. Controlled access to highly sensitive areas. Trained and drilled in counter terrorism practices. Maintained qualifications and proficiency in weapons use. Investigated crimes. Performed undercover assignments. Wrote reports and testified in court as necessary. Supply Officer for weapons, ammunition and munitions.

October 1989 to April 1993; 60 hours per week; Police Officer, Gustine Police Department, 3456 Main Street, Gustine, WI 09876; Supervisor: Lt. D. Goode, (555) 555-5555

Enforced felony and misdemeanor laws of Wisconsin. Apprehended, detained, arrested and interviewed suspects and witnesses; prepared and processed reports; maintained fitness and weapons qualifications.

July 1985-February 1989; 45 hours/week; Training Sergeant, E-6; promoted August 1985; Aviano Security Unit, PO Box 111, FPO NY 22222; Supervisor: 1st Lt. J. Guy, DSN 111-2222.

HRSC Resume 6-3 (Police) continued

Scheduled training and maintained training records for all law enforcement personnel assigned to the Unit. Scheduled and operated weapons ranges and fitness tests. Trained incoming personnel, react teams, perimeter guards on security and protection procedures and techniques.

TRAINING/EDUCATION:

AA Criminal Justice, Central Illinois University, May 1988
Certified in Biological and Chemical Anti-Terrorism Techniques

SUPPLEMENTAL DATA

SHERRI M. LEVAN
SSN: XXX-XX-XXXX

1.Lowest Grade Acceptable: GS-6 2.Highest Grade Held: GS-06; 2 years, 3 months
Federal Employment Status: Career status 3.Military Service/Veterans' Preference:
Honorable Discharge (July 1985-Feb 1989, USA)
Campaign badges/expeditionary medals: N/A
Retired military: No
Veterans' Preference: N/A

HRSC Resume 6-4 (WG)

RICHARD P. JONES
SSN: XXX-XX-XXXX

3456 Generic Street
Potomac, MD 88888
Home Telephone No: (301) 000-0000
Work Telephone No: (301) 123-4567
E-Mail address: none
Vacancy Announcement Number: XXXX

SUMMARY OF SKILLS:

Rigger, Maintenance Mechanic (carpentry, electrical, plumbing, painting). Work leader. Read schematic diagrams. Flooring: wood, linoleum, carpet. Electrical: switches and plugs, basic wiring. Plumbing: faucets, pipes, fixtures and fire sprinklers. Operate cranes and forklifts. Work planner and inspector.

EXPERIENCE

Nine years experience in the trades - apprentice to work leader.

July 1996 to March 1997; 40 hours per week; Maintenance Mechanic Leader WL-4749-10; Smithsonian Institute, 1111 Mall Ave., Washington DC, 12345; Supervisor: J. McGuire (202) 123-4567

Lead 9 employees working in all trades including: plumbing, painting, electrical (facilities), carpentry. Prioritize work, make assignments through oral instruction and sketches and assigning tools. Inspect and approved work or direct re-work. Tracked hours spent on each job and input into DBASE tracking system. In supervisor's absence, approve leave, maintain overtime log, counsel and take disciplinary action. Ensure all work done in accordance with Museum and OSHA safety requirements.

May 1992 to June 1996; 40 hours per week; Rigger/Maintenance Mechanic, WG-5210-10 (promoted 9/94); Smithsonian Institute, 1111 Mall Ave., Washington DC 12345; Supervisor: L. S. Walker, (202) 123-0987

Used forklifts, cranes, skids and rollers to safely move priceless museum exhibits. Assisted other trades in carpentry, plumbing, painting, and electrical work. Installed door alarms. Prepared all kinds of surfaces for work. Laid linoleum and carpet. Repaired wood floors, carpet and furniture. Installed door alarms. Wired switches and repaired plugs. Replaced piping, faucets and fixtures in plumbing.

HRSC Resume 6–4 (WG) continued

March 1988-April 1992; 40 hours per week; Rigger Apprentice, WT-5210-8; Portsmouth Naval Shipyard, Portsmouth, NH 98765; Supervisor: S. Barnett, (207) 456-7890

Lifted, moved and positioned heavy objects and loads (machines and large structural parts.) Selected equipment. Estimated sizes, weights and equipment capacities. Ensured safety. Used cranes, chainfalls, skids, rollers, jacks, forklifts to move all types of ship equipment. Qualified signalman for cranes.

TRAINING/EDUCATION

HS graduate - 1987; Residential Electricity, Drywall, Refrigeration and A/C, Regulated Waste Disposal, Certificate; Certificate in Industrial Blueprints

SUPPLEMENTAL DATA

RICHARD P. JONES
SSN: XXX-XX-XXXX

1.Lowest Grade Acceptable: WG-08 2.Highest Grade Held: WL-10; 8 months
Federal Employment Status: Career 3.Military Service/Veterans' Preference: N/A

Before sending your resume, verify that you have prepared it in accordance with HRSC instructions. You will be notified of receipt within two weeks.

> *Caution:* HRSC warns that unscannable resumes will be destroyed!

Military Resumes: Transition Assistance Online (TAOnline)

Military personnel who separate or retire from the service face a host of problems in their transition back to civilian employment. Many of these people haven't experienced life outside the military environment for a long time, and many have never experienced civilian employment at all. They will discover quickly that the two worlds are vastly different. Behavior, etiquette, structure, even language differ sharply between the two cultures: in private industry, a leader *manages;* in military service, a leader *commands.* And subordinates in a bank are not likely to salute a passing executive! These illustrations serve to point up some of the challenges facing former military personnel as they re-enter private life. They often need special help in making this daunting transition.

Among the resume sites we explored, we came across an online service called Transition Assistance Online, or TAOnline, which is just for transitioning military job seekers (see Figure 6.2).

Figure 6.2

The Transition Assistance Online home page at http://www.taonline.com.

TAOnline, which began in January 1997, was founded jointly by a company called DI-USA, Inc., and the Army Times Publishing Company. DI-USA, Inc., is a successful software publishing company, which was started by military veterans Richard Scott Rodriguez and Rocky Gillette along with Bob Lindsey, a nonveteran. Bob Lindsey, vice president and CFO of DI-USA, Inc., explains the unusual history of the company:

> DI-USA is primarily a software Internet company. It was founded in Florida by three partners, two who were former military officers. It began as Divers International-USA, Inc., with a subsidiary division in Cozumel, Mexico, called Divers International-Mexico, S.A. The president is Scott Rodriguez; the vice president is G. Roderick Gillette. The company was originally formed to provide scuba and snorkeling tours to cruise ship passengers visiting the Mexican island of Cozumel.
>
> The company received many resumes from veterans seeking employment because times were tougher economically then. The resumes were not of the highest quality, nor did they portray the finest qualities of the "best of the best": men and women who were disciplined, dependable, educated, and well trained. These individuals were quite accomplished but never had the need to write a resume in the military. The idea of a resume writer designed for transitioning military took shape, and so an idea was born—Transition Assistance Software (TAS)—to help these fellow veterans seeking employment in the civilian job market. Subsequently, an Internet resume bank for military was conceived from these resumes.
>
> In early 1996, DI-USA set up its first Web site at **www.di-usa.com** to promote its TAS software. In late 1996, Rocky Gillette, recognizing the growing importance of the Internet and the World Wide Web as a job seeking and hiring tool, developed a partnership with the Army Times Publishing Company (ATPCO) to produce Transition Assistance Online (TAO). TAOnline, at **www.taonline.com**, was launched in January 1997 and has been growing ever since, logging over a quarter of a million hits per month in June of 1998.

TAO offers separating service members, veterans, spouses, dependents, and DoD federal civilian employees, advice on their second careers in the Transition Information Center (**www.taonline.com/ticindex.html**). Users can submit their resumes to a password-protected resume database, which means that only employers who have registered with TAOnline can view their resumes. Separating members can also seek relocation assistance, career-fair information, continuing education advice, and so on. Chris Gillette, VP for Marketing and Business Development at DI-USA, adds:

> Users can search thousands of jobs posted by hundreds of employers that have signed up with TAO. Employers, including Airborne Express, BDM/Vinnell, Cintas, Circuit City, Hughes, Litton PRC,

Procter & Gamble, Manpower, Wang, and so on, have signed up to post nationwide job openings, search the resume database, and advertise. Employers can also leverage their exposure by simultaneously publishing their print advertisements in the Army Times's numerous print publications that include the *Army Times, Navy Times, Federal Times*, and so on.

The Army Times Publishing Company (ATPCO), a family-run entity, was recently purchased by Gannett, Inc., owners of *USA Today*. Bob Lindsey told us that DI-USA, ATPCO, and Gannett are entering into a new era of cooperation to provide the best possible services to job seekers and employers.

TAS Software

TAS 3.0 software is sold at military exchanges worldwide (see Figure 6.3). The software's name originated with the Transition Assistance Program (TAP) offices that were springing up on bases around the country as a result of the massive drawdowns taking place in the US military at that time.

Figure 6.3

The first screen of TAS software.

We reviewed the software and found TAS to be an excellent resource not only for transitioning military personnel, but for any job seeker. TAS is easy to use and organized in a logical manner. It contains sample resume and cover-letter formats and a Job Search Organizer to help keep the whole process on track. A financial planner is included in the package to assist with the economic aspects of looking for work. The "Lethal Job Hunting Guide" provides tips and advice for tackling the sometimes-overwhelming task of finding and keeping a job.

In addition, the software affords the capability to print federal application forms, such as SF-171 and OF-612, as well as the Veterans' Preference form, SF-15, to assist separating US military service members and veterans seeking civilian and federal employment.

You can purchase TAS 3.0 on CD-ROM in all US military base exchanges around the world or from the Army Times Publishing Company's Web site, Military City Online, at the following address:

www.militarycity.com

Of tremendous help to veterans is the MOS/Military Skills Translator included in the TAS software package. MOS stands for Military Occupation Series. MOS is the job title given to jobs in the armed forces. When veterans leave the service and enter the civilian labor market, they need to know what their military jobs are called in civilian terms. Sometimes the translation is fairly obvious. For example, MOS titles often contain the word *specialist*, a term not often used in civilian parlance; therefore, an administrative support specialist in MOS terms becomes an administrative clerk, a clerk typist, or a clerk general when translated into civilian terms.

Your DD-214 automatically converts your MOS to an occupational code—which is taken from the Federal Dictionary of Occupational Titles (DOT)—that translates into a civilian job title. The DOT is available online in sections that go throughout the alphabet, as shown in the following three addresses:

http://www.immigration-usa.com/dot_a1.html
http://www.immigration-usa.com/dot_b1.html
http://www.immigration-usa.com/dot_c1.html

The letter of the alphabet preceding the **1** in the address is the letter that starts your section. For example, **a1.html** brings up the section containing codes for the titles Abalone Diver to Acupuncturist and more; **b1.html** brings up the section containing codes for Boat Builder, Budget Clerk, and Bricklayer; at **c1.html**, you may find codes for CPA, Carpenter, and so on.

You can also contact any State Employment Service office for help in translating your MOS. In each of these offices nationwide, you will find a Local Veteran's Employment Representative (LVER), whose job is to assist veterans with employment. Al Harris is an LVER in the San Bernardino office of the State of California Employment Development Department. He does job development and placement with area veterans and assists them with other veteran services. Harris says:

> Your Local Veteran's Employment Representative will help you find training, benefit information, and local job market information. The representative can also assist you in translating your military occupational specialty into civilian terms. Military job titles can be confusing to people in the private sector, so the representative helps vets with this first step in transitioning into the civilian labor market.

According to TAOnline, more than 300,000 armed forces personnel will transition out of military service in a year, so it is no wonder they receive so much attention. The site is a comprehensive resource that contains not only job postings, but also company profiles and tips on resume writing and job hunting. TAOnline also accepts resumes from the dependents and spouses of military veterans.

Job seekers are not charged for posting resumes. You follow the guidelines for creating a scannable resume (see Chapter 3) and then save it in ASCII text, the required format of TAOnline. You can transmit your resume by sending it e-mail or conventional mail, by completing the template form at the Web site, or by using the TAS software found in all base exchanges worldwide.

Your resume is put in a database that is searchable by more than 500 employers who subscribe to TAOnline. Chris Gillette, VP for Marketing and Business Development at DI-USA, Inc., explains:

> Employers are able, for a minimal fee, to search the TAO resume bank. TAO uses the advanced, indexed-based search engine Excite for Web Servers™ to give its users access to a sophisticated keyword or concept-based search engine.

To search for your resume, employers enter their login ID and password and then select whether to search the TAOnline resume database, the partial Defense Outplacement Referral System (DORS) resume database, or both databases. Employers then choose whether to conduct a keyword or concept-based search. The employers enter the word(s) or text of their query and start the search. Depending on the query, the search can take from seconds to a few minutes (for the TAOnline Alternate Search Engine).

The results of the search are displayed in confidence groups that use a percentage (80 percent, 100 percent, and so on). Percentage scores with a red icon next to them show a high confidence in the match between your resume and the employer's search; those scores with a black icon show a lower confidence in the match. The employer then clicks on the Displayed Contact Information option for each responsive resume to view it or print it out.

Resumes are retained in the TAOnline system for 90 days. If you want to renew your resume posting after 90 days, simply resubmit the resume.

Now let's look at some sample resumes taken from the Transition Assistance Software (see TAS Resumes 6–5, 6–6, 6–7, 6–8, 6–9, and 6–10).

TAS Resume 6-5

ROY TAYLOR
2111 HIGHTOWER STREET #2B
HUNTSVILLE, ALABAMA 35801
(205) 456-2578
e-mail: sam@abcom.net

OBJECTIVE:
A career position in systems analysis and design.

PROFESSIONAL PROFILE:
Eight years of specialized experience in operations research, systems analysis and nuclear logistics. Proven experience in systems management and concept design. TOP SECRET CLEARANCE.

EDUCATION:
Master of Quantitative Analysis, 1994
Massachusetts Institute of Technology.

Bachelor of Science, Operations Research, 1984
United States Military Academy.

PROFESSIONAL EXPERIENCE:
September 1992 - Present Operations Research Analyst, Dept. of Defense
Responsible for quantitative analysis and simulation modeling of missile logistics systems. Manager of an automation program within the directorate. Developed courses in new missile distribution concept that resulted in a savings of $700,000.

July 1989 - June 1992 Evaluation Team Chief, US Army
Supervised a 7-man nuclear inspection team. Evaluated all nuclear units in three European countries. Developed and administered a budget of $430,000. Published a quarterly evaluation newsletter. Successfully presented community (politically sensitive) deficiencies to senior NATO officers.

January 1986 - June 1989 Emergency Operations Officer, US Army
Directed a four-man team responsible for executing presidential orders for nuclear weapons in central Europe. Commanded and controlled nuclear weapons during emergency situations. Initiated communication procedures that greatly increased security of unit.

11/01/84 - 12/31/86 Executive Officer, US Army
Second-in-command of a 170-man Ordnance Company. Responsible for maintenance and security of several nuclear storage sites. Supervised 5 officers and 30 soldiers. Received "No Deficiency" inspection ratings (highest) from Defense Nuclear Agency.

TAS Resume 6–5 continued

July 1983 - October 1984 Platoon Leader, US Army
Directly supervised 34 soldiers. Maintained and accounted for 36 vehicles and $300,000 of equipment. Designed a cross-training program which tripled the manpower available for a sensitive communication project.

Availability Date: 08/01/97

References available upon request.

TAS Resume 6-6

BARRY W. ABSHIRE
1711 THIRD AVENUE
NEW YORK, NEW YORK 10128
(212)761-1123

OBJECTIVE: A career in international sales and marketing.

EDUCATION:
Candidate for MBA in Marketing, 1998,
Harvard Business School, Cambridge, Massachusetts.

BS in Aerospace Engineering, 1991,
US Military Academy, West Point, New York.

Additional Military Schooling:
- US Army Parachute School - US Army Pathfinder School
- US Army Basic Infantry Officer - US Army Ranger School

PROFESSIONAL EXPERIENCE:

July 1996 - August 1996 MARKETING REPRESENTATIVE, DACOR. Summer Internship. Traveled throughout Caribbean, set-up three new dealerships, established 10 joint marketing and advertising projects, trained dealers and sold $150,000 worth of SCUBA equipment. Won "1996" Summer Internship Achievement Award.

January 1985 - June 1996 LOGISTICS OFFICER, US ARMY
Manager of supplies, ammunition, and maintenance for a 400 man unit. Controlled a budget of $1.5 million.

July 1993 - December 1995 COMPANY EXECUTIVE OFFICER, US ARMY. Second-in-command of an Infantry Company. Responsible for logistics and administration. Passed all Inspector General inspections. Accounted for $2 million of government equipment.

January 1992 - June 1993 RIFLE PLATOON LEADER, US ARMY. Leader of a 41-man light-infantry platoon. Managed training and welfare of the unit. Platoon was ranked number one out of 16 platoons. Accounted for $300,000 in equipment.

ACTIVITIES:
American Marketing Society, President, Harvard Business School
Cambridge SCUBA Diving Club, Officer
US Army Reserves, Captain

Secret Clearance

TAS Resume 6-7

STEVEN K. HIGGINS
487 Cypress Drive
Rialto, California 52576
(714) 971-9773

CAREER OBJECTIVE:
A leadership and managerial position in the communications field, focusing on the areas of public, media and community relations. Especially interested in environmental affairs and issues.

EXPERIENCE: Major, United State Army.

01/01/93 - Present
Public Affairs Officer, US Army
Handled public affairs matters for 7th Infantry Division of 14,000 men. Planned and coordinated the military and civilian-news media coverage, including Operation Desert Storm. Supervised and coordinated public relations for exercises and operations in the Philippines, Turkey and Honduras. Drafted news releases and stories, conducted press briefings and interviews, and supervised military photo-journalists. Developed and implemented a new media training program. Worked with all major national and international print and telecommunication news agencies.

06/16/86 - 05/31/88
Company Commander, US Army
Responsible for 160 soldiers assigned to a headquarters company. Established a training and evaluation program for the company's men and women working in more than a dozen different job specialties. The program resulted in a 100% pass rate in occupational skills testing. Controlled and accounted for equipment worth more than $3 million.

05/16/84 - 06/15/86
Executive Officer, US Army
Supervised 25 personnel charged with the supply storage and security of weapons, ammunition, vehicles, fuel equipment at an Army training center. Accountable for $6.3 million in supplies.

02/01/83 - 05/15/84
Training Officer, US Army
Directed the training of 460 basic training personnel. Planned and executed all instructional activities during a rigorous 8 week course. Successfully graduated over 5,000 trainees.

10/01/78 - 11/31/80 Platoon Leader, US Army
Gained extensive leadership and management experience. Supervised 41 personnel and managed nearly $1 million in equipment and assets.

TAS Resume 6-7 continued

EDUCATION:
Master of Public Administration, 1982, University of Colorado.
Bachelor of Science, Civil Engineering, 1978, University of Texas.
Public Affairs Officer Course, 1988, Defense Information School.

References available upon request.

TAS Resume 6-8

RAVI L. MULLENS
3251 RHINO DRIVE
KINGSPORT, TENNESSEE 37663
(615) 727-1998

OBJECTIVE:
A technical career position in the electronics industry.

PROFESSIONAL PROFILE:
3/93-7/96 PETTY OFFICER FIRST CLASS, US NAVY
Missile Technician Nuclear Submarine, Kings Bay, Georgia
Supervised, operated and performed maintenance on submarine weapon systems. Responsible for maintaining electrical circuitry of system, performed complex repairs and tests of circuitry. Maintained a 93% operational rate of all electronic weapon systems during three 6 month deployments.

6/94-1/93 PETTY OFFICER SECOND CLASS, US NAVY
Missile Maintenance Technician, Groton, Connecticut
Performed intermediate level maintenance on electric/hydraulic powered missile launching systems and equipment. Conducted firing and tests of missile system weekly. Installed explosive components in missiles and operated handling equipment to transport missiles. Tested and repaired electric circuitry and magnetic amplifier.

3/82-6/84 PETTY OFFICER THIRD CLASS, US NAVY
Torpedoman's Mate, Nuclear Submarine, Kings Bay, Georgia
Conducted maintenance on torpedoes and anti-submarine rockets. Operated and maintained firing systems, electrical system and test equipment. Qualified as shipboard safety inspector and cruise-missile technician.

EDUCATION:
Graduated Naval Torpedo, Electrician and various Electronic Technical Schools.

Graduated Hollywood High School, 1982, Hollywood, California.

INTERESTS:
Computers, swimming and golf.

Top Secret Clearance

References available upon request.

TAS Resume 6-9

EDDIE MORTON
2131 KING GEORGE DRIVE
DALLAS, TEXAS 23452
(214) 871-5732

OBJECTIVE:
A position as a Law Enforcement Officer.

PROFESSIONAL PROFILE:
- Armed Forces Police Training Instructor
- Traffic Accident Investigator
- Small Arms Instructor
- Game Warden

RELATED EXPERIENCE:
- Six years of military police experience.
- Performed criminal investigations for one year.
- Conducted physical security assessments of Naval ports.
- Instructed security forces in small arms training for two years.
- Auto theft investigator for one year

EMPLOYMENT HISTORY:
January 1993 - Present Master at Arms Norfolk Navy Base, Norfolk, Virginia
October 1991 - January 1993 Police Officer Naval Air Station, Key West, Florida

EDUCATION:
Military Police and Shore Patrol Training Courses and Schools.
Graduated Fort Hunt High School, 3.4 GPA, 1984, Fairfax, Virginia

INTERESTS:
Computers, auto repair and karate (black belt).

References available upon request.

CURRENTLY AVAILABLE FOR EMPLOYMENT

TAS Resume 6-10

GUS S. ORTIZ
8266 49th STREET #765
MIAMI, FLORIDA 33166
305-598-1864

OBJECTIVE: An aircraft-mechanic position in the civil aviation industry.

LICENSE:
Airframe and Power Plant License Number A&P 598-68-3454.

EDUCATION:
USAF Basic Jet Aircraft Mechanic Course.
USAF Aircraft Technician Course.
USAF C-1 30 Airplane General Course.
USAF Flight Control Rigging Course.
USAF Canopy Rigging Course.
Graduated Groveton High School, Alexandria, Virginia.

PROFESSIONAL EXPERIENCE:
- Maintenance and Shop Work on Power Plants.
- Engine Shop Services Q.E.C.
- Trouble Shooting.
- Mounting and Dismounting of Engines.
- Reversers.
- Removal and Installation of Flight Controls & Major Components.
- Rigging Canopies.
- Wheels and Brakes.
- Structural Repairs.
- Sheet Metal Work.
- Interior Conversion.
- Line Maintenance.
- C Checks and D Checks.

EXPERIENCED WITH: C-130, Boeing 707s and 737s; Douglas DC8s, DC9s and DC10s

EMPLOYMENT HISTORY:
04/10/90-03/14/92 AIRCRAFT MECHANIC, IAL, Miami, Florida.
07/24/81-02/28/89 AIRCRAFT MECHANIC, USAF, Homestead AFB, Florida.

PERSONAL:
Fluent Spanish and English.

Top Secret clearance
Available for employment immediately

Part I: Electronic Resumes

College Graduates and Recent Alumni: BridgePath

Many sites on the Internet contain information of interest to college students. You can find advice on careers, college majors, schools, and universities; you can locate alumni associations; you can even take virtual tours of college campuses. However, many people access college Internet sites to use their placement services. The best online recruiting service we found for college students and alumni is BridgePath (see Figure 6.4). You can find BridgePath at the following address:

http://www.bridgepath.com

Figure 6.4

The BridgePath home page.

BridgePath was founded by Auren Hoffman and Scott Bonds, both consultants with strong backgrounds in design and development of Web database systems and Internet technologies. They cofounded Kyber Systems, a Web database consulting firm, and the *Internet Herald*, a "Generation X" Web magazine.

Headquartered in San Francisco, BridgePath's mission is to increase employment opportunities for college students, recent graduates, and new alumni. BridgePath looks for applicants with less than ten years of experience. BridgePath calls these applicants "the most recently educated, dynamic, and cutting-edge segment of the workforce." BridgePath markets its services directly to recent graduates and alumni by visiting colleges and making their presence known at places where alumni and students are likely to be.

Mel Ochoa is BridgePath's Director of Public Relations and Communications. He is a recent alumnus of the University of California, Berkeley. He explains the company's focus on recent graduates:

Many of our clients are looking for young alumni because, in the age of automation, young alumni and recent graduates are becoming more important. They are being taught more specific skill sets in school than previous generations, and they have a better technological base at a younger age. Roughly 90 percent of college graduates can use MS Word, Excel, Access, the Internet, and e-mail. These qualified job seekers save the employer high training costs.

BridgePath works with career centers, student organizations, young alumni groups, and alumni organizations. BridgePath also has partnerships with major sites on the Internet, including Student Advantage, which is the number one student site on the Internet. All these are effective marketing tools. The word-of-mouth approach is also very successful for us.

Besides targeting college graduates and alumni, BridgePath focuses on passive job seekers, those people who are not inclined or don't have the time to go through the process of actively sending out applications and then searching through many databases to find jobs. These people are often employed and don't want their current employers to know they are looking elsewhere. Mel Ochoa explains:

Passive job seekers are people who are happy with their current job and who do not actively look in want ads on a regular basis. However, they are keeping abreast of what is on the horizon, ready to snag any offer that is too good to pass up. While classified ads tend to attract active job seekers (because the job seeker must work at constantly scanning the paper), BridgePath attracts passive job seekers because it doesn't require tedious searching on the part of the job candidate.

This is not to say, however, that BridgePath does not cater to active job seekers or job seekers with more than ten years' experience. Some of our clients are interested in these job seekers as well, and our database reflects this. BridgePath focuses on both active and passive job seekers.

A major difference between BridgePath and other services is that it is not simply a bulletin board of job openings. Rather, BridgePath enables employers to e-mail job and internship announcements directly to students based on their skills and interests. Consequently, BridgePath collects detailed information—on which employers search—when you register. Another difference is also noteworthy: BridgePath does *not* collect resumes. Instead, you are notified of an employer's interest in you, and you send your own resume via e-mail directly to the employer.

How BridgePath Works

You sign up for BridgePath's services by visiting its Web site and using your e-mail address. You fill out an online questionnaire that includes questions about where you want to work, what your major field of study is, what industries you are interested in, and what skills you have. This process takes five to ten minutes. BridgePath needs your e-mail address so that employers can contact you when suitable openings occur. Of course, you must check your e-mail often and respond to the announcements that interest you. When an employer has an opening, it uses pull-down menus to select its desired criteria. According to Mel Ochoa, these criteria include the following options:

- ✔ **Graduation date and/or years of experience**

- ✔ **Location:** the job candidate's current location or a desired location

- ✔ **University attended**

- ✔ **Degrees held:** BA, BS, MBA, JD, MA, MS, MD, Ph.D. (BridgePath also works with community colleges, so AA/AS degrees are also in the criteria.)

- ✔ **Major or concentrations studied**

- ✔ **Foreign language skills**

- ✔ **GPA**

- ✔ **Citizenship status**

- ✔ **Computer skills:** proficiency levels for programming, administration, databases

- ✔ **Interests and functions:** types of jobs the candidate is interested in

- ✔ **Type of work:** full-time, internship, temporary, and contractor

- ✔ **Company size:** start-up, small, medium, or large corporation

- ✔ **Customized criteria:** additional criteria to be added on a case-by-case basis

A very important feature of BridgePath is that your privacy is preserved until a suitable employer is interested in your qualifications. Employers search blind resumes, which means that your name and other contact information is shielded. When an interesting candidate is selected, the company forwards an e-mail to the person. According to BridgePath, the process works this way:

> As openings occur, recruiters decide which types of students they are looking for. Then recruiters visit our Web page and log in. Our easy-to-use interface lets recruiters tailor their search based on location, student interest by industry and job function, major field of study, and more than 20 other searchable criteria. Once their search is finished, recruiters are informed of how many students matched their criteria. Recruiters are not given students' personal information at this point. Then recruiters type a personal e-mail, alerting targeted students of a job or internship opening. After e-mails have been sent, it's up to the students to decide whether to submit their resumes via e-mail. Most importantly, students receive e-mails only from employers who are interested in them.

Employers are charged per e-mail, so it is in their best interest to target their searches carefully. Thus you are likely to get only serious inquiries. But BridgePath is service oriented to the employer as well as the job seeker. According to Mel Ochoa, BridgePath offers the following four services to employers:

- ✔ **BridgePath Weekly:** BridgePath sends out resumes of all its new and available candidates to clients (employers) each week. A client receives only the resumes of candidates who match the company's criteria; therefore, the client doesn't have to waste time reviewing unqualified resumes.

- ✔ **BridgePath Hunter:** This is BridgePath's traditional recruiter service. BridgePath gets paid only per hire and receives 20 percent of the placement fee that a client collects or 20 percent of the retainer. BridgePath screens the candidates' resumes thoroughly and forwards the top candidates on to the clients. BridgePath can also combine the screening process with preliminary interviews for 30 percent of the placement fee or 30 percent of the retainer.

- ✔ **BridgePath Direct:** BridgePath sends e-mail job announcements directly to job seekers who match a client's criteria. BridgePath charges the employer per announcement sent ($225.00), regardless of the number of recipients. Job seekers send their resumes directly to the client (employer).

- ✔ **BridgePath Slate:** BridgePath compiles a slate of 7 to 15 candidates who have been screened by experts and determined to fit the job opening. These candidates are fully guaranteed. If a client is not satisfied, BridgePath will refund its money.

Remember, BridgePath's services are *free* to the job seeker. Besides its basic service, BridgePath provides other assistance to job seekers at its site. One exceptional service is Resume Path, a useful tool that enables job seekers to send their resumes instantly to over 200 companies free of charge. You simply paste your resume into BridgePath's site and then send it electronically.

In addition, you can post your resume to a service called Resume Review (courtesy of Delphi Forums) and have it critiqued by others. With this service, you can also offer your advice to other resume writers. In the "Get a Job!" section of the BridgePath site, you can find job-hunting advice, employment opportunities, and interactive career discussions.

This combination of services to students and employers makes for a good success rate. Mel Ochoa explains this point by saying:

> Our success rate is very high because of the personal attention we give to job seekers and employers. Since job seekers create highly detailed personal profiles, BridgePath is the most comprehensive tool for clients to quickly and easily find the best candidates. BridgePath prescreens all of its candidates and forwards only those that are the most qualified for the specific position. Thus, our success rate is high because the candidates are the ones whom employers are specifically looking for, and the jobs are ones that job seekers have specifically said they want.

Because you will be sending your resume to employers through BridgePath, we asked Mel Ochoa for advice on writing a winning resume. He says:

> The most important thing to remember when writing a resume is that this is your chance to give an employer a snapshot of your qualifications and personality and to make yourself stand out in a crowd of other job seekers. However, a resume should not be a life history or an autobiography.

Ochoa offers these points to keep in mind when you write a resume:

- ✔ The resume should not be longer than a page. You can have two pages only if you have years of appropriate experience.

- ✔ Include necessary and relevant information to the job you are applying for. For example, although you may list a variety of previous positions, you should go into detail only about the ones that pertain to the job for which you are applying.

- ✔ Emphasize the duties, responsibilities, and accomplishments that you had in a position and include the dates you worked.

✔ Action phrases help to get the point across.

✔ You can also list skills or hobbies that may not be reflected in your job experience.

✔ Although you should not include information regarding high school, you can list relevant educational experiences, such as college or courses that have made you better qualified for the position.

And remember BridgePath's slogan: "Let the jobs find you!"

Whether you are a veteran, a college student, or a federal employee, many sites on the Internet can help you with your job search. You can also find services that target other specific groups, such as older workers, youth workers, and certain ethnic groups. The fact is, you can find a niche for just about any kind of job seeker on the Internet. Explore. Find your place. A special site is waiting for you.

Chapter 7

Posting Your Resume to Usenet Resume Newsgroups

Newsgroups are an early way of getting your resume on the Internet. They are not as important in job search as resume banks on the World Wide Web are today, but they remain useful—particularly for job searches limited to one city or state.

If you're familiar with newsgroups, jump ahead to the section "Preparing Your Resume for Newsgroups." If not, you'll find the background information you need to know in the next section.

Newsgroups Are Electronic Bulletin Boards

Usenet newsgroups were on the Internet before there was a World Wide Web. Think of a newsgroup as the electronic equivalent of a bulletin board in your local grocery store or on your college campus. Let's say your dog is missing. You can post a message about your dog on a bulletin board for people to read as they pass by. If someone has seen your dog, that person can copy down your telephone number and call you to report where your dog may be. Another person with a dog of the same breed can leave you a message to tell you about some available puppies. And because bulletin boards are visible to anyone who passes by, another person may write graffiti on your posting.

Newsgroups function in the same way as bulletin boards, and they are *the* bargain on the Internet because you have no charges for reading, placing, or responding to a posting—other than, of course, the regular cost of your Internet service provider.

Newsgroups are transmitted electronically around the world on Usenet (User's Network). Usenet newsgroups number in the thousands, and they are identified by topic. Some of the newsgroups are serious discussions on serious topics; others are just for fun; still others are frank, explicit discussions of adult topics. No one group is in charge of Usenet as a whole.

Just because you have Internet access doesn't mean you have access to Usenet newsgroups. And even if your Internet service provider affords access to Usenet, you still may not have access to all the thousands of newsgroups.

Newsgroups are identified with a [word] dot [word] and [word] dot [word] dot [word] format. The words may be abbreviated, as in the following example: `biz.jobs.offered`. This is a popular newsgroup for listing business jobs.

In a newsgroup, you'll see the postings (also known as *articles*) that can be as recent as five minutes old or as dated as several months old, depending on how many postings the group receives. In addition to the date, each posting is identified by its subject (or title) line. You decide which posting you want to read by its subject line.

When you select a particular posting to read, look for the return address of the poster. The return address may be in the upper-left corner in two lines, such as the following example:

```
fjandt
(at igc.apc.org)
```

To send an e-mail message to that person, you type the following address:

```
fjandt@igc.apc.org
```

Some newsgroup readers may have a reply function, which enables the reader to send a reply to the whole group or just to the original poster. If you reply to the whole group, your message will be public for anyone to read as a reply. If you reply to the original poster, your e-mail message goes only to the poster.

If you have no experience with newsgroups, one place to begin is the following newsgroup, which provides articles on how to best use newsgroups:

`news.announce.newusers`

Preparing Your Resume for Newsgroups

Getting your resume ready for a newsgroup posting is easy as long as you use a little creativity. Because so many newsgroups are on the Internet today, you have to make sure that your resume stands out. The next two sections give you some advice about preparing your resume for the newsgroups.

The Subject Line

Remember that newsgroup postings are identified by their subject (or title) line. An employer decides which postings to read by their subject lines. Too many applicants throw an opportunity away by entering overused or mundane words for the subject line, such as Resume or Resume for Registered Nurse. When an employer scans hundreds of resumes listed by subject line, the catchy ones get looked at first:

HIGHLY SKILLED, DEDICATED, COMPASSIONATE REGISTERED NURSE

Don't decide simply to throw out a few words that are related to your particular field. This approach is just not wise. You want to somehow distinguish yourself from the rest of the throng and at the same time give the employer a reason to want to read your resume instead of all the others in the newsgroup.

You can use a few creative ideas with the subject line to catch an employer's attention. For example, put your subject in capital letters or surround it with asterisks. Use angle brackets (> <) as arrows pointing to your subject line. Use adjectives. Put spaces and backslash marks between titles or terms. Be bold! Use attention-getting words, such as *talented, innovative, ambitious,* and *creative*. Each of the following lines contains a subject line that uses these ideas to catch the attention of an employer:

WRITER / MANAGER / ANALYST / V. QUALIFIED / CURIOUS

TALENTED, GIFTED, AMBITIOUS COMPUTER SCIENTIST

==============TOP SALES POSITION WANTED================

*****>>>>>>CREATIVE FREELANCE PHOTOGRAPHER<<<<<<*****

INNOVATIVE PR PROFESSIONAL>>>>>PROVEN TRACK RECORD

Compare the innovative subject lines with these common ones:

> entry-level psych research position
>
> Systems/software
>
> Management
>
> proj. 1dr/rdbms/client-server/imaging

A creative subject line grabs the employer's attention and invites the individual to look at your resume. Use the subject line with flair! Become a standout in that endless field of boring one-liners. You'll get noticed.

> ***Caution:*** Don't use anything too funny or off-color.

ASCII (or Plain) Text

You submit your resumes to newsgroups via e-mail. Every e-mail program supports ASCII (American Standard Code for Information Interchange). ASCII text is straight text; in other words, it has no indents, no centering, **no bold text,** <u>no underlines</u>, *no italics,* no color, no tables, no graphics, no pictures—just text. And the standard limit for the number of letters or spaces on a line is 70.

Even with these limitations, you can easily prepare an attractive resume for posting in newsgroups by following these guidelines:

- ✔ Build your resume in your word processor.

- ✔ Because you can't indent or use the centerline feature, space everything as you type it and then save the file. If you don't use spacing, everything will be left-aligned when you cut and paste it.

- ✔ Because you can't use bold text or italics, use uppercase and line breaks effectively.

- ✔ Double-check that no line exceeds 70 characters in length.

- ✔ Typographical errors and misspellings are deadly in a resume. Remember to do a spell check. Save your resume as a text (ASCII) file.

- ✔ When you're ready to post your resume to a newsgroup, cut and paste it directly into the body of your message.

- ✔ Check your work by sending a copy to your own e-mail address.

Chapter 7: Posting Your Resume to Usenet Resume Newsgroups

Resume Newsgroups

The Internet has many newsgroups that are dedicated to posting resumes. You can post your resume in these newsgroups at no cost. Most of the jobs and resume newsgroups serve a defined geographical area or a specific industry (see Table 7.1). If you live in one of the geographical regions listed in Table 7.1 or if you want to work in that location, use the newsgroup that is listed.

TABLE 7.1 RESUME USENET GROUPS

Type of Newsgroup	Newsgroup Name
General:	
Appropriate for most resumes	misc.jobs.resumes
Countries:	
Israel	israel.jobs.resumes
United Kingdom	uk.jobs.wanted
U.S. States:	
Florida	fl.jobs.resumes
Illinois	il.jobs.resumes
Pennsylvania	pa.jobs.wanted
Cities:	
Houston	houston.jobs.wanted
New York City	nyc.jobs.wanted
Pittsburgh	pgh.jobs.wanted
Philadelphia	phl.jobs.wanted
Portland, OR	pdaxs.jobs.resumes
	pdaxs.jobs.wanted
Quebec City, Canada	qc.jobs.wanted
St. Louis	stl.jobs.resumes
San Francisco Bay area	ba.jobs.resumes
San Diego	sdnet.jobs.wanted
Seattle	seattle.jobs.wanted
Industry:	
Biological industry	bionet.jobs.wanted
Medical sales	alt.medical.sales.jobs.resumes

Some newsgroups contain job-vacancy postings as well as some resumes. We suggest that you read the postings first to determine whether the newsgroup is an appropriate place to post your resume. Most of these are geographic newsgroups, discernable by the first part of the address: **seattle.jobs.offered** is for jobs in the Seattle area; **vegas.jobs** is for finding opportunities in Las Vegas; and so on. Several others in Table 7.2 are for more general offerings: **misc.jobs.contract** is for applicants looking for contract work; **misc.jobs.offered** is a site containing a variety of offerings.

Part I: Electronic Resumes

TABLE 7.2 JOB LISTING USENET GROUPS

akr.jobs	il.jobs.offered	oh.jobs
alabama.jobs	in.jobs	ont.jobs
alt.jobs	israel.jobs.offered	ott.jobs
atl.jobs	ithaca.jobs	pa.jobs.offered
atl.resumes	jobs.offered	pgh.jobs.offered
austin.jobs	kc.jobs	phl.jobs.offered
az.jobs	la.jobs	sac.jobs
ba.jobs	mi.jobs	sat.jobs
ba.jobs.contract	milw.jobs	seattle.jobs.offered
ba.jobs.offered	misc.jobs	tor.jobs
bc.jobs	misc.jobs.contract	triangle.jobs
biz.jobs.offered	misc.jobs.contracts	tx.jobs
ca.jobs	misc.jobs.offered	uk.jobs
can.jobs	ne.jobs	uk.jobs.contract
cle.jobs	nebr.jobs	uk.jobs.offered
cmh.jobs	nh.jobs	us.jobs
co.jobs	niagara.jobs	us.jobs.offered
ct.jobs	nj.jobs	us.jobs.offered.contract
dc.jobs	ny.jobs	us.jobs.resumes
de.markt.jobs	nyc.jobs	ut.jobs
dfw.jobs	nyc.jobs.offered	va.jobs
fl.jobs	nz.jobs	vegas.jobs
houston.jobs.offered	oc.jobs	

Submitting Your Resume

Even if you don't have access to these newsgroups, you can still post your resume there by using one of the resume data banks that will post your resume in newsgroups when you submit your resume to them. By using newsgroups, you are getting your resume out where others can see it, even if you can't see it yourself. The following list includes some of the resume banks that provide this service. These banks are fully described with their URL addresses in Part II.

✔ **HeadHunter.Net:** Resumes from all career fields are posted to newsgroups and other Internet sites.

✔ **JobCenter:** Resumes from all career fields are posted to your choice of Usenet newsgroups once every other week.

✔ **MedZilla™:** Abstracts of health-care resumes are posted without identifying information. MedZilla also serves as a contact to protect the identity of the job seeker.

✔ **VirtualResume:** Resumes from all career fields are posted and appear under the job seeker's own name and e-mail address.

A few sites used to provide e-mail to any newsgroup available on the sites. These mail-to-news gateways became abused and overloaded and are no longer available or are not publicly announced. If you find a service of this sort, ask permission before you use it or publish its address.

Special Considerations

The nature of Usenet newsgroups creates two unique factors for you to consider. First, newsgroup postings are labeled by date. Remember that the postings can be as recent as five minutes old or as dated as several months old, depending on how many postings the group receives. Because of the volume of resumes posted to newsgroups, your resume will either be purged or filtered by most browsers within less than a week. In an active, popular resume newsgroup, you may need to consider reposting your resume when it is no longer available on the newsgroup or when you change your resume.

Second, newsgroups are public, which means that anyone—a resume data bank, for example—can copy your resume from the newsgroup. This access can be both an advantage and a disadvantage. When you're a job seeker, you may want your resume in as many places as possible to increase the probability that an employer will find you. On the other hand, you may not want your resume so easily available in so many places.

Dr. Frank Heasley of MedZilla cautions that a job seeker who posts a resume with identifying information in a newsgroup assumes the risks of getting spammed with junk e-mail, being stalked, being approached by con artists who use information from the resume to gain trust and take advantage of the job seeker at a vulnerable time, and risking identity theft. Perpetrators can actually use resume information to apply for new identification papers and then use these papers to open credit-card accounts or commit other crimes.

And consider the following risk with a hypothetical resume service: Lee's Resume Service wants to increase the size of its database to entice more corporate subscribers. Lee copies your resume from a newsgroup and adds it to his resume data bank. Lee does not delete resumes from his database, so one year later your resume is still available at Lee's Resume Service. After this much time, your resume is no longer accurate, and you may not want it publicly available. By now, your resume could be in several other data banks as well. Because of the free access to newsgroups, no one can ever know how many resumes are available on the Internet. Yours may be in several resume data banks at the same time.

We recommend that you add the line "Last updated on *date*" to a resume posted in a newsgroup. At least this one line ensures that an employer knows whether your resume is current.

Posting your resume in a newsgroup is called a passive posting because you never know who—if anyone—has read your resume. You never know when it is read, where it is read, nor why it is read. With a passive posting, all you can do is wait to be contacted.

Posting your resume in a newsgroup costs nothing and takes very little time; however, this kind of posting is not as likely to result in an offer of employment as the more active methods.

The following resumes were taken from several Usenet newsgroups. We include them here so that you can see what they look like and understand some of the problems associated with them. Our comments appear at the end of each resume.

Sample Resume 7-1

Date : June 16 1998
  Name : Ben James
  Address : Some Block, Some Address, Pitam Pura,
    Delhi, Delhi 110085
  Country : India
  Phone # : 000-000- 0000
   Email : xxx@xxxxx.xxx
              Resume

SUMMARY OF QUALIFICATIONS

* Diploma in Merchant Banking and Financial Services from Institute of
Chartered Financial Analyst of India (ICFAI)
* Honours Diploma in Software Engineering from Aptech, New Delhi
* B.Com from Delhi University
* Persuing MBA Finance
* Enjoy my work and consistently strive to achieve the best results in tasks
assigned to me

RELAVANT SKILLS & EXPERIENCE(About Eight Years Experience in the field of
Finance)

Presently Working as a Assistant Manager Credit Control with Some Company Ltd.
(from 30-04-XX till date)

Responsible for the entire Credit Function- Credit Verification, Rating,
Revenue Assurance- BILLING and COLLECTIONS.
Continuous Monitoring, review and formulation of Credit Policies towards Direct
Parties and Franchisees and to take necessary action so that the Payments and
the 'TDS Certificates' are received from them within a stipulated period of
time
Settlement of Claims etc, with the parties, if any.
Designing and Preparing various MIS reports for the Management..
Worked as a Credit Control Officer with Some Company (INDIA) LTD. (from 3-08-
XX TO 30/4/XX)

Periodic monitoring of Sundry Debtors and to take such necessary action with a
view to ensure that the parties make Payments within a reasonable/stipulated
period of time.
To keep a strict vigil on those parties to whom sales are being made against
'C' and 'ST-I' forms with a view to ensure that these are received from them
within a reasonable period.
Preparing weekly reports showing Partywise amounts outstandings for more than
one month and action taken for early settlement of dues and various other MIS

Sample Resume 7-1 continued

reports for the Director

Worked as an Accountant cum Computer Programmer with Any Firm & Associates for more than one and half years (from 1-01-XX to 31/7/XX)

Worked as an Accountant with Another Company Pvt. Ltd. for three and a half years (from 1-05-XXto 31/12/XX)

MY BELIEF

I strongly believe that hard work has no substitute. I always enjoy my work and constantly strive to enthuse dedication and commitment to the work in myself and my team. I strongly belive that one who can beat the clock, can beat the world.

Ben James

> *COMMENTS:*
> *Poorly spaced. Misspellings(!) Not much information in the way of skills. Confusing acronyms. Interesting "My Belief" statement. Fresh take on Personal Statement.*

Sample Resume 7-2

Evelyn Stumpf
000 Some Street
Some City, Some State XXXXX
(000)000-0000

Position: PHYSICAL THERAPY TECH

Resume:

===================

OBJECTIVE
To obtain a growth position with a Physical Therapy Clinic in Western State

HIGHLIGHTS OF QUALIFICATIONS
-Excellent teacher/trainer; patient and effective when working with a wide range of personalities.
-Over 13 years of professional experience with the public.
-Proven skill in perserving to solve customer problems.
-Self-motivated and confident in making independent decisions.
-Very well organized and able to meet deadlines.

SKILLS
Patient Educator,Supervising,Managing,Team Building,Data Processing,Planning,Communication,Implementing,Trouble Shooting

RELEVANT EXPERIENCE
Excellent patient educator trained in the techniques of active and passive range of motion exercise, massage therapy, paraffin wax therapy, ultrasonic therapy, gait training , muscle strength training and post operative wound care.

Effectively supervised and trained junior personnel most of whom had no previous patient care experience and oversaw all requirements needed to support over 600 patients visits per month.

Accurately maintained and managed an annual fiscal budget of over $62,000 , ensured optimal stocking levels for over 950 consumable items.

Revised, orgainzed and prepared statndard operating procedure manuals for Medical Surgical Clinic areas, and maintained, managed and improved patient care processing procedures while at the same time reducing manhours. This resulted in the department receiving the highest customer service satisfaction rating among Air Force Medical Facilites, conducted by an outside data processing firm.

Mediated between management and staff to maintain harmonious working relations and maximized work performance.

Sample Resume 7-2 continued

Initiated, coordinated and taught a New Prenatal Education Program for expectant mothers for over 28,000 patients annually for over a period of three years.

Computer skills include Windows 95, MS DOS, MS WORD, WORD PERFECT 5.0/6.1, COMPOSITE HEALTH CARE SYSTEM (CHCS) and AMBULATORY DATA SYSTEM (ADS).

EMPLOYMENT HISTORY
Apr XX-Present   Night Patient Supervisor, Some Military Hospital
Some City, Some State
Sep 94-Apr 97   Medical Surgical Clinic Supervisor, Same Military Hospital,
                 Same City, Same State
May 94-Sep 94   Hospital Corps School, A Military Clinic in WA
Jun 93-May 94   Line Supervisor, An Air Force Base in U.S.
May 89-Jun 93   Technician and Line Supervisor, A Military Base in U.S.

EDUCATION
         Currently working on Associates of Science, A Particular University
         (68 credits)
1987   Presidential Senior High School, Ft. Collins, CO High School Diploma
1989   Aviation Course, Some City, MN(1200 hrs)
1994   Hospital Corps Course, Some Military Base, US (800 hours)

COMMENTS:
Lots of good skills information. Scanner-friendly. Nicely laid out, but some problems with indenting. Some spelling mistakes! Gender-specific language (manhours) is inappropriate.

Sample Resume 7-3

Subject: Resume: Health Care Executive, Sales, Operations and Start-up Experience
From: person@xxx.xxx (Person's Name (via JobCenter))
Date: 1998/06/12
Message-ID: <6lrnoi$k0r@news9.noc.netcom.net>
Newsgroups: alt.medical.sales.jobs.resumes,houston.jobs.wanted

Article Segment 1 of 2
(Get All 2 Segments)

Name: Jobseeker
Company: (none specified)
E-mail: person@xxx.xxx
Phone: 000-000-0000
Location: Lakewood, FL

JOBSEEKER

WORK EXPERIENCE

1997 - Present   Northwest Diabetes Resources, Sequim, WA
Director, New Business Development Services

Responsible for researching, analyzing, coordinating and implementing
new business opportunities for Some Company, a physician practice management
company focused exclusively on oncology treatment.

* Developed and implemented Juvenile Diabetes program in 6 of 16
existing
practice locations
* Increased physician count by 55%
* Initiated hospital partnership program to create Comprehensive
Juvenile Diabetes Centers at Some Company practice locations
* Developed genetic testing program for Company's practice network

19XX – 19XX Some Software Company, Topeka, KS
Vice President National Accounts

A founder of SSC, Inc., a start-up company, providing
comprehensive "managed care" service for all office technology.
Services included hardware repair and maintenance and software and
network support.

* Developed company start-up facilities and operational infrastructure
* Developed, tested and modified the consultative sales model

Sample Resume 7-3 continued

* Authored field training programs and marketing tools
* Recruited and managed the sales team in the initial test market
* Recruited regional sales management personnel
* Sold and managed implementation of the top five SSC accounts, generating 60% of the companies total revenues
* Established strategic alliances with comparable business to business partners
* Recruited and managed the network of national preferred service providers

19XX – 19XX Technical Solutions, Inc., Kansas City, KS
President/CEO

Founder of Technical Solutions, Inc., a data transcription service that provided data conversion for legal and medical firms

* Developed and implemented business plan and obtained $2 million in private funding
* Directed all company business management activities, including property leases, insurance, legal and medical forms, office equipment acquisitions and leases.
* Developed all company operational policies and procedures, including human resources, inventory tracking, sales and sales training
* Developed all company promotional materials and alliance partner collateral
* Managed expenses
* Recruited and managed sales force, exceeding year one and two revenue plans by 60%
* Established strategic alliance with largest legal and medical firms in 3 states

(Get Next Article Segment)

> **COMMENT:**
> *Resume too long, as required posting in two segments. However, lots of good skills information. Nicely laid out. Easy to read, despite length.*

Sample Resume 7-4

Subject: Resume: Biological laboratory technician or similar career opportunities
From: xxx@xxx.xxx
Date: 1998/06/03
Newsgroups:
misc.jobs.resumes,alt.medical.sales.jobs.resumes,bionet.jobs.wanted,pa.jobs.wanted

Article Segment 1 of 2
(Get All 2 Segments)

Name: Alan Davidson
Company: (none specified)
E-mail: xxx@xxx.xxx
Phone: (555) 555-5555
Location: Northeast United States

Alan Davidson
Temporary Address:
1111 South Bliss Drive
Four Corners, TN
Phone: (555) 555-5555

Permanent Address:
PO BOX XXXX
Five Corners, TN
Phone: (555) 555-5555

Objective:
   To obtain a full-time position and establish a career with advancement possibilities. Also, to undergo any required training needed to ensure maximum proficiency in the designated work field.

Education:
   Sept. 1994- May 1998   BS: Biology
                Some Tennessee College

Total credits currently scheduled (Spring 19XX): 18.0
Total credits earned: 124.0
Total credits earned toward graduation: 142.0
Total credits- 300 & 400 level courses: 42.0
Cumulative quality point average: 3.273
Major quality point average: 3.442

Internships and Presentations:
   Physical Therapy Internship:
   Observed and examined both in- patient and out-patient physical

Sample Resume 7-4 continued

therapy in a hospital environment. Researched a specific disease, Guillane Barre, and presented a case study on it.
   Seminar:
   Presented with many topics outlined by fellow students. Researched and presented a lecture on Multiple Sclerosis.

Research:
   Research in Biology:
   In Spring 1998, I was placed in charge of designing and operating a new neurophysiology laboratory at Some Tennessee College. This is an independent study program. One topic that will be studied is nerve transmission within the green frog. Other research interests will be performed, however these have not be isolated. The experiments designed in this lab will be utilized in upcoming courses.

Work Experience:
   Sales Associate: Ritzy department store. Learned merchandising and worked with people directly to establish a better rapport. Responsible for opening and closing terminals, and handling the receiving area. (1 year)
   Water Safety Instructor: Planned and taught many American Red Cross approved swim and water safety lessons. Additionally worked as a lifeguard and assistant pool manager. (5 years)
   Work Study: Worked directly with a professor performing clerical duties. Other responsibilities include setting up laboratories and performing trial experiments. (1 year)

Personal Interests and Organizations*:
-Learning new things   -Outdoor Recreation   -Racquetball
-Writing   -Studying / Tutoring -Swimming / Teaching swim lessons
-Exploring the Internet   -Community involvement
*STC Martial Arts Club (Vice Pres: 1 year, Treasurer: 1 year)
*STC Swimming & Diving Club (Pres: 3 years)
*Delta Sigma Phi Fraternity (Secretary: 1 year, Philanthropic Chairman: 2 years)

Related Courses and Laboratories:
   ** All courses have additional hours in laboratory.
   ^ Classes currently enrolled in.

Biology:
-Human Anatomy & Physiology I & II**   -A&P of Speech and Hearing
-Parasitology** -Biology I & II**   -General Ecology**   -Immunology
-Neural Science -Human Physiology -Microbiology**
-Animal Physiology**   -Biological Seminar I & II -Genetics

Sample Resume 7-4 continued

-Comparative Vertebrate Anatomy**   -Physical Therapy Internship
-Histology**   ^Molecular Biology**   ^Biological Instrumentation**

Chemistry and Physics:
-Intro Chemistry I & II** -Organic Chemistry I & II**   -Physics I & II**

(Get Next Article Segment)

> *COMMENT:*
> *Objective is vague, not mentioning position desired. Unnecessary listing of credits earned, attempted, and so on. It is more appropriate to list relevant course work. Very confusing use of symbols to designate course work, which is also misplaced in the resume. Haphazard layout. Resume is too long, needing two segments to list completely.*

Sample Resume 7-5

Jessica Lewis
1111 Fisher
Harrisburg, PA
home: 555-555-5555
or: 111-111-1111
email: xxx@xxx.xxx

OBJECTIVE: A secretarial/office management position where my organizational, creative and computer skills would be used to run an efficient and professional office.

EXPERIENCE: 19XX – 19XX   Ready Concrete Company   Harrisburg, PA
OFFICE MANAGER
Responsible for all payroll, new hire and termination paper work. Hired and supervised office help. Designed and implemented new database forms. Performed drug testing. Installed new computer hardware and software. Processed daily work orders. Purchased material. Prepared reports. Programmed, answered and maintained a multi-line phone system. Produced monthly invoices. Managed field office with up to 50 employees. Resolved problems with vendors, suppliers and the home office.

EDUCATION: Some Eastern Community College, Pittsburgh, PA
ASSOCIATES DEGREE
Dean's List, Who's Who of College Students, and Treasurer of sorority

Skills: I am proficient in the following computer programs: Q&A versions 4 & 5, Win95, Windows 3.1, Carbon Copy, Norton Utilities, Excel, Pathminder, Print Shop and DOS 6.2.

I am able to operate the following office machines: typewriter (40 WPM), personal computer, fax, modem/fax, copier, dot matrix and inkjet printers, multi-line phone system, and communication/radio system.

COMMUNITY
ACTIVITIES: Cub Scout den leader, President of Assumption School Board, Band Booster Secretary

Sample Resume 7–5 continued

nursery and VBS teacher, organized a can drive fund-raiser and spearheaded a spring fund-raiser.

> *COMMENTS:*
> *Lots of data for scanning. Use of personal pronouns not advised. Bulleted short statements rather than full sentences are recommended. Community activities not job-related and contain unfamiliar acronym.*

Part I: Electronic Resumes ....

Sample Resume 7-6

Evan Thomas
65 Kaiser Street
Longmont, CO
xxx@xxx.xxx

Objective:

Combine the skills developed during my teaching career with my building experience to become a contributing member of a project management team working for a successful construction company in the greater Denver area.

Employment History:

12/97 - 2/98, Assistant Project Manager, Bass Construction Corp., Denver, CO
    Developed 78K renovation proposal for Safe Medical Center, Denver, CO
    Tracked 4.7M rehab to flrs. 16-24. Rock Solid Insurance Building, Denver,
    Generated RFI's, Submittal Transmittals, AIA G702 Documents,
    work schedule, invoices, purchase orders and value engineering
    meeting minutes.

8/XX - 6/XX, Teacher and Choir Director, Longmont High School, Longmont, CO
    Taught tenth grade Math and eleventh grade Physics
    Coached boys swimming. Directed Choir
8/82 - 6/83, Teacher and Coach, Some High School, Denver, CO
    Taught twelfth grade Chemistry and seventh grade Science
    Coached varsity and junior varsity swimming
8/78 - 6/82, Teacher and Coach, Some Other School, Phoenix, AZ
Taught ninth grade Earth Science and energy efficient home
    construction.
    Coached boys varsity soccer.

Summers 78 - 97, Independent Contractor.
    General Contractor, Construction Supervisor and Builder.
    Floor-plan layout, frame construction, insulation, roof, sidewall,
    interior finish.

Education:

Master of Education, Major University, Phoenix, AZ
BS in Education, College in Colorado

Additional Skills:

Systems: Win95, MacOS.

Sample Resume 7-6 continued

Software: Microsoft Office, Microsoft Project, Prolog Manager, Claris Works.

> ***COMMENTS:***
> *Uneven margins. Lots of nouns for scanning. Some stale experience–back to 1978! Irrelevant last position.*

Sample Resume 7-7

Name: Elizabeth Reed
Company: (none specified)
E-mail: xxx@xxx.xxx
Phone: (555) 555-5555

OBJECTIVE

A career in human resources that will utilize my skills and offer challenging work opportunities and continued personal growth.

EDUCATION

Northern California University   Dec 19XX
Department of Liberal Studies. Emphasis in the Nature of Language. Course work: Presently taking classes to obtain a certificate in Human Resource Management.

WORK EXPERIENCE

Some Unknown Company, Sacramento, CA   July 19XX- Present
Human Resource Assistant   Responsible for coordinating benefit packages as well as workers compensation claims. Implement pension plans for union workers. Develop strategies to improve efficiency of deliveries. Input information for shipping confirmations. Correlate invoices for accounts   receivable. Answer phone lines by utilizing a switchboard to transfer calls to employees.

Happy Times Elementary School, Sacramento, CA Jan. 19XX - April 19XX
Teacher's Aide   Worked in a Third Grade Hyperactive Class. Assisted in maintaining order and an active learning environment. Conducted verbal and   written spelling tests. Helped students who had difficulties learning the new   vocabulary. Illustrated the concepts of math to children using manipulatives to help them learn about multiplication and division. Formed reading groups to help utilize the scaffolding effect.

Anytime Leisure Sales, Sacramento, CA 19XX – 19XX
Receptionist: Reorganized files to maintain efficiency in a fast paced environment. Answered phones and typed various business letters. Had the opportunity to   interact with customers daily.

Good Times Productions Visalia, CA 19XX – 19XX
Helped organize group events as well as developed the schedules that correlated with each event. Kept a record of the participants in each group. Accessed information via the Internet.

Sample Resume 7-7 continued

COMPUTER SKILLS
Functional knowledge in Macintosh (Mac OS), PC (Windows 95/NT), most business applications, the UNIX operating system (Telnet, FTP, C-shell programming) and ability to utilize the Internet as an important search tool for information.

> *COMMENTS:*
> *Nicely worded and laid out. Some problems with spacing. Need to spell out what "most business applications" means. The more information, the better for a scanner.*

Part I: Electronic Resumes

Sample Resume 7-8

Name: Gloria Atterbury
Company: (none specified)
E-mail: xxx@xxx.xxx
Phone: (555) 555-5555
Location: Durham/Raleigh, NC

Gloria Atterbury

Objective: To utilize my vast knowledge and successful educational experience in planning and organizing multifaceted, complex activities in which professional growth and personal contributions are the norm.

EMPLOYMENT SUMMARY:

Some Eastern Community College   -   1987 -   Teach basic speech courses; advise students; and serve on   committees.

University of Another Eastern State   -   1990 -   1991
       Taught mass lecture Public Speaking course; supervised graduate teaching associates; and advised all communication majors.
Community College   -   1986 - 1987; 75 - 77   Taught Fundamentals of Speech, Oral Interpretation, Public   Speaking, and Developmental English; advised students; served   on committees.
A State College   -   1979 - 1980
         Served as Director of College Recruitment.

ACADEMIC PREPARATION:
M.A.T,   Speech A Southern University
M.Ed.,   Elementary Education, Same Southern University
 B.A.,   Speech and Drama, Different Southern School
Ph.D. Studies, Speech and Theatre Education, An Eastern University

DISTINCTIONS AND AWARDS:
Returning Doctoral Candidate Fellowship, Alma Mater University
Fellowships to Western and Eastern Universities
        Graduate Teaching Associateships, Some Southern University
Teacher Recognition Award, SGA, NOVA

Sample Resume 7-8 continued

AFFILIATIONS:

Nationwide Communication Association
College Teachers Speech Communication Association

> ***COMMENTS:***
> *Objective is vague and needlessly wordy. What position is desired? Applicant did not allow for 70-character line rule, giving a haphazard appearance. Problems with spacing. Appropriate list of affiliations, if position sought is teaching. An academic CV would be more appropriate for this candidate.*

Sample Resume 7-9

Subject: Resume: PC SUPPORT / HELPDESK
From: JobBankUSA@data.jobbankusa.com
Date: 1998/06/04
Message-ID: <06040854571000051614@data.jobbankusa.com>
Newsgroups: misc.jobs.resumes,us.jobs.resumes

Position: PC SUPPORT / HELPDESK
City/State/Zip: FARNHAM - SURREY - ENGLAND, AK GU9 7DA
Location: CA
Relocate: Y
Years Exp: 2/3
Salary:
Salary Type: HR
Position Type: PC

Resume:

===================

SUMMARY

An enterprising, confident person, keen to succeed and prepared to work long hours, having a wide knowledge base of experience gained from diverse areas. Able to work well with people, both alone and within a team situation, to give presentations to large international groups and to converse well with people who are not confident in the English language. A comprehensive range of interpersonal skills has been acquired through working within a multilingual and multinational environment. TEFL Certificate awarded by Cambridge University on the 19 May 1995. A versatile trainer of language and computer skills, as well a competent technician.

EDUCATION
Secondary schooling
9/1983 - 7/1985 Montgomery el Alamein, Winchester. (UK Boarding)
9/1985 - 4/1988 Wavell School, Farnborough (UK)
Subjects Studied: All foundation subjects, including computer studies, plus options in:
            Physics; Chemistry; Biology; Drama and Geography.

WORK EXPERIENCE
14/4/97 - present   Mobil Plastics - Helpdesk/support Specialist
This work entails network administration, software support and training for all of the Company's European Users in both the English and French languages. Hardware and software application and upgrade installation and testing, repair work, including, when necessary, negotiating the most cost-effective solution and ordering replacement parts, and the administration required, logging and report writing etc, to ensure the smooth

Sample Resume 7-9 continued

running of the Helpdesk/SCS environment. The Company has large numbers of desktops, laptops, network and local printers, which has enabled extensive experience to be gained on a wide range of hardware and software systems. In the event of system crashes, I am part of the Mobil ADP team that visits users to reconfigure local systems and individual machines.

Since my employment, the Company has installed a new NT4 operating system with Lotus Notes Mail and I am a major contributor to the international roll-out of these products. I am in charge of the primary helpdesk.

Office Software: Microsoft Office 4.2;4.3; 95 & 97
Lotus 123
Word Perfect
Gear 4.2, (CD Writing)software
        Operating Systems: Windows 3.1 and 3.11
Windows 95 and 97
Windows NT
AS 400

Mail Software: Profs/Winoffis
CC-Mail
Lotus Notes
Internet E-Mail Network Systems: Novell 3.12
Novell 4.1
NT Server

Technical Training Courses
Computer-Based Training appreciation course   - 3 days
Excel basic course   - 2 days
Beginner's Graphics   - 3 days
Understanding Quality Assurance   -5 days
Access Database starter course   -2 days
AS 400 an introduction   -3 days
Networks - an environment   -2 days

1/6/95 -10/4/97   Short-Term Contracts
· First-level Help Desk for software applications and hardware. Supporting users by resolving problems with software applications (Helpdesk function).
· Eurocontrol, Central Flow Management Unit. Providing technical support to update and maintain the Access database of member States' operational functional units and to perform quality reviews on the technical documentation. In addition, assisted in the training of new staff to permit them to build confidence on the new PCs, in both English and French.
· Using various software drawing packages to produce commercial promotional material.

Sample Resume 7-9 continued

· Eurocontrol, working for EATCHIP Planning Division as a technical assistant to support the production of various EATCHIP documentation, including completed deliverable documents for distribution to member nations. Resolution of problems that staff experienced with MS Office, including all applications therein, Windows (3.1 and 95) and Corel Draw.
· Working in a Belgian Computer Company performing various data entry tasks, including project planning using MS Project, translation work, document formatting, production of presentation material and producing reports for the French Director. This position entailed the full use of Microsoft Office (French).
· Editing and formatting Eurocontrol documents to satisfy the EATCHIP documentation requirements, using MSOffice, and producing presentation material using Power Point and Corel Draw.

Independent Teacher
Working as an English Language Teacher for three schools in the Brussels region enabled me to continue to meet a wide variety of people of all ages and vocations, attend functions with students to assist them with their professional work and in their assimilation into an English environment.

16/5/1994 - 31/3/95   Ceran International Language School (English Department)
Tasks covered the organisation of students in both academic and social activities, performing the day to day office work, assisting the students with their English studies, including giving private lessons, using the computer to set timetables for the students and researching individual background information as requested. In addition, supported the creation and maintenance of the English Language Computer Based Training(CBT) packages. The students ranged in age from 14 to over 70 and represented a spectrum of nationalities with a very wide range of vocations. Organisation and supervision of evening group activities and daytime discussion groups.

The work/study situation at Ceran, , have resulted in the following:
· French and German - aural and oral, fluent; written and comprehension fair;
· Japanese and Flemish - reasonable conversational level
· Spanish - basic conversation.

I left Ceran after studying for nearly a year as I felt that it was to utilise my skills in a more constructive way. I applied for and passed the entrance tests of grammar construction and personality, and was then accepted on the Teaching English as a Foreign Language (TEFL) Course which was successfully completed on the 19 May 1995.

1/2/1991 - 11/3/1994   Contract Work - Self Employed
· Designed and implemented a database for a small antique restoration company to assist with their stock control, supplier evaluations, address of both customers and suppliers and the day to day financial transactions. This was carried out using the spreadsheet package Excel.
· Designed and produced forms and templates for an estate agent. These were used for potential purchaser requirements and details, for the surveyors on their site visits and

Sample Resume 7-9 continued

to input property details for circulation to prospective purchasers. Set up a database to cross relate the templates and forms with the potential purchasers. This was all performed on an IBM compatible machine. Weekly updating the computer files and records.

· Technical assistant with a small UK-based IT Company in Brussels. This included typing letters, reports and responses to calls for tender using the processors Word and Word Perfect. Designing charts and graphs using the drawing packages Corel Draw and Freelance, designing the presentation and incorporating textual and graphical formats, and the creation and updating of the accounting spreadsheets using the package Excel. Updating the Access database and creation of simple databases.

INTERESTS   Languages; Badminton; Snooker; Swimming; Travel; Computing and Electronics (built up my own computer).

> *COMMENTS:*
> *Resume was cross-posted to a newsgroup list by a resume database, making the candidate anonymous. Resume is excessively long and wordy. Summary should concentrate on skills, as well as personal qualities. Inappropriate use of personal pronouns. Unnecessary listing of short-term training courses. Way too much information here, even for a resume scanner!*

Chapter 8

Overview of the Resume Banks

The main way to get your resume on the Internet is to post your resume in one or more resume banks. Resume banks collect and make resume information accessible to employers.

Internet resume postings are from professionals in high-tech and engineering fields as well as from professionals in health care, financial, sales, and marketing fields. Some resume postings are from recent college graduates, and some are from people separating from the military. Some are entry level, and some are from experienced executives. The 82 resume banks we describe in this book total more than an amazing three million resumes. If you want your resume to be among them, you'll need the information in this chapter, where you'll read about the various types of resume banks available. In Part II, you'll find a detailed description of the resume banks to help you decide where you want to post your resume.

Submitting Your Resume

Each resume bank Web page explains how to submit your resume. Some banks ask you to submit your resume via e-mail; however, more banks ask you to complete an online form with information about yourself and then to cut and paste your resume into the Web form.

Some resume banks require the job seeker and the employer to fill out similar forms that ask questions about languages spoken, highest degree obtained, and the like. This information results in better matches between what the job seeker has to offer and what the employer is looking for.

If you don't want to use a computer to submit your resume online, you can find resume banks that will enter your resume for you. For example, the Transition Assistance Online resume bank accepts paper resumes from separating US military; Online Opportunities will enter your paper resume for a $5.00 fee; and JobExchange, medsearch, and Online Career Center will enter your paper resume for a $15.00 fee.

Passive Posting

Some resume banks are similar to the Usenet newsgroups because they simply provide an online presence. These data banks store and make your resume available for employers to search. Unfortunately, like the resume newsgroups, you will never know whether anyone reads your resume. You are passively waiting for employers to contact you.

After your resume has been successfully posted at this type of resume bank, you are dependent on the employer for the next step. The employer must go to that resume bank and select your resume. A few of these resume banks organize resumes only by category so that the employer has to look at each resume under a category heading. Most data banks, however, offer an employer a chance to search the text of your resume by keywords. The sophistication of the search program varies from data bank to data bank. For example, jobEngine has a sophisticated search engine—developed by I-Search Inc.—which presents the employer with a list that ranks the most appropriate candidate first.

All searches of the large CareerPath resume bank are done by staffing specialists who contact job seekers by e-mail to ensure privacy and then fax qualified and interested candidates' resumes to the employer. They guarantee at least five interested and qualified applicants for each search or the employer is not charged.

Interactive Data Banks

Unlike passive data banks, some resume banks can interact with you in important ways. Some give you feedback about the number of times your resume was reviewed. Contract Employment Weekly, for example, notifies job seekers by e-mail about who viewed and/or downloaded their resumes and when they did so. And The Job Resource enables you to see who has requested your resume and when.

Some data banks have software that monitors job and resume postings and automatically notifies the employer and the job seeker when a match occurs. CareerCast, Career Shop, CareerWeb, HealthCareerWeb, PassportAccess,

SelectJOBS, and Transition Assistance Online all notify employers on a regular basis of any resumes that match the skills requested by the employer. DiversiLink automatically notifies the job seeker of jobs as they are posted.

Careerfile, JobOptions, JobCenter Employment Services, Inc., medsearch, The Monster Board, and Online Career Center notify both employers and job seekers. These resume banks e-mail resumes that match a list of criteria to employers, and they notify job seekers of job openings that match their skills.

Public or Confidential?

Just as Usenet resume newsgroups are open to the world to read, so are some of the resume banks; therefore, anyone can find your current address, phone number, e-mail address, and even your employment history. This access to information means that anyone can find you, record your address, and try to sell you something in the future. This free access also means that your current employer may discover that you're on the job market.

By having free access to resumes, some employers and resume data banks may also copy your resume and add it to their data banks. For example, such resume banks as CareerCast, InstaMatch Resume Database, and Net-Temps use spiders or robots to search out resumes to add to their data banks. Because of programs and data banks such as these, duplicate resume postings account for an estimated 20–30 percent of Internet resumes.

Although these resume banks promote this free exchange of information as an advantage to employers, other resume banks promote just the opposite: *not* adding resumes to their data banks from newsgroups and other resume banks. This viewpoint reflects an ongoing discussion among Human Resource professionals about the aging of resumes. Some of these professionals believe that new resumes represent people who are actively on the job market and older resumes represent people who are likely to have already found employment. Other Human Resource professionals accept all resumes regardless of age under the principle that everyone is always looking for a better job.

Nonetheless, even if the resume bank accepts only new resumes, only a few of these resume banks, such as MedZilla™ and SIRC, contact the poster or verify any information.

Many of the resume banks do offer some degree of confidentiality. Some guarantee that access to resumes is limited to their subscribers, who can access the resumes only with a password; however, your current employer may be one of the subscribers! Other resume banks offer other kinds of confidentiality. PursuitNet Online, for example, enables job seekers to indicate any employer to which they don't want to send a resume.

Some resume banks offer a confidential listing. For example, job seekers can request confidentiality on Canadian Resume Centre, JobOptions, Minorities' Job Bank, The Monster Board, SEEK, Virtual Job Fair, VirtualResume, and Western New York Resumes. Typically, a confidential listing means that your resume has no contact information; therefore, you are limited to using your resume only for applying for posted positions, not for advertising your availability for positions.

If confidentiality is important to you, you may want to use the resume banks that limit their data banks to anonymous profiles. The data bank secures your permission before your resume and identifying information is released to an employer. In CareerSite, for example, employers can see only the job seeker's profile when they search the data bank. If the employer indicates an interest, CareerSite sends the job seeker a message that requests permission to release the job seeker's identity and resume.

BridgePath resumes are not open for general viewing. Employers search for specific criteria and send e-mail announcements to anonymous e-mail addresses. The job seekers decide whether to respond or ignore the announcements they receive. BridgePath sends out over 10,000 job-announcement e-mails per day. BridgePath can be particularly attractive to passive job seekers—employed workers who don't want anyone to know they are open to new opportunities.

CareerPath places priority on job-seeker privacy as well. Only CareerPath.com specialists search the resume bank and contact job seekers for permission by e-mail before faxing the candidate's resume to the employer. And CareerMagazine does not send resumes to employers; instead, it notifies job seekers by e-mail of job openings that match their skills and requirements.

Another way to conceal your identity is to use one of the recruiter or headhunter resume banks. EasyResume™ is a search firm for software engineering professionals. EasyResume matches jobs with job seekers and then contacts the job seeker to discuss the position. Similarly, JobLynx is a resume bank that is limited to headhunters. The headhunters contact the job seeker directly.

The London-based PeopleBank The Employment Network uses a structured curriculum vitae (CV) without any identifying or contact information. PeopleBank contacts the job seeker, describes the position and employer, and only then releases personal details to the employer.

Resume Mailing Services

Some people do mass mailings of their resumes to companies they believe may be hiring. This process is expensive: think about how much it costs in time and money to print and mail 200 resumes! Job-search professionals try to discourage this strategy largely because it's rarely effective and always expensive.

Now you have an electronic equivalent that is simple, quick, and much less expensive. Internet resume mailing services use the power of the Internet to distribute your resume to hundreds of employers and recruiters who have indicated that they want to receive resumes from the service. There is no charge to the employers.

Resume Blaster! sends your resume to over 1,000 recruiters nationwide for $49.00–$89.00. ResumeXPRESS! sends your resume to thousands of employers, recruiters, and online resume data banks for $89.95. ResumeXPRESS! also maintains your resume in its resume data bank for one year.

Other resume banks offer this service as an option to their other services. BridgePath, for example, offers ResumePath, which e-mails resumes to over 200 companies. And EngineeringJobs.com offers an optional resume e-mailing to 250 headhunters for a $35.00 fee.

Resume mailing services distribute your resume for a fee that is much less than what you would have spent in postage alone. However, you shouldn't rely only on this strategy.

Evaluating Resume Banks

Even if posting your resume is free, you are still investing your time. You want your resume to be seen by potential employers; therefore, you need to evaluate the resume banks carefully and decide which ones are most appropriate for you.

In Part II, you'll find our descriptions of the resume banks. We collected the information about the resume banks in April 1998 by an e-mail questionnaire. (Those questions that were not answered by the bank are not shown.) In our descriptions, we tried to maintain as much of the original language of the person who completed our questionnaire as possible so that you can tell what the bank thinks is important. For example, is confidentiality a priority? Does the bank provide job-search tips? You can also determine how helpful the bank will be if you encounter a problem.

Under the name of each resume bank, we have listed a description of its primary geographical area, the employment fields or job classifications of the majority of the resumes it holds, and our rating of the site from one star to five stars. In making our assessment, we considered the following factors:

- Stability of the sponsorship or ownership

- Cost to the job seeker

- Cost to employers

- Ratio of the number of resumes held to the number of employers who use the database

- Ratio of the number of resumes held to the number of daily hits on the resumes

- Confidentiality available to the job seeker

- Sophistication of the search options

- Technology to notify job seeker and employer of matches

- Overall ease of entering the resume and using the site

- Other aspects that help the job seeker, such as career information

- Unique, special features

As you review these descriptions, keep the guidelines that are discussed in the next sections in mind. The guidelines will help you evaluate which resume banks will best serve your interests.

Stability

Resume banks are a new service. As early as 1984, the search firm Lee Johnson International was receiving resumes via FidoNet, which linked Bulletin Board Systems. In 1989, Gonyea & Associates created the first career-guidance agency to operate 100 percent online. JobOptions, formerly E.span, began its online recruitment service in 1991 but didn't start accepting resumes until 1995. In 1992, Online Career Center (OCC) started accepting resumes. In Part II, we've identified about 10 resume banks established in 1994 and about 20 in each of 1995, 1996, and 1997.

Only a few resume banks have been offering their service for more than a few years. Look to see whether a resume bank with a longer history has kept up to date with technology and services. You can also check to see whether a newer resume bank is starting to be competitive and has gotten employer interest.

Major Corporate Sponsor

Most corporate ownership of resume banks has been by major advertising and publishing corporations. Some resume banks, including ones with strong capital backing, have closed their doors, however. Look at the owners or sponsors, their experience, and the year the resume banks started accepting resumes. You should also consider how important the maintaining of resume and job banks is to their major corporate activity. Table 8.1 lists the major corporate sponsor of several resume banks and the year the bank started accepting resumes.

TABLE 8.1 MAJOR CORPORATE SPONSORS OF RESUME BANKS

Corporate Sponsor	Resume Bank	Year
Adams Media	CareerCity	1997
Bernard Hodes Advertising	The Insurance Career Center	1994
Bernard Hodes Advertising	CareerMosaic	1995
BSA Advertising (world's largest privately held, multi-office recruitment advertising agency)	CareerMart	1997
CareerPath.com (financial backing by Knight-Ridder, New York Times Company, Times Mirror Company, Tribune Company, The Washington Post Company, Cox Interactive Media, Gannett Company, and Hearst Corporation)	CareerPath	1997
DI-USA, Inc. and Army Times Publishing Company (Gannett)	Transition Assistance Online	1996
Gund Business Enterprises, Inc.	JobOptions	1995
Landmark Communications (owner of 43 newspapers and The Weather Channel)	CareerWeb	1995
Landmark Communications	HealthCareerWeb	1997
Lycos, Inc.	Tripod Resume Builder	1995
TMP Worldwide (world's largest yellow-page advertising agency and the largest recruitment advertising agency)	Online Career Center	1992
TMP Worldwide	medsearch	1993
TMP Worldwide	The Monster Board	1995
Ziff-Davis Publications	jobEngine	1997

Geographic Coverage Area

Consider the resume bank's geographic coverage area: global, specific countries, or regions. Although the Internet is global in nature, few resume banks have a global presence. CareerMosaic and Online Career Center (OCC) are two exceptions. Most resume banks specialize in one country. The majority of banks serve the United States. Within the United States, some resume banks have a defined geographic focus. This focus offers a definite plus if you want to work in that area. Table 8.2 lists several resume banks by their geographic areas.

TABLE 8.2 GEOGRAPHICAL LOCATIONS OF RESUME BANKS

Area	Resume Banks
Global:	
Asia, Australia, Canada, France, Hong Kong, Japan, United Kingdom, United States	CareerMosaic
Africa, Asia/South Pacific, Australia, Canada, Central America, Europe, Mexico, Middle East, Scandinavia, South America, United States	Online Career Center (OCC)
Countries:	
Australia	The Australian Resume Server, Computer People, SEEK
Canada	Canadian Resume Centre, JobNet
Ireland	The Irish Jobs Page
United Kingdom	JobServe, PeopleBank The Employment Network
Areas in the United States:	
Eastern Pennsylvania, Northern Delaware, and Southwestern New Jersey	America's TV JobNetwork
Colorado	Colorado Online Job Connection
US Northwest and British Columbia, Canada	Jobs Northwest
Ohio	Ohio Careers Resource Center
Philadelphia	Online Opportunities
California's Silicon Valley	Resume-Net
Western New York state	Western New York Resumes

Kinds of Resumes in the Data Bank

Are the resumes in the data bank specialized and in the field where you are seeking employment? Does the resume bank accept resumes from all career fields? General data banks are used by employers seeking employees with a wider range of experience. Specialized data banks are used by employers with clearly defined, specific needs. Table 8.3 gives examples of specialized resume banks.

TABLE 8.3 SPECIALIZED RESUME BANKS

Specialty	Resume Bank
Recent college graduates	BridgePath, The Job Resource, JOBTRAK
Entertainment	Showbizjobs
Executive	PursuitNet Online, SIRC
Federal government	HRSC
Healthcare	HealthCareerWeb, medsearch, MedZilla, National NurseSearch
Hospitality	Hospitality Net Virtual Job Exchange
Insurance	The Insurance Career Center (part of CareerMosaic)
Military, separating	Transition Assistance Online
Minorities	DiversiLink (Hispanic engineers), Minorities' Job Bank
Passive job seeker	BridgePath, SkillSearch
Sports and recreation	Online Sports Career Center

The ten largest resume banks, the number of resumes they have on file, the length of time the resumes remain online, and their focus at the time of our survey in April 1998 are included in Table 8.4. Read these numbers carefully. A resume bank may have 100,000 resumes, but only 20,000 of them may have been received in the past 90 days.

TABLE 8.4 THE TEN LARGEST RESUME BANKS

Resume Bank	Number of Resumes	Length of Time Posted	Specialty
CareerMart	540,000*	6 months	All fields
The Monster Board	340,000	12 months	All fields
Net-Temps	225,000	30 days	All fields
PassportAccess	151,989	indefinitely	High tech
JOBTRAK	150,000	3 months	College graduates
CareerSite	140,500	indefinitely	All fields
CareerPath	130,000	6 months	All fields
BridgePath	120,000	6 months	All fields
jobEngine	100,000	60 days	High tech
Virtual Job Fair	100,000	90 days	High tech

*Total number of resumes. People can post resumes in multiple categories and states.

Ratio of Resumes to Corporate Subscribers

Compare the number of resumes that a resume bank has online to the number of corporate subscribers and employers it has. Keep in mind, however, that some resume banks are open without registration to any employer, so the ratio can't be calculated for them. In our survey, some resume banks did not provide the information to calculate this ratio. Table 8.5 lists some resume banks that have the most favorable ratio of employers to resumes.

TABLE 8.5 RATIO OF RESUMES TO EMPLOYERS

Resume Bank	Resumes/Employers
JOBTRAK	150,000/320,000*
JobNet	2,500/5,000
Careerfile	30,000/20,000
JobCenter Employment Services, Inc.	21,000/13,500
Job Link USA	1,500/600
CareerMosaic	60,000/20,000
Insurance Career Center	2,500/700
The JobExchange	45,000/11,000
ResumeXPRESS!	4,000/1,000
Contract Engineering	450/107

*Number of employers who have posted positions since 1988.

Ratio of Resumes to Daily Page Hits

In our survey, some resume banks did not provide the information to calculate the ratio of resumes to daily page hits. Table 8.6 lists some resume banks that have the most favorable ratio of daily page hits to resumes.

TABLE 8.6 RATIO OF RESUMES TO DAILY PAGE HITS

Resume Bank	Resumes/Daily Page Hits
SelectJOBS	28,000/20 million per month
ORASEARCH	700/10,000
HeadHunter.NET	35,000/400,000
Resume-Net	400/3,000
Worldwide Resume/Talent Bank	5,000/1 million per month
Job Center Employment Services, Inc.	21,000/50,000
Lasting Impressions	500/1,100
A+ On-line Resumes	50/5,000 per month
SIRC	500/1,000
CareerMosaic	60,000/130,000

Fees

Consider what fees are charged by the resume bank. Are corporate subscribers and employers charged? Is the job seeker charged?

Many of the resume banks with the most favorable ratio of employers to resumes and of page hits to resumes are free or inexpensive to employers. Neither CareerMosaic nor HeadHunter.NET charges the job seeker or the employer. Careerfile does not charge the job seeker; instead, employers view the candidates' profiles and then decide whether to order the full resume for a fee of $6.95. JobCenter Employment Services, Inc., charges the job seeker $5.00 for six months of notifications of employment matches. JobCenter charges employers $15.00 per week with a two-week minimum per advertisement. The JobExchange charges employers $22.00 per resume download online and has no charge for the job seeker.

JobLynx charges $39.85 to post a resume for 90 days, but if you are not presented with employment opportunities during two consecutive 90-day periods, JobLynx will refund 50 percent of the fee.

In general, we found that job seekers are reluctant to use resume banks that charge a fee—particularly a very expensive one—unless the resume bank is highly specialized. If users go to a general job bank, they don't want to pay anything. A basic rule of thumb: The more expensive a resume bank, the less attractive it is to employers and job seekers.

Length of Time Online

Review the length of time resumes remain online before the job seekers can update or renew them. The shorter the period of time that resumes remain online, the more recent—and more desirable—the resumes. Most data banks retain resumes for six months before renewal is required; however, many data banks retain their resumes indefinitely, although some of these banks offer searches based on the length of time the resume has been in the data bank. Table 8.7 lists some of the data banks that have short time periods before renewal is required.

TABLE 8.7 RENEWAL PERIODS

Resume Bank	Renewal Period
DICE High Tech Jobs Online—Announce Availability	30 days
Net-Temps	30 days
Resume-Net	1 month
Science Professional Network	7 weeks
jobEngine	60 days
Saludos Career Web	60 days
Virtual Job Fair	60 days
Hospitality Net Virtual Job Exchange	2 months
CareerCast	90 days
Careerfile	90 days
CareerWeb	90 days
Contract Engineering	3 months
EngineeringJobs.com	3 months
HeadHunter.NET	90 days
HealthCareerWeb	90 days
JobLynx	90 days
JOBTRAK	3 months
Lasting Impressions	3 months
Ohio Careers Resource Center	3 months

Online Help

What help is available if you have problems submitting your resume? Many of the resume banks offer an FAQ (frequently asked questions) page or e-mail assistance. Some offer more complete help in the entire job-search process, as shown in Table 8.8.

TABLE 8.8 ONLINE HELP

Resume Bank	Online Help
BridgePath	Advice section and weekly e-mail career newsletter
CareerAvenue	Help files and monthly career advice column
CareerMagazine	Articles section; 85,000 downloaded in a month
CareerWeb	Articles and career inventory test
HealthCareerWeb	Articles and career inventory test
The JobExchange	Online advice and references from the site's participating newspapers
JOBTRAK	Award-winning resume guide
SEEK	Resources to assist job seekers in all aspects of the job-search process
Transition Assistance Online (TAO)	Job hunting and resume writing resources

Special Features

Look for any special features that may be helpful to you. CareerMart, for example, offers a chat room in which job seekers can speak with employers in real time over the Internet.

Resume banks offer an exciting new way to match the job with the job seeker. Always remember, however, that submitting your resume to a resume bank is only part of your overall job-search process. Applying directly to employers via online resume forms and e-mail is another part. Following up on e-mail correspondence from employers is one more. And, as we have shown you in Part I of this book, crafting a winning resume is key to the entire process of online job search.

Part II

Resume Banks

In Part II, we offer descriptions of several resume banks—Web sites that collect and make resumes accessible to employers. We suggest that you review Chapter 8, which presents an overview of these resume banks, before you begin your search for where you'd like to post your resume. We rated the sites based on the following criteria:

- ✔ **Outstanding site (★ ★ ★ ★ ★):** Meets all the criteria established in Chapter 8 with some outstanding features.

- ✔ **Good site (★ ★ ★ ★):** Meets all the criteria established in Chapter 8.

- ✔ **Average site (★ ★ ★):** Satisfactorily meets most of the criteria established in Chapter 8.

- ✔ **Fair site (★ ★):** Satisfactorily meets some of the criteria established in Chapter 8.

- ✔ **Poor site (★):** Not recommended.

A+ On-line Resumes

USA
All Career Fields
Rating: ★ ★

A+ On-line Resumes converts your resume to HTML and posts it on the World Wide Web with a specific Internet address (URL). It registers the URL with the most popular search engines using your name, job type, and *resume* as keywords.

- **URL:** `http://ol-resume.com`

- **Ownership/sponsorship:** Merilee Kern.

- Started accepting resumes in 1995.

- **Approximate number of resumes online in April 1998:** 50.

- Resumes are accepted in all career fields.

- **Total number of corporate subscribers/employers:** one (currently seeking).

- Of corporate subscribers/employers, 100 percent are staffing firms.

- **Fee structure for corporate subscribers/employers:** $25.00 per job listing, per month.

- **Methods and rules for submitting resumes:** Preferred method is via e-mail as a text or Word document, or you can create online at `http://ol-resume.com/create.htm`.

- **Percentage of resumes received is as follows:**

  39 percent: e-mail
  1 percent: diskette
  60 percent: Web form

- 100 percent of resumes received from individuals.

- **Limits on length:** Prices based on a two-page word processed document. A $3.00 surcharge applies for each additional page.

- **Format:** General template used for all unless specific requests are made.

- **Fees for person submitting resume are as follows:**

  3 months: $ 40.00
  6 months: $ 60.00
  9 months: $ 80.00
  12 months: $100.00

- Resumes remain online based on preceding payment terms.

- **Procedures for updating/renewing:** e-mail request; no charge if within reason.

- It is not possible to limit who can see a resume, although A+ On-line Resumes can render the resume confidential (see `http://ol-resume.com/conf.htm`).

- It is not possible to shield a resume from being viewed by a current employer.

- **Assistance provided to the person submitting a resume:** A comprehensive document that includes tips and techniques for online job hunting is provided upon notification of upload.

- **Search options available to employers viewing resumes:** Keyword via search index server by job category or by state.

- **Average number of daily hits on resumes:** 5,000 on home page per month.

- **Other distinguishing factors:** Small database provides clients with a higher probability of their resume's being found and read. The company has been in business since 1995, so most employers, recruiters, and others visit the site on a regular basis.

America's Employers

USA

All Career Fields

Rating: ★ ★ ★ ½

Career Relocation Corporation is a network of independent career consultants who are experts in outplacement and career develpment throughout the United States. All the consultants have experience assisting displaced and relocated workers.

- **URL:** http://www.americasemployers.com

- **Ownership/sponsorship:** Career Relocation Corporation of America.

- **Started accepting resumes in:** 1997

- **Approximate number of resumes online in April 1998:** 48,000.

- Resumes are accepted in all career fields.

- **Total number of corporate subscribers/employers:** 315

- **Of corporate subscribers/employers, the percentages include the following:**

    80 percent: direct-hire employers
    10 percent: staffing firms
    10 percent: contract/consulting firms

- **Fee structure for corporate subscribers/employers:** $5,000/year.

- **Methods and rules for submitting resumes:** Online form in Resume Bank section of site.

- 100 percent of resumes received by Web form.

- **Percentage of resumes received is as follows:**

    80 percent: individuals
    20 percent: outplacement firms

- No limits on length.

- **Format specified:** Online form must be followed.

- No fees to person submitting resume.

- Resumes remain online 90 days, or longer if individual renews.

- **Procedures for updating/renewing:** online form update/renewal.

- It is possible to limit who can see a resume.

- It is possible to shield a resume from being viewed by a current employer.

- **Assistance provided to the person submitting a resume:** online instructions.

- **Search options available to employers viewing resumes:** skills matching.

- **Technology to match jobs to resumes and e-mail resumes to clients:** Site has online Job Finder, which matches resumes to jobs in the database.

- **Average number of daily hits on resumes:** over 100,000.

- **Special features:** Resumes are confidential.

Part II: Resume Banks

America's TV JobNetwork

Eastern Pennsylvania,
Northern Delaware,
Southwestern New Jersey
All Career Fields
Rating: ★ ★

This site is promoted by its own TV show in the tri-state area of Eastern Pennsylvania, Northern Delaware, and Southwestern New Jersey.

- **URL:** http://www.tvjobnet.com

- **Ownership/sponsorship:** Owned and produced by America's InterActive Production Network:

    America's TV JobNetwork
    P.O. Box 289
    Pennsauken, NJ 08110

- Started accepting resumes in 1996.

- Resumes are accepted in over 130 job classifications. Resumes can be listed in up to three classifications.

- **Total number of corporate subscribers/employers:** Free site to employers; any employer can search resumes.

- **Fee structure for corporate subscribers/employers:** none.

- **Methods and rules for submitting resumes:** Must be submitted with payment (major credit cards accepted). Accepts clean, scannable copy of your resume by mail.

- **Approximate percentage of resumes received is as follows:**

    20 percent: e-mail
    50 percent: fax
    25 percent: other paper (job fairs, mailings)
    5 percent: Web form

- 100 percent of resumes received from individuals.

- No limits on length.

- **Format:** open.

- **Fees for person submitting resume are as follows:**

    $19.95 for six-month listing
    $39.95 for six-month anonymous listing of your resume without a name, address, or phone number

- Resumes remain online six months.

- **Procedures for updating/renewing:** Contact company/Webmaster.

- It is possible to limit who can see a resume if you use the anonymous option.

- It is possible to shield a resume from being viewed by a current employer if you use the anonymous option.

- No assistance is provided to the person submitting a resume.

- **Search options available to employers viewing resumes:** Search by job classification.

- **Technology to match jobs to resumes and e-mail resumes to clients:** none at present. All responses are forwarded to America's TV JobNetwork via phone, fax, mail, or e-mail. The company contacts you with all responses received.

- **Other distinguishing factors:** Site promoted locally by TV show.

Part II: Resume Banks

The Australian Resume Server

Australia
All Career Fields
Rating: ★ ★ ★

The Australian Resume Server was established in August 1995 as a resource for job seekers wanting to work in Australia. The site enables job seekers to upload their resumes into the Australian Resume Server's database and enables employers and agencies to search the database. Job seekers also have the option of having an HTML resume home page.

- **URL:** `http://www.herenow.com.au/`

- **Ownership/sponsorship:** Owned by resume-writing consultancy `me@here.now`.

- Started accepting resumes in 1995.

- **Approximate number of resumes online in April 1998:** 2,500.

- Resumes are in all career fields.

- **Total number of corporate subscribers/employers:** 250.

- **Of corporate subscribers/employers, the percentages include the following:**

    30 percent: direct-hire employers
    30 percent: staffing firms
    30 percent: contract/consulting firms
    10 percent: other

- **Fee structure for corporate subscribers/employers:** small annual subscription fee.

- **Methods and rules for submitting resumes:** You can submit resume text or URL to a Web resume on another server. Uploading and linking are free for job seekers.

- 100 percent of resumes are received by Web form.

- **Approximate percentage of resumes received is as follows:**

    70 percent: individuals
    20 percent: colleges or universities
    10 percent: outplacement firms

- No limits on length.

- **Format:** open.

- No fees for person submitting resume. The service is free for job seekers.

- Resumes remain online as long as the job seeker wants.

- **Procedures for updating/renewing:** Job seeker is issued a password for updates, renewal, and deletion.

- It is possible to limit who can see your resume. Details are kept in a secure area and are available only to subscribers.

- It is not possible to shield a resume from being viewed by a current employer.

- **Assistance provided to the person submitting a resume:** pointers for resume writing on the Web.

- **Search options available to employers viewing resumes:** free-form text, areas of Australia where you want to work, languages spoken, and citizenship/residency status.

- No technology to match jobs to resumes and e-mail resumes to clients.

- **Average number of daily hits on resumes:** 100–200.

- **Special features:** Service available to Australian job seekers or job seekers from overseas wanting to work in Australia.

- **Other distinguishing factors:** One of Australia's longest running Internet employment sites. Highly regarded by industry and industry groups.

BridgePath

USA

All Career Fields

Specializes in College Graduates with Up to Ten Years' Experience

Rating: ★ ★ ★ ★ ★

BridgePath was founded in 1996 by two UC Berkeley graduates, Auren Hoffman and Scott Bonds. It specializes in students and recent graduates.

- **URL:** `http://www.bridgepath.com`

- **Ownership/sponsorship:**

    BridgePath
    562 Mission Street, Suite 350
    San Francisco, Calif. 94105
    (415) 512-1900

- Started accepting resumes in 1996.

- **Approximate number of resumes online in April 1998:** BridgePath has over 120,000 job seekers in its database and is adding approximately 3,000 more per week. It has several key services for job seekers. First, job seekers can create a personal profile by entering detailed information into numerous parameters on the Web site. This process enables you to create an expanded resume online instead of pasting in your existing resume. Second, BridgePath has a service called ResumePath, where you can instantaneously e-mail your resumes to over 200 companies.

- Resumes are in all career fields.

- **Total number of corporate subscribers/employers:** The company has hundreds of employers to whom it sends announcements on a regular basis.

- **Of corporate subscribers/employers, the percentages include the following:**

    70 percent: direct-hire employers
    25 percent: staffing firms
     5 percent: other

- **Fee structure for corporate subscribers/employers:** BridgePath has three different options for employers. First, it can provide a slate of candidates who meet specific requirements and criteria for under $1,000. Second, it can provide a full recruiting service for 20 percent of the employee's first year's salary. Third, employers can pay per e-mail that they send to job seekers who meet their criteria.

- **Methods and rules for submitting resumes:** Job seekers visit the Web site, located at `http://www.bridgepath.com` and enter their detailed personal information online. They do not need to visit the site continually except to update their information periodically. Instead, they are contacted via e-mail when a job opportunity that matches their qualifications arises. With BridgePath, job seekers let the jobs they're interested in find them.

- 100 percent of resumes received by Web form. All the job seekers visit the Web site and enter their detailed personal information online.

- **Percentage of resumes received is as follows:**

    95 percent: individuals
     1 percent: colleges or universities
     4 percent: outplacement firms

- Job seekers are directed to the site due to the Web presence and because of partnerships with other major sites on the Internet, including Student Advantage, the number one student site on the Internet. BridgePath also has partnerships with CyberGold, Vault Reports, and University Wire.

- BridgePath puts no limit on the amount of information that job seekers can enter into the Web site. BridgePath has numerous parameters and many options to add information not covered. Job seekers can also paste a resume of any length into the ResumePath feature.

- **Format:** The company does not specify a format for the resume, but it does have specific questions that may require you to select from a number of options.

- No fees for person submitting resume.

- **Length of time resumes remain online:** BridgePath deactivates accounts with bad e-mail addresses or those that do not log in at least once every six months.

- **Procedures for updating/renewing:** Job seekers can visit the site at `http://www.bridgepath.com` and update their information at any time.

- It is possible to limit who can see a resume. All job-seeker information is confidential. Employers search for specific criteria and send e-mail announcements to anonymous e-mail addresses. Job seekers can choose to respond or ignore announcements that they receive.

- **Is shielding a resume from being viewed by a current employer possible?** Yes and no. BridgePath can shield the resume from an employer who admits to its identity but not to one who attempts to gain access without revealing who it is.

- **Assistance provided to the person submitting a resume:** BridgePath has made the online procedure as simple as possible. Job seekers create their own personal profile with the click of a mouse. If, however, they have technical problems, they can reach the technical assistants in the main office.

- **Search options available to employers viewing resumes:** With the click of a mouse, employers search the database by using the same criteria that job seekers use to create their personal profiles. For example, with BridgePath's extensive database, employers can conduct a detailed search for a person who has two years of working experience, who is proficient in C++ and Java, who can speak fluent Cantonese, who is interested in the financial services industry, who has studied computer science, who has over a 3.3 GPA, and who wants to work in Dallas.

- **Technology to match jobs to resumes and e-mail resumes to clients:** BridgePath uses Internet-based WWW technologies in conjunction with expert systems to perform matches.

- **Average number of daily hits on resumes:** The company doesn't post the resumes for general viewing at this time. It sends out over 10,000 job announcement e-mails per day.

- **Special features:** BridgePath also offers an advice section that provides answers to difficult questions regarding career options and choices. Questions range from "What do I want out of a job?" to "What is going on in the job market right now?" The company also sends a weekly career newsletter with useful job-searching tips, job humor, and Vault Reports information via e-mail.

- **Other distinguishing factors:** BridgePath focuses on passive job seekers and job seekers with up to ten years of experience. Young alumni are the most recently educated, dynamic, and cutting-edge segment of the work force; and in this age of automation, these job seekers are becoming more important. They are being taught more specific skill sets in school than previous generations were, and they have a better technological base at a younger age.

- Roughly 90 percent of college graduates can use MS Word, Excel, Access, the Internet, and e-mail. These qualified job seekers save employers high training costs.

- Young alumni and recent graduates are also the most difficult group for companies to access because there are thousands of university career centers, making a search process monstrous, and most job-placement agencies require candidates to have at least ten years of experience. BridgePath understands the growing demand for these job candidates, so it has centralized the recruitment process to make it easier for clients to connect with recent graduates.

- BridgePath also focuses on passive job seekers—those who are happy with their current jobs and who do not actively look in want ads on a regular basis. BridgePath is effective for these passive job seekers because it sends out e-mail announcements when a job possibility arises.

Canadian Resume Centre

Canada
All Career Fields
Rating: ★ ★

The resumes at this site are from Canadians or people who want to work in Canada.

- **URL:** `http://www.nas.net/~resume` or `http://www.Netaccess.on.ca/~resume/`

- **Ownership/sponsorship:** private company:

    The Canadian Resume Centre
    P.O. Box 81060
    Fiddlers Green Postal Outlet
    Ancaster, Ontario, Canada
    L9G 4X1
    Fax: (519) 759-1735

- Started accepting resumes in 1997.

- **Approximate number of resumes online in April 1998:** 250.

- Resumes are accepted in all career fields.

- **Total number of corporate subscribers/employers:** no tabulation.

- **Of corporate subscribers/employers, the percentages include the following:**

    25 percent: direct-hire employers
    75 percent: staffing firms

- **Fee structure for corporate subscribers/employers:** no fee.

- **Methods and rules for submitting resumes:** Fill out form onscreen, paste text/resume, and send.

- **For a confidential resume, complete the profile:** job title, years of experience, education, keywords to describe what you do (as many as you want), achievements/responsibilities, geographic preference, position desired, subject line (usually your job title or last position), salary, industry, and how you would like to be contacted when an employer wants to see your complete resume.

- **Percentage of resumes received is as follows:**

    75 percent: e-mail/Web form
    10 percent: fax
    15 percent: mail

- 100 percent of resumes received from individuals.

- No limits on length.

- **Format specified:** e-mail your resume directly to resume@netaccess.on.ca. The company accepts only the following formats: txt, doc, rtf, or wp. Resumes can also be faxed or mailed.

- **Fees for person submitting resume are as follows:**

    $25.00 (Canadian): nonconfidential, e-mailed
    $40.00 (Canadian): nonconfidential, mailed or faxed
    $50.00 (Canadian): confidential

- Resumes remain online for six months.

- **Procedures for updating/renewing:** You can change or delete your resume at any time by informing the company by e-mail, fax, or mail.

- It is possible to limit who can see a resume. Confidential resumes are recommended.

- It is possible to shield a resume from being viewed by a current employer. Confidential resumes are recommended.

- **Assistance provided to the person submitting a resume:** Fill out the form onscreen; fairly straightforward.

- **Search options available to employers viewing resumes:** Keyword search only. Searches a resume but sees only the profile with no personal/company information for confidential resumes.

- **Technology to match jobs to resumes and e-mail resumes to clients:** permission needed to e-mail resume to clients.

- **Average number of daily hits on resumes:** 46 per month.

- **Special features:** confidential resumes. (Employers leave contact information, and the job seeker decides whether to send a resume.)

- **Other distinguishing factors:**

    Primarily for Canadian job seekers and those wanting to work in Canada.

    Section for employers to post jobs: $25.00 (Canadian) for three months.

Career Avenue

USA
All Career Fields
Rating: ★ ★ ★

Career Avenue was developed by Human Resource managers who have many years of experience filling positions within their respective companies.

- **URL:** http://www.careeravenue.com

- **Ownership/sponsorship:** Owned by Internet Advertising, Inc., San Antonio, Texas.

- Started accepting resumes in 1995.

- **Approximate number of resumes online in April 1998:** 2,100.

- Career Avenue encourages the posting of resumes and positions regardless of the specialty or field.

- **Total number of corporate subscribers/employers:** 124.

- **Of corporate subscribers/employers, the percentages include the following:**

  75 percent: direct-hire employers
  10 percent: staffing firms
  15 percent: contract/consulting firms

- **Fee structure for corporate subscribers/employers:** $30.00 for three months unlimited resume access and job posting.

- **Methods and rules for submitting resumes:** The company has two methods: ASCII and formatted resume input. All resumes are maintained for a period of six months. The site does not accept resumes attached to e-mail messages.

- 100 percent of resumes received through site submission.

- **Percentage of resumes received is as follows:**

  99 percent: individuals
  1 percent: other

- No limits on length.

- **Format:** Format is suggested through the site's instructions. You can locate many ways to find assistance in writing a resume on the site.

- No fees for person submitting resume.

- Resumes remain online for six months.

- **Procedures for updating/renewing:** Career Avenue enables job seekers to delete their resume at will. The process includes the assignment of a resume identification number at the time the resume is posted. You use this number and an assigned password to delete or edit the resume.

- It is not possible at this time to limit who can see a resume.

- It is not possible at this time to shield a resume from being viewed by a current employer.

- **Assistance provided to the person submitting a resume:** Significant assistance through the site's many Help pages and through a professional resume writer affiliated with the site.

- **Search options available to employers viewing resumes:** A powerful search engine that features Boolean search operators and other typical search methods (quotation marks, plus and minus signs, and so on) is available.

- **Technology to match jobs to resumes and e-mail resumes to clients:** none at this time.

- **Average number of daily hits on resumes:** approximately 200.

- **Special features:** Significant Help files and a career-advice column that changes monthly. In addition, the site is hosted by a professional in Human Resources. Questions are answered from individuals as time and volume allow.

- **Other distinguishing factors:** simple and inexpensive. Career Avenue offers an alternative to the monster sites while offering a significant amount of career advice and help in looking for a job. The site is offered as a service to those seeking jobs as well as to the employers.

CareerCast

USA
All Career Fields
Rating: ★ ★ ★

CareerCast's ResCast resume database is made up of two kinds of resumes: those that are posted directly to its site and those that its Spider acquires while searching the entire Internet.

- **URL:** http://www.careercast.com

- **Ownership/sponsorship:** private ownership, (312) 944-7171.

- Started accepting resumes in 1997.

- **Approximate number of resumes online in April 1998:** 20,000. The resumes are purged every 60 days.

- Resumes are in all career fields.

- **Total number of corporate subscribers/employers:** 57 clients, 200 users.

- **Of corporate subscribers/employers, the percentages include the following:**

  80 percent: direct-hire employers
  10 percent: staffing firms
  10 percent: contract/consulting firms

- **Fee structure for corporate subscribers/employers with a resume database is as follows:**

  With automated job-postings contract: no additional cost

  Without automated job-postings contract: $600.00 for six months

  For one-year access: $1,000

- **Methods and rules for submitting resumes:** CareerCast's resume database is made up of direct resume postings from thousands of candidates visiting the site. Additionally, thousands of additional resumes are data mined from hundreds of Web sites and Usenet groups and added to the database. ResCast's advanced resume Spider identifies and catalogs these sites, downloads the resumes, and performs the clean-up of the resumes to identify and purge duplicate resumes.

- **Percentage of resumes received is as follows:**

  25 percent: e-mail
  25 percent: Web form
  50 percent: Robot/Spider technology

- **Percentage of resumes received comes from the following sources:**

  50 percent: individuals
  50 percent: Robot/Spider technology

- No limits on length.

- **Format:** In the Web form; however, the company accepts any attachment.

- No fees to person submitting resume.

- Resumes remain online 90 days.
- **Procedures for updating/renewing:** e-mail notification after 90 days.
- It is not possible to limit who can see a resume; however, the database is password protected and accessed only by licensed recruiters.
- It is not possible to shield a resume from being viewed by a current employer.
- **Assistance provided to the person submitting a resume:** Web form or attachment, no restrictions.
- **Search options available to employers viewing resumes:** CareerCast has the most intelligent searching capabilities for resumes on the Internet. The search is a real-time, concept-based search, providing topic searching and synonym/thesaurus facilities. The relevancy ranking of search results places the best matching results first. Searches can be made for any combination of skills, education, geographic location, company names, and so on. ResCast also enables recruiters to pull resumes from the database into their desktop PC for offline search and management. The resumes can also be imported directly into the leading resume-management systems, such as Restrac, Resumix, and others.
- **Technology to match jobs to resumes and e-mail resumes to clients:** CareerCast's JobBot agent provides an e-mail Push facility that automatically notifies recruiters about new resumes that match their search criteria while they are offline. CareerCast is releasing its E-mail Job & Resume Agent in the summer of 1998. Resumes will be e-mailed to recruiters, and jobs will be e-mailed to candidates according to the search criteria.
- **Average number of daily hits on resumes:** No exact figure is for release; however, only 200 users are licensed to access the database.
- **Special features:** CareerCast's Robot technology intelligently and proactively pulls in thousands of resumes from other sites. All resumes are converted by the system into clean and formatted straight text. The resumes can then be imported directly into any leading, industry-recognized automated resume-management system.
- **Other distinguishing factors include the following:**

    For the job seeker: Most licensed recruiters who access the database are corporate recruiters from such companies as Microsoft, Lucent Technologies, Northrop Grumman, Monsanto, Unisys, and SAIC—to name a few. A low percentage of the clients are third-party recruiters.

    For the recruiter: The combination of the Robot technology, CareerCast's ranking-based search engine, and the price make CareerCast a good buy for any company.

CareerCity

USA
All Career Fields
Rating: ★ ★

CareerCity is a Lycos Top Five Percent Web site and is ranked number four among all Career Web sites on the content of its magazine. CareerCity is an Internet Business Network Master site and an Excellence in Electronic Recruiting award winner.

Part II: Resume Banks

- **URL:** `http://www.careercity.com`

- **Ownership/sponsorship:** Adams Media.

- Started accepting resumes in 1997.

- **Approximate number of resumes online in April 1998:** 24,000.

- Resumes are in all career fields.

- **Of corporate subscribers/employers, the percentages include the following:**

  60 percent: direct-hire employers
  40 percent: staffing firms

- **Methods and rules for submitting resumes:** Go to `www.careercity.com/res` and submit via that Web page. Resumes not accepted by e-mail.

- 100 percent of resumes are received by Web form.

- 100 percent of resumes are received from individuals.

- No limits on length.

- **Format:** must be entered on Web.

- No fees to person submitting resume.

- Resumes remain online 3–5 months.

- **Procedures for updating/renewing:** Log in via Web by using name and password.

- It is possible to limit who can see a resume.

- It is possible to shield a resume from being viewed by a current employer.

- **Assistance provided to the person submitting a resume:** e-mail assistance and sample resumes onsite.

- **Search options available to employers viewing resumes:** keyword, occupational category, level of experience, willingness to relocate.

- **Special features:** career advice from one of the largest print publishers in the field.

Careerfile

USA
All Career Fields
Rating: ★ ★ ★ ★

Careerfile offers a unique service to job seekers and employers. Job seekers register a profile. Employers search the profiles for free and can request the complete resume for a small fee. Careerfile was named as an Infoseek select site and is one of Tripod's top 22 career sites.

- **URL:** `http://www.careerfile.com`

- **Ownership/sponsorship:** Search and Placement Services, Inc.

- Started accepting resumes in 1996.

- **Approximate number of resumes online in April 1998:** Careerfile adds and deletes resumes regularly to keep the database current. Active resumes at any one time average about 30,000.

- Resumes are in all career fields.

- **Total number of corporate subscribers/employers:** 20,000.

- **Of corporate subscribers/employers, the percentages include the following:**

  85 percent: direct-hire employers
  15 percent: staffing firms and contract/consulting firms

- **Fee structure for corporate subscribers/employers:** Careerfile offers free employer listings in its popular industry/state directory and free browsing of its candidates' career profiles. Careerfile operates like a library, where candidates can keep their credentials (not their identities) in constant circulation to be reviewed by employers specifically searching for their skills. After employers see credentials that interest them, that candidate's full profile or resume can be ordered for a nominal fee of $6.95. Careerfile charges no up-front or subscription fees and has no obligation to buy. This policy makes this service the "employer's first-stop recruitment resource."™

- **Methods and rules for submitting resumes:** Free registration. Candidates fill out a one-time summary of their career credentials, which they can update regularly and must review every 90 days. The contact data and full resume is given out only to those employers who are interested enough to pay a nominal fee. Only registered employers can browse the candidates' career profiles.

- 100 percent of resumes are received by Web form.

- 100 percent of career profiles are completed by the candidate directly online at the Web site. Approximately ten percent are college students. The logon records indicate that several major outplacement companies are having their clients list with Careerfile.

- Length is limited. Fields are defined to make summaries easy and quick to search and review.

- **Format:** last two jobs, special skills, education, desired job title, and location.

- No fees to person submitting resume.

- Resumes remain online 90 days unless renewed.

- **Procedures for updating/renewing:** A copy of the profile is sent out to the candidate every time an employer of interest to the job seeker registers and every 90 days or by special request so that the candidate has an opportunity to update the profile.

- It is possible to limit who can see a resume. Only registered employers can review the resume. Careerfile also limits who can see the identity of the candidate, but it keeps the qualifications summary in constant circulation.

- Shielding a resume from being viewed by a current employer is possible to the extent that an employer would have to specifically request and pay for a candidate's contact information to learn who it is.

- **Assistance provided to the person submitting a resume:** The resume summary form is easy to complete and asks for all the pertinent information.

- **Search options available to employers viewing resumes:** The free search enables employers to be very specific about required and desired attributes, such as location, salary range, special skills, desired industry, and so on.

- **Technology to match jobs to resumes and e-mail resumes to clients:** proprietary program.

- **Average number of daily hits on resumes:** 12,000.

- **Special features:**

  Authentic data: All the candidates and employers have registered for Careerfile's service; they are not simply "mined" from the Web in general.

  Preview-before-you-buy feature for employers: No restriction on access to profiles gives candidates greater exposure and makes Careerfile the "employer's first-stop recruitment resource."

- **Distinguishing factor:** Careerfile's free Persistent Search™ feature instantly notifies candidates whenever an employer that matches the job seeker's interests for industry and location registers in Careerfile. Similarly, Persistent Search sends employers new profiles of candidates who match the search criteria they have entered in the last 30 days™.

CareerMagazine

USA
Computer, Engineering, Manufacturing, Finance, Sales, and Retail
Rating: ★ ★ ★

CareerMagazine was launched in 1994 on the World Wide Web.

- **URL:** http://www.careermag.com
- **Ownership/sponsorship:** service is provided by NCS, Inc., a privately held corporation.
- Started accepting resumes in 1994.
- **Approximate number of resumes online in April 1998:** 18,000.
- Resumes are primarily in IT/MIS, computer/data processing, sales/marketing, accounting/finance, engineering, insurance, manufacturing, and retail.
- **Total number of corporate subscribers/employers:** 600.
- **Of corporate subscribers/employers, the percentages include the following:**

  30 percent direct-hire employers
  52 percent staffing firms
  7 percent contract/consulting firms
  11 percent other (products and services)

- **Fee structure for corporate subscribers/employers include the following range of services:**

  A single job order for $95.00 for 42 days

  An unlimited posting package including a company profile for $8,900 for one year

- **Methods and rules for submitting resumes:** online form; follow the instructions.
- 100 percent of resumes are received by Web form.
- **Percentage of resumes received comes from the following sources:**

  80 percent individuals
  10 percent outplacement firms
  10 percent colleges or universities
  (This area is growing because of new programs.)

- No limits on length.
- **Format:** Web form.
- No fees to person submitting resume. Current promotion is free.

- Resumes remain online six months to one year.

- **Procedures for updating/renewing:** Web interface with user name and password.

- It is not possible to limit who can see a resume because it is a searchable database.

- It is possible to shield a resume from being viewed by a current employer by using a confidential program.

- **Assistance provided to the person submitting a resume:** e-mail/phone number if the directions do not work.

- **Search options available to employers viewing resumes:** relational database: search by location, skill, and title.

- **Technology to match jobs to resumes and e-mail resumes to clients:** JobNotes is CareerMagazine's e-mail notification to candidates of available job openings that match their skills and requirements. After being notified via e-mail, the candidates go to their Web interfaces in CareerMagazine and get the full, detailed information on the matching job openings.

- From a recruitment perspective, the company does not send candidate resumes to clients. This decision is not based on a programming issue; rather, CareerMagazine feels that sending out resumes without the job seeker's permission raises ethical issues.

- **Average number of daily hits on resumes:** Of the entire site, resumes are the second most frequently hit portion.

- **Special features:** Relational database makes searching easy. Users' feedback tells CareerMagazine that this feature is very helpful when the time to find resumes is short.

- **Distinguishing factors:** Articles section (called Career "Magazine") offers a range of articles about legal issues, interviewing, diversity, and so on. This section also features the On Campus section. Downloaded 85,000 articles in March 1998.

CareerMart

USA
All Career Fields
Rating: ★ ★ ★ ★ ★

CareerMart is a service of BSA Advertising, the world's largest privately held, multioffice recruitment advertising agency. With 540,000 resumes online, CareerMart is the largest resume data bank.

- **URL:** `http://www.careermart.com`

- **Ownership/sponsorship:** BSA CareerMart.

- Started accepting resumes in 1997.

- **Approximate number of resumes online in April 1998:** 540,000. This number is correct, but please keep in mind that people can post their resumes in multiple categories and multiple states.

- Resumes are accepted in all career fields. CareerMart has over 40 different categories in which applicants can post their resumes.

- Staffing firms are not allowed to search the resume database.

- **Fee structure for corporate subscribers/employers:** $100.00 per month per state/category.

- **Methods and rules for submitting resumes:** The posting criteria are simple. Applicants have to select the state in which they want to work and the category that best fits their skill sets. Multiple states/categories can be selected.

- The majority of resumes are received from e-mails.

- No limits on length.

- **Format:** easy-to-follow instructions.

- No fees to person submitting resume.

- Resumes remain online for six months.

- **Procedures for updating/renewing:** Log on to the Post Resume field and enter your first name and last name; then click the Submit button, which brings up your resume for editing and renewing.

- It is not possible to limit who can see a resume.

- It is not possible to shield a resume from being viewed by a current employer.

- **Assistance provided to the person submitting a resume:** directions, tech support number, and e-mail support address.

- **Search options available to employers viewing resumes:** categories, states, keywords.

- **Technology to match jobs to resumes and e-mail resumes to clients:** Using the latest Push technology, the e-mail agent instantly matches applicants with jobs.

- **Special features:** employment chat rooms, audio banners, video banners, virtual job fairs.

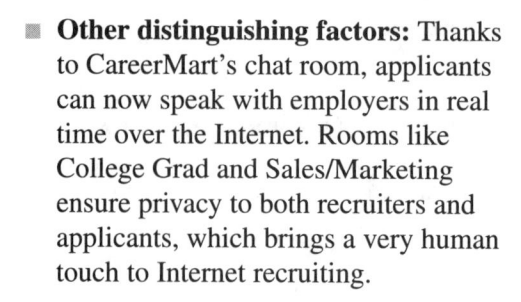

- **Other distinguishing factors:** Thanks to CareerMart's chat room, applicants can now speak with employers in real time over the Internet. Rooms like College Grad and Sales/Marketing ensure privacy to both recruiters and applicants, which brings a very human touch to Internet recruiting.

CareerMosaic

Global
All Career Fields
Rating: ★ ★ ★ ★

CareerMosaic is a long-standing employment site on the World Wide Web. CareerMosaic houses several main sections: Employers section, which profiles companies; J.O.B.S. database; Online Job Fairs; Resource Center; CollegeConnection; and ResumeCM. The CareerMosaic International Gateway provides links to CareerMosaic sites in Asia, Australia, Canada, France, Hong Kong, Japan, and the UK.

- **URL:** `http://www.careermosaic.com`

- **Ownership/sponsorship:** Bernard Hodes Advertising.

- Started accepting resumes in 1995.

- **Approximate number of resumes online in April 1998:** 60,000. The resumes are never older than four months.

- Resumes are accepted in all career fields.

- **Total number of corporate subscribers/employers:** 20,000.

- **Fee structure for corporate subscribers/employers:** no cost.

- **Methods and rules for submitting resumes:** ASCII format.
- 100 percent of resumes received by Web form.
- 100 percent of resumes received from individuals.
- No limits on length.
- **Format:** ASCII format.
- No fees to person submitting resume.
- Resumes remain online for four months.
- **Procedures for updating/renewing:** must resubmit.
- It is not possible to limit who can see a resume.
- It is not possible to shield a resume from being viewed by a current employer.
- **Assistance provided to the person submitting a resume:** online instructions.
- **Search options available to employers viewing resumes:** keyword searches.
- **Technology to match jobs to resumes and e-mail resumes to clients:** none.
- **Average number of daily hits on resumes:** 130,000.
- **Distinguishing factors:** Resumes are always fresh and current; they are never older than four months.

CareerPath

USA
All Career Fields
Rating: ★ ★ ★ ★

CareerPath was cofounded in October 1995 by *The Boston Globe, Chicago Tribune, Los Angeles Times, The New York Times, San Jose Mercury-News,* and *The Washington Post* to post their combined 35,000 job-vacancy announcements on the Internet. In May 1996, two other newspapers joined. Later that summer, the list of cooperating newspapers had grown to 19. Today, CareerPath offers job seekers the greatest number of the most current jobs available from the Help Wanted ads of the nation's leading newspapers and from the Web sites of leading employers. In late 1997, CareerPath started accepting resumes. Within a few months, it became one of the largest sites for resumes on the Internet.

- **URL:** `http://www.careerpath.com`
- **Ownership/sponsorship:** *The Boston Globe, Chicago Tribune, Los Angeles Times, The New York Times, San Jose Mercury-News,* and *The Washington Post*. Financial backing is provided by Knight-Ridder, New York Times Company, Times Mirror Company, Tribune Company, The Washington Post Company, Cox Interactive Media, Gannett Company, and Hearst Corporation. CareerPath's corporate headquarters is located at

    523 West 6th Street, Suite 515
    Los Angeles, CA 90014
    Phone: (213) 996-0202
    Fax: (213) 623-0244

- Started accepting resumes in fourth quarter 1997.
- **Approximate number of resumes online in April 1998:** 130,000.
- Resumes are accepted in all job classifications.

- **Total number of corporate subscribers/employers:** More than 250 employers have used the Resume Connection since it went "live" in January 1998.

- **Of corporate subscribers/employers, the percentages include the following:**

    90 percent: direct-hire employers
    5 percent: staffing firms
    5 percent: contract/consulting firms

- **Fee structure for corporate subscribers/employers:** Employers are charged a flat fee for each job search completed by CareerPath's staffing specialists. Employers are guaranteed at least five interested and qualified applicants for each search, or they are not charged for the search.

- **Methods and rules for submitting resumes:** Job seekers follow the step-by-step process on CareerPath's Resume Connection to prepare a searchable resume.

- **Percentage of resumes received is as follows:**

    97 percent: Web form
    3 percent: job fairs of affiliated newspapers

- 100 percent of resumes received from individuals.

- **Limits on length:** No limit on employment history. The Resume Connection form prompts users to fill in necessary data.

- **Format:** Format is specified by the Resume Connection interactive form.

- No fees to person submitting resume.

- Resumes remain online for six months.

- **Procedures for updating/renewing:** Resumes can be updated by the job seekers whenever they want. Those with resumes online are notified that their resumes will be made inactive when they've been unchanged on the site for six months. If at this time the job seekers want to keep their resumes in Resume Connection, they simply need to access the Edit view of their resumes on CareerPath to keep them actively searchable.

- It is possible to limit who can see a resume. No employer will see a job seeker's resume unless that job seeker has given permission for it to be viewed by that particular employer.

- It is also possible to shield a resume from being viewed by a current employer because of the protection given by the need for permission.

- **Assistance provided to the person submitting a resume:** Resume Connection's interactive format walks job seekers through the process, step by step.

- **Search options available to employers viewing resumes:** Staffing specialists at CareerPath work with employers to identify staffing needs and to create search methodologies that cull only those resumes that fit their unique recruiting needs.

- **Technology to match jobs to resumes and e-mail resumes to clients:** All resume searches are performed by CareerPath staffing specialists, who contact job seekers via e-mail (to ensure privacy) and then fax qualified and interested candidates' resumes to the employer.

- **Special features:** Job-seeker privacy is the number-one priority for CareerPath; therefore, no resume is forwarded to any employer without the expressed permission of the job seeker. Also, the staffing specialists ensure that employers receive only those resumes that fit their staffing needs.

- **Other features on the site include the following:**

    Job database: Job seekers can search (by using keywords) more than 60 newspapers from across the United States. These newspapers post jobs from their classified sections on CareerPath every week, with an average of nearly 300,000 jobs per day, none more than two weeks old.

    CareerPathEXTRA: Jobs listed on corporate Web sites are searchable on CareerPath, so job seekers who are interested in a particular company also have searchable access to jobs on the Web, in addition to those from newspapers across the United States.

    Employer profiles: In-depth employer information is available on CareerPath, with links to corporate Web sites when applicable.

    Resources: The finest job-hunting strategies and tips have been aggregated on CareerPath for use by job seekers.

- **Other distinguishing factors:** A clear, concise, and intuitive design interface ensures that the job seeker can access CareerPath's information quickly and easily.

Career Shop

USA
Financial, Management,
Sales, Technology
Rating: ★ ★ ★

Career Shop features local online Job Fairs—each with complete job and resume-database access—in more than 40 cities. Local online Job Fairs enable employers to target their Internet recruiting efforts geographically.

- **URL:** `http://www.careershop.com`

- **Ownership/sponsorship:** privately owned.

- Started accepting resumes in 1996.

- **Approximate number of resumes online in April 1998:** 12,000.

- Resumes can be posted into 24 categories, which include accounting/bookkeeping, data processing/programming, technical, engineering, sales/marketing/advertising, financial, and management.

- **Total number of corporate subscribers/employers:** 400.

- **Of corporate subscribers/employers, the percentages include the following:**

    50 percent: direct-hire employers
    50 percent: staffing firms

- **The fee structure for corporate subscribers/employers includes the following:**

    Free: resume posting and job searches
    $295.00/month: Internet recruiter membership
    $495.00/month: online Job Fair city page

Part II: Resume Banks

- **Methods and rules for submitting resumes:** Simple to use resume-posting page. If applicants have an existing resume, most of the resume-entry process can be done by cutting and pasting from their word processing software.

- **Percentage of resumes received comes from the following sources:**

  10 percent: e-mail
  90 percent: Web form

- 100 percent of resumes received from individuals.

- No limits on length.

- **Format:** Each applicant must use a format to enter contact information and some specifics regarding objectives and background. The specifics include name, address, phone number, fax number, e-mail address, career objective, years experience, and degree. The body of the applicant's resume can be pasted directly from the word processing software into the resume window. The entire resume entry process normally takes less than ten minutes.

- **Fees to person submitting resume:** Career Shop charges no fee to post a resume. The applicants can also post their resumes in more than one of the resume categories at no charge.

- **Length of time resumes remain online:** Resumes remain active in the database for up to 120 days and can be updated or deleted at any time. When applicants update their resumes, the expiration date is automatically extended to 120 days from the date of update.

- **Procedures for updating/renewing:** Applicants can log in and update their resume at any time.

- It is not possible at this time to limit who can see a resume. The employer customers can view any resume in the database through the Applicant search section.

- It is not possible to shield a resume from being viewed by a current employer. However, applicants can enter their resumes under the name Confidential and not include the name of their current employers if they feel this step is necessary.

- **Assistance provided to the person submitting a resume:** Applicants can e-mail Career Shop at any time for assistance.

- **Search options available to employers viewing resumes:** Employers can search up to three resume categories at one time by using any of the following search criteria: Preferred State, Degree Required, Keywords, And/Or Logic, Whole Words Only, or Any Part of Word.

- **Technology to match jobs to resumes and e-mail resumes to clients:** Career Shop's automated Resume Match service is provided to all employers who subscribe to the site. This service matches resumes entered in the database to all active job postings. Any matches are automatically e-mailed directly to the employer who posted the position. The Resume Match process runs Sunday through Thursday every week and is free to all applicants posting their resumes in Career Shop.

- **Special features:** In addition to free resume posting and free job searches, applicants will find the local Job Fair pages extremely beneficial. Career Shop has over 40 online Job Fair pages that feature local and national employers' job openings.

CareerSite

USA
All Career Fields
Rating: ★ ★ ★ ★

CareerSite members create a profile when they register as members. Prospective employers see only this profile when they search the candidate database. When an employer views profiles and indicates an interest in them, CareerSite sends the members a message that advises them of the employer's interest and requests permission to release their identities and resumes.

- **URL:** `http://www.careersite.com`
- **Ownership/sponsorship:** private.
- Started accepting resumes in 1996.
- **Approximate number of resumes online in April 1998:** 140,500.
- Resumes are in all career fields.
- **Total number of corporate subscribers/employers:** approximately 450.
- **Of corporate subscribers/employers, the percentages include the following:**

    95 percent: direct-hire employers
    5 percent: staffing/recruiting firms

- **Fee structure for corporate subscribers/employers include the following packages:**

    Six-month contract at $775.00: five 30-day job postings; includes company profile, unlimited searching of candidate pool, and a desktop recruiting office.

    One-year contract: posts 25 jobs or more; includes company profile, unlimited searches, multiple desktop recruiting offices, link to home page.

- **Methods and rules for submitting resumes:** Job seekers simply sign up with a profile, which contain an overview of their interests, qualifications and skills, and both a text version and an Adobe PDF (portable document format) file of their resume, which enables employers to view the fully formatted document. Job seekers need a copy of Adobe's Acrobat Reader software to view the PDF version of their resumes. If they don't already have a copy, they can download the latest version for free from Adobe at this site.
- 100 percent of resumes received by e-mail.
- 100 percent of resumes received from individuals.
- No limits on length.
- **Format:** open.
- No fees to person submitting resume.
- **Length of time resumes remain online:** The job seekers are usually employed and looking for the "right" job, so they continue to update their resumes as they continue their search, and they don't remove them. CareerSite believes that you need to be in a constant job hunt; you never know when you will find a new job, so the resumes are never removed.
- **Procedures for updating/renewing:** Online and very easy; with one click, your resume is on the system.
- **It is possible to limit who can see a resume:** All candidates have total confidentiality; they release their resumes when they know who wants to review them. Candidates create a profile of their credentials, skills, and what they want in their next job for any

searching company, but their personal contact information is withheld. The job seeker is always in full control of all personal information.

- It is also possible to shield a resume from being viewed by a current employer.

- **Assistance provided to the person submitting a resume:** CareerSite does not offer resume-writing services.

- **Search options available to employers viewing resumes:** Employers can search on anything. CareerSite has a flexible system that helps employers find the "right" person for the jobs. Employers can search by occupation, location, industry, skills, education, and any qualification that are necessary (in general, skills are used for the qualifications). Salary, benefits, type of employment, amount of travel, and amount of experience are also searchable.

- **Technology to match jobs to resumes and e-mail resumes to clients:** CareerSite has developed a third-generation technology, called SmartMatch, that matches candidates with jobs. All responses are e-mailed to the employer, either to a direct e-mail address or to the employer's resume-collection system. Employers are able to review responding resumes, cover letters, and profiles online with their CareerSite's desktop recruiting office. Along with modifying jobs, deactivating jobs, and adding job, employers have full control of their postings from any computer with Internet access.

- **Average number of daily hits on resumes:** over 300,000 individual visitors each month.

- **Special features:** CareerSite messages candidates weekly with jobs that match what they are seeking.

- **Other distinguishing factors:** CareerSite searches and matches on a 50,000-synonym knowledge base; therefore, when different terminology is used, all matching words and phrases aren't missed in the search.

- **Details to know about CareerSite:**

    Has a desktop recruiting-management system

    Is able to reach the passive job seeker

    Automatically updates all jobs directly from a database or subscriber Web site

    Cross-posts to other contracted recruitment sites

    Automatically acknowledges all replies by e-mail

    Requires no installation, upkeep, or update of software

    Has a search engine that can be used on any company's Web employment site with that subscriber's look, customized to the company's specs

    Accommodates multiple users with one ID and password or multiple passwords under one ID

    Accommodates any number of users who can access the same information from any computer at one time

    Posts all jobs with an HTML look, which is professional and easy to read

- CareerSite is a technology company that provides solutions to Internet recruiting and posts jobs. It works with a company's existing system(s) to create a smooth transition for employment. CareerSite works with the Human Resources department and the Information Technology (IT) department to make the process easy for all.

CareerWeb

USA
Information Technology,
Engineering, and Business
Rating: ★ ★ ★

CareerWeb specializes in professional, technical, and managerial jobs in engineering, information systems, telecommunications, marketing, accounting, health care, and many other fields. CareerWeb was given *PC Magazine's* award for being in the top 100 sites on the Web. CareerWeb also received recognition from WebCrawler as one of the best sites on the Web, and it was awarded a 1997 Excellence in the Electronic Recruiting Industry (EERI) award.

- **URL:** http://www.careerweb.com

- **Ownership/sponsorship:** a subsidiary of Landmark Communications, which is the owner of The Weather Channel, 43 newspapers, and other media interests.

- Started accepting resumes in 1995.

- **Approximate number of resumes online in April 1998:** 18,700; all resumes have been listed within the last 90 days and represent active job seekers in the following fields:

    30 percent: computer
    20 percent: engineering and science
    19 percent: management and administration
    14 percent: sales and marketing
    11 percent: miscellaneous disciplines

- **Total number of corporate subscribers/employers:** 300.

- **Of corporate subscribers/employers, the percentages include the following:**

    93 percent: direct-hire employers
    2 percent: staffing firms
    5 percent: contract/consulting firms

- **Fee structure for corporate subscribers/employers:** Rates are categorized in packages (available annually and in three- and six-month terms) and a la carte.

- **The Gold Package is an annual fee of $3,900 with an additional monthly fee of $300.00, which includes the following:**

    Unlimited job postings
    Unlimited resume searching
    Company profile page
    Link to corporate Web site from profile page
    Live e-mail link from job listings
    Account-manager access, which permits online management of job listings and reporting

- **The Silver Package is an annual fee of $2,900 with an additional monthly fee of $300.00, which includes the following:**

    Unlimited job postings
    Company profile page
    Link to corporate Web site from profile page
    Live e-mail link from job listings
    Account-manager access, which permits online management of job listings and reporting

- **The Bronze Package is an annual fee of $1,900 with an additional monthly fee of $300.00, which includes the following:**

    Unlimited job postings
    Live e-mail link from job listings
    Account-manager access, which permits online management of job listings and reporting

- **A la carte costs include the following:**

    Single job postings
    $135.00 for 30 days
    Profile pages
    $2,000 annual fee
    Resume database access
    $2,000 annual fee

- The CareerWeb resume database includes resumes in many disciplines and is searchable by job category, keyword, city, state, country, and date listed.

- **Methods and rules for submitting resumes:** 100 percent of resumes are received by Web form. Job seekers may submit resumes via the CareerWeb online resume form or by cutting and pasting their resumes into the database form. All resumes include contact information, skill classification categories, and cover letter. All resumes listed on CareerWeb are received via Web form; however, employers can receive resumes via fax, e-mail, or postal mail.

- 100 percent of resumes are received from individuals. CareerWeb does not take free resumes from newsgroups because it cannot guarantee the quality or availability of these candidates.

- No limits on length.

- **Format:** No mandatory format; however, job seekers can use a resume-listing form as an optional submission method and guide.

- No fee to person submitting resume.

- Resumes remain online 90 days.

- **Procedures for updating/renewing:** Job seekers can update their resumes at any time by using the online form. An e-mail is sent to candidates on the 80th day that their resumes are online. The e-mail message informs them that their resumes will be on CareerWeb for 10 more days and invites them to resubmit their resumes before they are taken offline.

- It is not possible to limit who can see a resume because all client employers who have purchased a resume-database access or a CareerWeb package including resume-database access can view the resumes.

- It is not possible to shield a resume from being viewed by a current employer. CareerWeb has made a policy decision *not* to attempt to restrict access to resumes from certain companies specified by the job seeker due to liability concerns. However, users do have the capability of submitting multiple resumes and the option of allowing their resumes to be searchable or not. CareerWeb recommends that users who want to keep their resumes from being seen by certain companies do the following: First, submit a full resume and specify that this resume is not to be searchable; job seekers can then use this resume when responding online to a job listing. Second, submit a second resume that has been edited to exclude personal details. This resume can then be searchable in the database.

- **Assistance provided to the person submitting a resume:** CareerWeb provides career-guidance information online.

- **Search options available to employers viewing resumes:** Employers can search resumes by date entered into the database, city, state, country, keyword, or category.

- **Technology to match jobs to resumes and e-mail resumes to clients:** CareerWeb is implementing Resume Finder, an agent function that searches for resumes that meet the criteria specified by a client; Resume Finder then e-mails newly added resumes to clients on a daily or weekly basis.

- **Average number of daily hits on resumes:** 1,500.

- **Special features:** CareerWeb provides Job Match, a free service that e-mails job seekers newly listed jobs that meet the job seeker's criteria. In addition, CareerWeb provides the following career resources for its job seekers: a bookstore, relocation information, a job-inventory test, Career Doctor articles, and employer profile pages.

- **Other distinguishing factors:** CareerWeb's focus is on matching professional, technical, and managerial job seekers with employers. Jobs and resumes are accepted only from CareerWeb members and candidates to guarantee high-quality experiences for all users of the service. CareerWeb does not collect free listings or resumes from newsgroups or other sites because it cannot guarantee the quality of such information. CareerWeb maintains a highly efficient Web site that is easily navigable and simple.

Colorado Online Job Connection

Colorado
Software Development
Rating: ★ ★

Peak Career Management, Inc., is a contingency search firm that has specialized in recruiting for software-development firms across the United States since 1995. Peak hosts the Colorado Online Job Connection (COJC), the premier regional career Web site for Colorado. The COJC received an Editors Choice Award from *Reader's Digest's* WWW subsidiary, LookSmart.

- **URL:** `http://www.jobsincolorado.com`

- **Ownership/sponsorship:** Peak Career Management, Inc.

- Started accepting resumes in January 1996.

- **Approximate number of resumes online in April 1998:** None online.

- Resumes are mainly in commercial software development.

- **Total number of corporate subscribers/employers:** 10 corporate subscribers in Colorado only.

- 100 percent of corporate subscribers/employers are direct-hire employers.

- **Fee structure for corporate subscribers/employers:** Employers are in Colorado or in the Rocky Mountain region. A 12-month subscription to the COJC is $2,400 with no other recruiting fees and includes the following:

   Minicompany Web page with employer's company's logo

   Link to employer's home page and e-mail address on its member-company page

   Up to 25 job posts per month on its job-openings pages

   Up to 25 jobs per month posted to various Internet newsgroups

- **Percentage of resumes received is as follows:**

    97 percent: e-mail
    1 percent: fax
    1 percent: other paper (job fairs, mailings)
    1 percent: newsgroups

- 100 percent of resumes received from individuals.

- **Format:** ASCII text.

- No fees to person submitting resume. Free to job seekers, but it does not post resumes online.

- **Length of time resumes remain online:** The resumes are never online with this service.

- **Procedures for updating/renewing:** send new resume.

- Is shielding a resume from being viewed by a current employer possible? The process of protecting identities is too difficult in any circumstance.

- **Average number of daily hits on resumes:** The COJC receives over 500 individual visitors per day.

- **Distinguishing factors:** The COJC is one of the few regional career Web sites serving Colorado and the Rocky Mountain region.

Computer People

Australia
Information Technology
Rating: ★ ★

Computer People describes itself as Australia's largest and most successful information technology services agency with a history of over 17 years in business.

- **URL:** `http://www.cpg.com.au/people/index.htm`

- **Ownership/sponsorship:** Computer Power Group.

- Started accepting resumes via Web in 1996.

- **Approximate number of resumes online in April 1998:** 60,000.

- Only information technology resumes are accepted.

- **Total number of corporate subscribers/employers:** 400 main customers throughout Australia, and other smaller customers.

- **Of corporate subscribers/employers, the percentages include the following:**

    95 percent: direct-hire employers
    5 percent: contract/consulting firms

- **Fee structure for corporate subscribers/employers:** Fee is based on placement of a candidate in a position.

- **Methods and rules for submitting resumes:** Anyone is free to submit over its Web page and via e-mail.

- **Percentage of resumes received from various sources is as follows:**

    90 percent: e-mail
    1 percent: fax
    1 percent: diskette
    8 percent: Web form

- **Percentage of resumes received from people is as follows:**

    90 percent: individuals
    10 percent: colleges or universities

- **Length:** No restrictions; the longer the better!

- **Format:** Open.
- No fees to person submitting resume.
- Resumes remain online indefinitely or until the candidates request that they be removed.
- **Procedures for updating/renewing:** via new submission over Web or via e-mail.
- It is possible to limit who can see a resume because the resume is visible only to the staff.
- It is possible to shield a resume from being viewed by a current employer because the resume is viewed by the staff only.
- **Assistance provided to the person submitting a resume:** Personal attention through branches throughout Australia and Asia.
- **Search options available to employers viewing resumes:** None; all searches are done by the staff.
- **Technology to match jobs to resumes and e-mail resumes to clients:** Internally developed MS Windows proprietary technology package.
- **Average number of daily hits on resumes:** 500.
- **Distinguishing factors:** Computer People is the largest IT employment agency in Australia, and it is a part of computer power group in association with Parity People and Equus.

Contract Employment Weekly

USA
Temporary Technical Jobs
Rating: ★ ★ ★ ★

Contract Employment Weekly has been the primary trade magazine serving the temporary technical industry since 1969. A technical temporary or contract employee is an individual who works for a contract service firm on temporary job assignment for that firm's client company. Approximately 550 contract offices advertise their current and anticipated job openings in *Contract Employment Weekly*.

- **URL:** http://www.ceweekly.com
- **Ownership/sponsorship:** C.E. Publications.
- Started accepting resumes in 1998.
- **Approximate number of resumes online in April, 1998:** 4,000–5,000.
- Resumes are in all engineering, IT/IS, and technical job classifications.
- **Total number of corporate subscribers/employers:** more than 500.
- Of corporate subscribers/employers, 100 percent are staffing firms, which include contract/consulting firms.
- **Fee structure for corporate subscribers/employers:** varies from $115.00/month to more than $350.00/week.
- **Methods and rules for submitting resumes:** You must be a subscriber.
- **Percentage of resumes received is as follows:**

    50 percent: e-mail
    10 percent: fax
    20 percent: other paper (job fairs, mailings)
    10 percent: diskette
    10 percent: Web form

- 100 percent of resumes are received from individuals.

- No limits on length.
- **Format:** open.
- **Fees to person submitting resume:** No fees, but you must be a subscriber.
- **Length of time resumes remain online:** As long as an individual is a subscriber (or you can deactivate the resume at the request of a subscriber).
- **Procedures for updating/renewing:** available.
- It is possible to limit who can see a resume.
- Shielding a resume from being viewed by a current employer is not possible if that employer is a current advertiser.
- **Assistance provided to the person submitting a resume:** Instructions are covered in both the *Subscriber's Manual* and online at the Web site. Phone assistance is also available. Subscribers can input or edit their own resumes online.
- **Search options available to employers viewing resumes:** search by keywords.
- **Technology to match jobs to resumes and e-mail resumes to clients:** None is available; instead, when online resumes are viewed by recruiters, Contract Employment Weekly e-mails to the subscribers that their resumes have been viewed or downloaded, and by whom.
- **Average number of daily hits on resumes:** 2,500–3,000.

Contract Engineering

USA
Engineering
Rating: ★ ★ ½

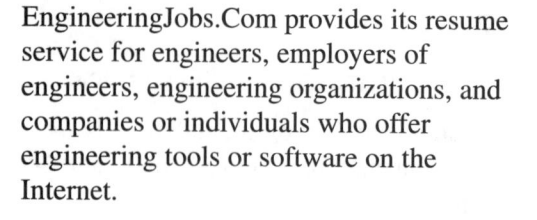

EngineeringJobs.Com provides its resume service for engineers, employers of engineers, engineering organizations, and companies or individuals who offer engineering tools or software on the Internet.

- **URL:** `http://www.ContractEngineering.com`
- **Ownership/sponsorship:** Engineering Jobs.
- Started accepting resumes in 1997.
- **Approximate number of resumes online in April 1998:** 450.
- **Resumes are all engineering related:** aeronautics, agricultural, automation, chemical, civil, electrical, environmental, geological, hydraulic, industrial/manufacturing, information tech/software, materials, mechanical, naval, nuclear, petroleum, solar, systems, and telecommunications/network.
- **Total number of corporate subscribers/employers:** 107.
- 100 percent of corporate subscribers/employers are contract/consulting firms.
- **Fee structure for corporate subscribers/employers:** free.
- **Methods and rules for submitting resumes:** submit at Web site.
- 100 percent of resumes received by Web form.
- 100 percent of resumes received from individuals.
- No limits on length.
- **Format:** Contract Engineering's listing is formatted; individual resumes are not.
- No fees to person submitting resume.
- Resumes remain online three months.

- **Procedures for updating/renewing:** submit new listing.

- It is not possible to limit who can see a resume.

- It is not possible to shield a resume from being viewed by a current employer.

- **Assistance provided to the person submitting a resume:** none available.

- **Search options available to employers viewing resumes:** scrolling through resumes organized by engineering discipline.

- **Technology to match jobs to resumes and e-mail resumes to clients:** none available.

- **Average number of daily hits on resumes:** This information is proprietary.

- **Other distinguishing factors:** probably the largest site on the Net specializing in contract engineering.

DICE High Tech Jobs Online

USA

IT or High Tech

Rating: ★ ★ ★ ½

DICE lists contract, full-time, and contract-to-hire positions in programming, systems administration, engineering, and other high-tech fields.

- **URL:** http://www.dice.com

- **Ownership/sponsorship:** Lloyd Linn and Diane Rickert (owners of D&L Online, Inc.)

- **Started accepting resumes in what year?** DICE actually has two ways of obtaining information from job seekers: Announce Availability, which asks for pertinent information online and is similar to a resume bank; and ResumeOnline, which is a secure place to post resumes because it is not indexed. DICE started to accept the Announce Availability forms in 1990 on the BBS and in 1995 on the Web. DICE accepted resumes on ResumeOnline in 1998. DICE's service is different from most others because of its Announce Availability.

- **Approximate number of resumes online in April 1998:** 8,500 on Announce Availability. ResumeOnline was new at this point.

- All resumes are IT or high tech in nature.

- **Total number of corporate subscribers/employers:** 1,400.

- 100 percent of DICE subscribers (customers) are third-party recruiters who place people in jobs outside their companies.

- **Fee structure for corporate subscribers/employers:** Prices start at $385.00 for multiple offices.

- **Methods and rules for submitting resumes:** Anyone can post a resume on DICE. It is a secure place to store a resume because DICE does not index it and send the information out to recruiters. DICE leaves that job to Announce Availability. The rule for Announce Availability is that the job seeker must be looking for work (either full time or contract) within the next three weeks.

Part II: Resume Banks

- 100 percent of resumes received from the DICE site by Web form.
- 100 percent of resumes received from individuals.
- No limits on length.
- **Format:** For Announce Availability, the format is specified by question. As for the resume, no special format is needed.
- No fees to person submitting resume.
- **Length of time resumes remain online:** Announce Availability is 30 days. ResumeOnline is unlimited as long as the job seekers touch their resumes at least once in a 30-day period.
- **Procedures for updating/renewing:** For Announce Availability, the job seekers call in to Customer Support. For ResumeOnline, they enter their JobTools account; then they can edit the resume.
- Is it possible to limit who can see a resume? Not for Announce Availability, but ResumeOnline can limit who sees a resume.
- Is shielding a resume from being viewed by a current employer possible? Yes for ResumeOnline.
- **Assistance provided to the person submitting a resume:** Job seekers will find an FAQ sheet; they can also call in or e-mail Customer Support.
- **Search options available to employers viewing resumes:** DICE customers can search the *Hotlist*—the form that is sent out daily with the information from Announce Availability—by entering keywords, dates, contract, or full time, among other search options.

- **Technology to match jobs to resumes and e-mail resumes to clients:** The *Hotlist* is sent out daily to the customers. In addition, an online search of the *Hotlist* is available to match the job seekers with employers.
- **Average number of daily hits on resumes:** Each company can look at the Announce Availability forms as much as it wants. The resumes on ResumeOnline are secure, however. Only when a job seeker wants to submit the resume is it looked at.
- **Special features:** DICE spends over $1,000,000 each year to advertise its service in national publications. Its service is an alternative to the Classifieds sections.
- **Other distinguishing factors:** DICE is available exclusively to companies who are third-party recruiters. The site contains jobs in information technology. DICE offers a metro search capability for several cities.
- For more information, go to the DICE home page and select **media room** on the left-hand side.

DiversiLink

USA
Hispanic Engineers
Rating: ★ ★ ★

The DiversiLink Web site is the career-development and job-posting Web site developed and managed by Innovative Human Resource Solutions (IHRS) for the Society of Hispanic Professional Engineers.

- **URL:** http://www.diversilink.com

- **Ownership/sponsorship:** Innovative Human Resources Solutions (IHRS) for the Society of Hispanic Professional Engineers (SHPE).

- Started accepting resumes in 1998.

- **Approximate number of resumes online in April 1998:** 500.

- Resumes are accepted in biology/biomedical engineering, chemical engineering, civil engineering, electrical engineering/electronics, environmental engineering, industrial engineering, materials science, mechanical engineering, business, arts, and other science or engineering fields.

- **Total number of corporate subscribers/employers:** 15.

- **Of corporate subscribers/employers, the percentages include the following:**

  75 percent: direct-hire employers
  25 percent: staffing firms

- **Fee structure for corporate subscribers/employers:** Access is free when job posting or other services are purchased.

- **Methods and rules for submitting resumes:** To input your resume, fill in each field completely, and cut and paste your scannable resume from your file into the Resume Drop. Make sure that the Resume Drop does not have any contact information at the beginning. The form can accept only ASCII format (text only with no bold type). DiversiLink will e-mail you the instructions to modify or delete your resume in the future.

- 100 percent of resumes received by Web form.

- 100 percent of resumes received from individuals.

- No limits on length.

- **Format:** contact information, education, objective, and resume.

- No fees to person submitting resume.

- Resumes remain online six months.

- **Procedures for updating/renewing:** resubmit updated resume.

- After a client pays for access, it is not possible to limit who can see a resume.

- It is not possible to shield a resume from being viewed by a current employer.

- **Assistance provided to the person submitting a resume:** Questions, suggestions, and problems are handled via e-mail.

- **Search options available to employers viewing resumes:** keyword, location (city, state), student/professional, degree, major, and date of resume.

- **Technology to match jobs to resumes and e-mail resumes to clients:** Search by major, keywords, and location. Employers can view the resumes online and then contact the DiversiLink staff to obtain access.

- **Special features:** listserve with hot jobs, resume update capability.

- **Other distinguishing factors:** Searchable job listings categorized by region. In June 1998, DiversiLink added a personal search agent that automatically sends job announcements as they are posted to interested individuals and according to individual preferences.

Part II: Resume Banks

EasyResume™

USA and Canada
Software Engineering
Rating: ★ ★ ★ ½

Lee Johnson International is a search firm that does employer-retained searches for software engineering professionals, primarily in the United States and Canada. The company specializes in leading-edge technologies such as object-oriented languages, connectivity, fuzzy logic, neural networks, distributed database internals, optimizing compilers, programming environments, GUIs, and multiprocessor operating systems internals. Lee Johnson International does not work in the MIS area.

- **URL:** http://www.dnai.com/~lji

- **Ownership/sponsorship:** Lee Johnson International, a division of Integrated Resource Search, Inc.

- Started accepting resumes in 1972 physically and in 1984 electronically via Fido.

- **Approximate number of resumes online in April 1998:** 5,789.

- Resumes are accepted from object-oriented software developers.

- **Total number of corporate subscribers/employers:** none (Lee Johnson International is a recruiting firm).

- **Fee structure for corporate subscribers/employers:** 25 percent of the candidate's annual salary when placed.

- **Methods and rules for submitting resumes:** e-mail to lji@dnai.com or fax to (510) 787-3191 (fine or detail mode).

- **Rules:** object-oriented software engineers only.

- **Percentage of resumes received is as follows:**

  98 percent: e-mail
  1 percent: other paper (job fairs, mailings)
  1 percent: newsgroups

- 100 percent of resumes received from individuals.

- **Length:** the longer the better.

- **Format:** ASCII text file or MS Word.

- No fees to person submitting resume.

- Resumes remain online forever. (Several people have called for a copy of the resumes they lost.)

- **Procedures for updating/renewing:** Lee Johnson International encourages people to update their resume annually. A resume prepared when you are still employed sounds a lot more positive.

- It is possible to limit who can see a resume because Lee Johnson International doesn't send out resumes without the candidates' permission. Its computer is not on any network.

- It is possible to shield a resume from being viewed by a current employer because Lee Johnson International gets the approval of a candidate first.

- **Assistance provided to the person submitting a resume:** Lee Johnson International's EasyResume outline is free at www.dnai.com/~lji.

- **Search options available to employers viewing resumes:** None; Lee Johnson International uses ZyIndex to search a resume.

- **Technology to match jobs to resumes and e-mail resumes to clients:** ZyIndex (full-text indexing).

- **Special features:** Lee Johnson International maintains a one-to-one relationship with its client companies and candidates. It does not mass-mail its resumes. It uses an OCR system and full-text database software that indexes every word in the resumes. When conducting a search, Lee Johnson International queries the database with a very complex Boolean search statement that gives only exact matches, so it doesn't waste your time. If your resume is retrieved, the company contacts you with a detailed description of the position and discusses the position with you.

EngineeringJobs.Com

USA

Engineering and Information Technology

Rating: ★ ★ ★ ★

EngineeringJobs.Com provides a free service for engineers, employers of engineers, engineering organizations, and companies or individuals who offer engineering tools or software on the Internet. The company also offers an optional resume distribution for a fee.

- **URL:** http://www.EngineeringJobs.com

- **Ownership/sponsorship:** Engineering Jobs.

- Started accepting resumes in 1996.

- **Approximate number of resumes online in April 1998:** 3,400.

- Accepts only engineering and information tech resumes, which are categorized by engineering discipline.

- **Total number of corporate subscribers/employers:** 1,451.

- **Of corporate subscribers/employers, the percentages include the following:**

  75 percent: direct-hire employers
  25 percent: staffing firms and recruiters (Several recruiters handle both permanent and contract positions.)

- **Fee structure for corporate subscribers/employers:** free access to resumes; $25.00/month for keyword searching.

- **Methods and rules for submitting resumes:** submitted by form at the Web site.

- 100 percent of resumes received by e-mail.

- 100 percent of resumes received from individuals.

- No limits on length.

- **Format specified:** EngineeringJobs.Com formats the resume listing from entry fields on its submission form. Actual full resumes, which are hyperlinked to the resume listings, are formatted by the job seeker.

- No fees to person submitting resume.

- Resumes remain online three months.

- **Procedures for updating/renewing:** Submit a new listing.

- It is not possible to limit who can see a resume.

- Shielding a resume from being viewed by a current employer is possible only by using an alias.

- **Assistance provided to the person submitting a resume:** none available.

- **Search options available to employers viewing resumes:** Employers can freely view the resumes posted on the Web, or they can do keyword searches for a fee.

- **Technology to match jobs to resumes and e-mail resumes to clients:** keyword searches.

- **Average number of daily hits on resumes:** not tracked.

- **Special features:** EngineeringJobs.Com also features listings of hundreds of recruiting agencies that specialize in engineering, IT, and high-tech employment. The company also features over a thousand hyperlinks to the engineering job pages of companies that directly employ engineers.

- **Other distinguishing factors:** For $35.00, EngineeringJobs.Com will send an engineering resume directly to 250 headhunters who specialize in engineering and IT jobs.

Entry Level Job Seeker Assistant

USA

Entry Level Only in All Career Fields

Rating: ★ ★ ★ ★

This site is for people who have never held a full-time, permanent job in their field or who have less than a year of nonacademic experience. The Entry Level Job Seeker Assistant does not accept resumes; instead, it contains links to your WWW resume. This site was featured in the June 1995 edition of *NetGuide* magazine and was the only WWW Job Seeker Assistant page to have a positive rating (out of nine pages reviewed for that article).

- **URL:** `http://members.aol.com/Dylander/jobhome.html`

- Started accepting resume URLs in 1994.

- **Approximate number of resume links in April 1998:** about 35–40 at any given time.

- Links to resumes in all job classifications are accepted. The resumes must be for entry-level job seekers. People who are changing fields but have many years of experience in their preceding field can classify as entry level.

- **Methods and rules for submitting resumes are as follows:**

  Put your resume into an HTML document format.

  Put this HTML resume on a WWW server.

  E-mail the URL of your WWW resume to the administrator of the Entry Level Job Seeker Assistant.

- 100 percent of resumes received from individuals.

- No limits on length.

- **Format:** To be linked, your resume must satisfy the following criteria:

  Must be readable by WWW text-only browsers

  No inlined graphics images

  No nondefault background coloring or images

No HTML 3.0+ commands or features (including TABLE)

No JAVA/ActiveX applets

No Netscape only/Microsoft Explorer only features

Must state clearly what field(s) you are interested in

- No fees to person submitting the resume link.

- **Length of time resume links remain active:** They remain active until the resumes can no longer be accessed; until they are changed so that they violate one of the format requirements; or until the owners tell the Entry Level Job Seeker Assistant administrator that they are no longer seeking employment.

- **Procedures for updating/renewing:** Resume owners maintain their own resumes at their leisure.

- **Average number of daily hits on resumes:** unknown because the site has no way to track this information.

- **Special features:** The site has a 100 percent text-based WWW page for quickness of downloading by Human Resource departments during normal business hours. The page includes a section of links to companies and other WWW resources that provide useful information for entry-level job seekers. The second section includes links to resumes of entry-level job seekers.

- **Other distinguishing factors:** All resumes are periodically checked. If the administrator gets a `file not found` error, the link to the resume is removed without warning. Resumes are checked before they are posted to make sure that they satisfy the required criteria. They are also spot checked to make sure that they stay that way. If you add graphics to your resume and the administrator catches the graphics, he will delete your link without warning. Resumes will also be checked for content to make sure that only those listing little or no non-academic experience are posted.

Future Access Employment Guide

USA
Information Technology,
Biotech, Sales, and Marketing
Rating: ★ ★ ★

Future Access is located in California's Silicon Valley.

- **URL:** `http://futureaccess.com/`

- **Ownership/sponsorship:** independently owned by

    Future Access
    PO Box 584
    Saratoga, CA 95071

- Started accepting resumes in 1994.

- **Approximate number of resumes online in April 1998:** 1,800.

- Resumes are primarily from biotech industry, hardware engineers, sales and marketing, software engineers, and miscellaneous.

- **Total number of corporate subscribers/employers:** approximately 500.

- **Fee structure for corporate subscribers/employers:** Non-subscription; resume access is free; job postings start at $10.00 per month.

Part II: Resume Banks

- **Methods and rules for submitting resumes:** Must supply basic information, including e-mail address.
- 100 percent of resumes received by Web form.
- 100 percent of resumes received from individuals.
- **Limits on length:** 3,000 characters.
- **Format:** free form.
- No fee to person submitting resume.
- Resumes remain online approximately six months.
- **Procedures for updating/renewing:** currently none.
- Is it possible to limit who can see a resume? Possible, but not limited.
- It is not possible to shield a resume from being viewed by a current employer.
- **Assistance provided to the person submitting a resume:** online Help.
- **Search options available to employers viewing resumes:** multiple keywords, country, state, city, Zip code, name, e-mail.
- **Technology to match jobs to resumes and e-mail resumes to clients:** none.
- **Average number of daily hits on resumes:** 600.
- **Distinguishing factors:** Many applicants are non-US residents, and many are willing to relocate.

HeadHunter.NET
USA
All Career Fields
Rating: ★★★★

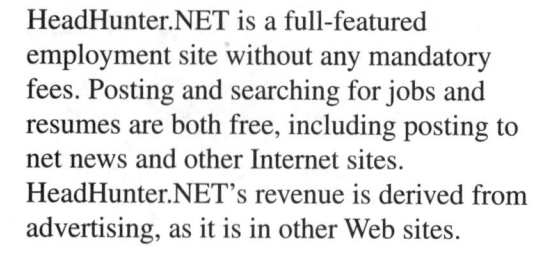

HeadHunter.NET is a full-featured employment site without any mandatory fees. Posting and searching for jobs and resumes are both free, including posting to net news and other Internet sites. HeadHunter.NET's revenue is derived from advertising, as it is in other Web sites.

- **URL:** `http://www.HeadHunter.NET/`
- **Ownership/sponsorship:** HeadHunter.NET.
- Started accepting resumes in 1996.
- **Approximate number of resumes online in April 1998:** 35,000 current resumes (less than 90 days old). Other sites may report higher numbers because they do not clean their databases as HeadHunter.NET does.
- Resumes are accepted in all career fields, which include over 100 industries.
- **Total number of corporate subscribers/employers:** 400.
- **Of corporate subscribers/employers, the percentages include the following:**

  50 percent: direct-hire employers
  25 percent: staffing firms
  25 percent: contract/consulting firms

- **Fee structure for corporate subscribers/employers:** Free access to resumes and free job posting.
- **Methods and rules for submitting resumes:** First you register; then the company sends you a password; and then you fill in an online Web form and press Submit.
- 100 percent of resumes received by Web form.
- **Percentage of resumes received is as follows:**

99 percent: individuals
1 percent: outplacement firms

- **Limits on length:** 6K.

- **Format:** Several fields on form; actual resume is text.

- No fees to person submitting resume.

- Resumes remain online 90 days.

- **Procedures for updating/renewing:** Visit at will and update any time.

- It is possible to limit the contact information so that the resume is "blind."

- It is not possible to shield a resume from being viewed by a current employer.

- **Assistance provided to the person submitting a resume:** form-based technical support.

- **Search options available to employers viewing resumes:** advanced form-based searching.

- **Technology to match jobs to resumes and e-mail resumes to clients:** None online now.

- **Average number of daily hits on resumes:** 250,000 resume-page views (400,000 hits); 500,000 total site-page views (800,000 hits).

- **Other distinguishing factors:** In an exit survey, 50 percent of HeadHunter.NET's resume posters report that the company helped them find a job. This percentage is much higher than normal for the Internet. HeadHunter.NET is the only large Internet recruiting site that allows free access to its resume database. Its users report that they have more success with this site than any other resume bank on the Net. The current record: a user was in the process of posting a resume when the phone rang three minutes later while she was still surfing the site!

HealthCareerWeb

USA
Health Care
Rating: ★ ★

HealthCareerWeb includes resumes in the health-care field. It is an affiliate site of CareerWeb.

- **URL:** `http://www.healthcareerweb.com`

- **Ownership/sponsorship:** An affiliate site of CareerWeb, a subsidiary of Landmark Communications, which is the owner of The Weather Channel, 43 newspapers, and other media interests.

- Started accepting resumes in 1997. HealthCareerWeb has been a pioneer in online recruiting within the health-care industry.

- **Approximate number of resumes online in April 1998:** Currently, HealthCareerWeb has 650 resumes in the resume database. All resumes have been listed within the last 90 days and represent active job seekers.

- The HealthCareerWeb resume database includes resumes from health-care professionals.

- **Total number of corporate subscribers/employers:** 58.

- 100 percent of corporate subscribers/employers are direct-hire employers.

- **Fee structure for corporate subscribers/employers:** Rates are categorized in packages and a la carte.

- **The Gold Package is an annual fee of $2,800 with an additional monthly fee of $300.00, which includes the following:**

Unlimited job postings
Unlimited resume searching
Company profile page
Link to Web site
Live e-mail link from job listings
Account-manager access, which permits online management of job listings and reporting
Cross-posted jobs on CareerWeb

- **The Silver Package is an annual fee of $1,800 with an additional monthly fee of $300.00, which includes the following:**

Unlimited job postings
Company profile page
Link to Web site
Live e-mail link from job listings
Account-manager access, which permits online management of job listings and reporting

- **The Bronze Package is an annual fee of $1,900 with an additional monthly fee of $300.00, which includes the following:**

Unlimited job postings
Live e-mail link from job listings
Account-manager access, which permits online management of job listings and reporting

- **A la carte costs include the following:**

Single job postings
  $80.00 for 30 days
  $35.00 additional to cross-post on CareerWeb

Profile pages
  $2,000 annual fee

Resume database access
  $1,000 annual fee
  $2,000 for access to both the HealthCareerWeb and CareerWeb resume data bank

- The HealthCareerWeb resume database includes resumes in many disciplines and is searchable by job category, keyword, city, state, country, and date listed.

- **Methods and rules for submitting resumes:** Job seekers can submit resumes via the HealthCareerWeb online resume form or by simply cutting and pasting their resumes into the database form. All resumes include contact information, skill categories, and cover letter.

- 100 percent of resumes are received by Web form. Employers can receive resumes via fax, e-mail, or postal mail.

- 100 percent of resumes are received from individuals. HealthCareerWeb does not take free resumes from newsgroups because it cannot guarantee the quality or availability of these candidates.

- No limits on length.

- **Format:** No mandatory format; however, you can use a resume listing form as an optional submission method and guide.

- No fees to person submitting resume.

- Resumes remain online 90 days.

- **Procedures for updating/renewing:** Job seekers can update their resumes at any time by using the online form. An e-mail is sent to candidates on the 80th day that their resume is online. The e-mail informs them that their resumes will be on HealthCareerWeb for only ten more days and invites them to resubmit their resumes.

- It is possible to limit who can see the resume because only client employers who have purchased a resume-database access or a HealthCareerWeb package including resume-database access can view resumes.

- **Shielding a resume from being viewed by a current employer is possible under the following circumstances:** HealthCareerWeb has made a policy decision *not* to attempt to restrict access to resumes from certain companies specified by the job seeker due to liability concerns. However, users do have the capability of submitting multiple resumes and the option of allowing their resumes to be searchable or not. HealthCareerWeb recommends that users who want to keep their resumes from being seen by certain companies do the following: First, submit a full resume and specify that this resume is not to be searchable; job seekers can then use this resume when responding online to a job listing. Second, submit a second resume that has been edited to exclude personal details. This resume can then be searchable in the database.

- **Assistance provided to the person submitting a resume:** HealthCareerWeb provides career-guidance information online and includes a bookstore, career-inventory test, and CareerDoctor articles.

- **Search options are available to employers viewing resumes:** Employers can search resumes by date entered into the database, city, state, country, keyword, or category.

- **Technology to match jobs to resumes and e-mail resumes to clients:** HealthCareerWeb is implementing Resume Finder, an agent function that searches for criteria specified by a client and e-mails new resumes to the client on a daily or weekly basis.

- **Average number of daily hits on resumes:** 40.

- **Special features:** HealthCareerWeb provides job seekers with such career resources as a bookstore, relocation information, a job-inventory test, CareerDoctor articles, and employer-profile pages. HealthCareerWeb also provides a free service that e-mails new job postings to job seekers based on their criteria.

- **Other distinguishing factors:** Jobs and resumes are accepted only from HealthCareerWeb members and candidates. It does not collect free listings or resumes from newsgroups or other sites because it cannot guarantee the quality of such information. Additionally, HealthCareerWeb maintains a highly efficient Web site that is easily navigable and simple.

Hospitality Net Virtual Job Exchange

Global
Hospitality
Rating: ★ ★ ★

The Hospitality Net Virtual Job Exchange serves the global hospitality and lodging industry on the Internet.

- **URL:** `http://www.hospitalitynet.nl/job/home.htm`

- **Ownership/sponsorship:** ownership by Hospitality Net.

- Started accepting resumes in 1995.

- **Approximate number of resumes online in April 1998:** more than 250.

Part II: Resume Banks

- **All resumes are in the following job classifications in the hospitality industry:** accounting, conference and banqueting, corporate office, food and beverage, sales and marketing, and rooms divisions.

- **Total number of corporate subscribers/employers:** greater than 10,000 registered users.

- **Of corporate subscribers/employers, the percentages include the following:**

    50 percent: direct-hire employers
    50 percent: contract/consulting firms

- **Fee structure for corporate subscribers/employers:** all free of charge.

- **Methods and rules for submitting resumes:** Resumes are submitted online by using an online form; there are no special rules.

- **Percentage of resumes received from sources is as follows:**

    1 percent: e-mail
    99 percent: Web form

- **Percentage of resumes received from people is as follows:**

    99 percent: individuals
    1 percent: other

- No limits on length.

- **Format:** Online form with name-and-address format specified; all other information is free text entries.

- No fees to person submitting resume.

- Resumes remain online two months.

- **Procedures for updating/renewing:** undergoing change in the new version of the Hospitality Net Web site.

- It is not possible to limit who can see a resume, but this feature is undergoing change in the new version of the Hospitality Net Web site.

- It is not possible to shield a resume from being viewed by a current employer, but this feature is undergoing change in the new version of the Hospitality Net Web site.

- **Assistance provided to the person submitting a resume:** easy-to-use resume registration form.

- **Search options available to employers viewing resumes:** All parts of the resume can be found by using the Hospitality Net search engine.

- **Technology to match jobs to resumes and e-mail resumes to clients:** Hospitality Net's extensive search engine.

- **Average number of daily hits on resumes:** more than 7,000 per day.

- **Special information:** At the time this information was provided, Hospitality Net Virtual Job Exchange was working on a completely new version of the Hospitality Net Web site, which was to have been available in June 1998. The new version of the Hospitality Net Web site will feature a new version of the Job Exchange, which will include the following features:

    An extensive registration process

    The opportunity to update or change your curriculum vitae (CV)

    The opportunity to register your CV in a private Job Exchange (limited access)

    The opportunity to refer to personal information (CV, experience, and so on) on your own Web site or Web page

- A new section of Hospitality Net, where all CVs can be found (The focus will be on four areas: technology, environment, sales and marketing, and human resources.)

- Because Hospitality Net Virtual Job Exchange is still working on the new Job Exchange, more new features will likely be added.

InstaMatch Resume Database

USA

All Career Fields

Rating: ★ ★ ★

Through various methods, InstaMatch adds 200 to 400 resumes (of both technical and nontechnical skills) weekly to its resume database. Each resume contains an e-mail address for instant e-mail to that job seeker.

- **URL:** `http://www.instamatch.com`

- **Ownership/sponsorship:** ProsperTech Group, Inc.

   2900 W. Anderson Lane #20-181
   Austin, TX 78757-1124
   http://www.prospertech.com

- Started accepting resumes in 1995.

- **Approximate number of resumes online in April 1998:** 10,000.

- Resumes are from almost every career field.

- **Total number of corporate subscribers/employers:** 400.

- **Of corporate subscribers/employers, the percentages include the following:**

   15 percent: direct-hire employers
   30 percent: contract/consulting firms
   50 percent: staffing firms
   5 percent: other

- **Fee structure for corporate subscribers/employers:** Each user must have an account. The fee structure for unlimited access to resumes is as follows:

   $ 14.00   for 1 week
   $ 48.00   for 1 month
   $138.00   for 3 months
   $268.00   for 6 months
   $488.00   for 12 months

- Multiuser discounts are available.

- **Methods and rules for submitting resumes:** InstaMatch Resume Database usually accepts resumes only from individuals. The resumes must have some form of contact information, and they must be text resumes only.

- **Percentage of resumes received by sources is as follows:**

   30 percent: e-mail
   5 percent: fax
   30 percent: newsgroups
   10 percent: other paper (job fairs, mailings)
   25 percent: robot and InstaMatch personnel

- **Percentage of resumes received from people is as follows:**

   30 percent: individuals
   70 percent: other

- No limits on length.

- **Format:** free-format text.

- No fees to person submitting resume.

- Resumes older than four months are deleted.

- **Procedures for updating/renewing:** Candidate sends text resume by e-mail to `resume@instamatch.com`.

- **Limit on who can see a resume:** A free demo enables a person to view ten resumes. Any further access requires a paid account. There are no restrictions for a paid account.

- It is not possible at this time to shield a resume from being viewed by a current employer. This feature is planned for a future release, however.

- **Assistance provided to the person submitting a resume:** Online Help and personal support, although any type of support from the professional staff is rarely required.

- **Search options available to employers viewing resumes:** All words in every resume are indexed. Full Boolean searches, phrases, and word-proximity searches are available. Geographic searches are available. InstaMatch Resume Database has a search engine specifically tailored for matching resumes to requirements.

- **Technology to match jobs to resumes and e-mail resumes to clients:** InstaMatch Resume Database is currently working on the development of this service.

- **Average number of daily hits on resumes:** 1,800.

- **Special features:**

  Highlighting of key search words

  Geographic search capabilities, including area code

  Capability of configuring screens to individual preferences

- Ranking of search results, with color coding to identify higher- from lower-ranking resumes

- **Other distinguishing factors:** A free demo is available.

The Insurance Career Center

USA

Insurance

Rating: ★ ★ ★ ★

The Insurance Career Center was founded in October 1995 as the first commercial Web site dedicated to insurance professionals. In May 1997, The Insurance Career Center became part of CareerMosaic.

- **URL:** `http://www.insjobs.com`

- **Ownership/sponsorship:** Bernard Hodes Advertising.

- Started accepting resumes in 1995.

- **Approximate number of resumes online in April 1998:** 2,500.

- **Resumes are fielded as follows:**

  Industry Groupings: Property and Casualty, Commercial Lines; Property and Casualty, Personal Lines; Life and Health; Other

  Title: Home Office Executive, Officer or Director; Home Office Staff; Regional Manager; Branch Manager; Manager; Supervisor; Staff Level; Support, Clerical; and Other

  Specific Skill: Actuary; Attorney; Accounting, Finance; Claims;

Consulting; Data Processing, Programming; Human Resources; Loss Control; Managing, Broker or Agent or Wholesale; Managing, Underwriting; Marketing, Broker, Agent, Wholesale; Marketing; Premium Audit; Production Underwriting; Producer, Broker, Agent; Program Development; Risk Management; Research; Reinsurance/Treaty; Sales, Other; Underwriting; and Other.

- **Total number of corporate subscribers/employers:** 700.

- **Of corporate subscribers/employers, the percentages include the following:**

  50 percent: direct-hire employers

  50 percent: staffing firms

- **Fee structure for corporate subscribers/employers:** no cost.

- **Methods and rules for submitting resumes:** Resume Builder: population of fields with ASCII-text resume at end of submission.

- 100 percent of resumes received by Web form.

- 100 percent of resumes received from individuals.

- No limits on length.

- **Format:** ASCII format.

- No fees to person submitting resume.

- **Length of time resumes remain online:** Resumes are managed by the users online for an unlimited time, unless they ask for resumes to be removed.

- **Procedures for updating/renewing:** online.

- It is not possible to limit who can see a resume.

- It is not possible to shield a resume from being viewed by a current employer.

- **Assistance provided to the person submitting a resume:** online instructions.

- **Search options available to employers viewing resumes:** Keyword searches; searches against any fielded data, including salary and location.

- No technology to match jobs to resumes and e-mail resumes to clients.

- **Average number of daily hits on resumes:** 17–18 percent of all page views are resumes.

- **Distinguishing factors:** Resumes are updated by candidates on an ongoing basis.

The Internet Job Locator

USA
All Career Fields
Rating: ★ ★

- **URL:** `http://www.joblocator.com/`

- **Ownership/sponsorship:** Travelers OnLine.

- Started accepting resumes in 1995.

- Resumes are accepted in all job classifications.

- **Approximate number of resumes online in April 1998:** 7,000–8,000, which are six months old or newer.

- The make-up of corporate subscribers/employers is confidential.

- **Fee structure for corporate subscribers/employers:** from $25.00 to $225.00.

- **Methods and rules for submitting resumes:** via Web only.

- 100 percent of resumes received by Web form and third-party software.

- **Percentage of resumes received is as follows:**

  99 percent: individuals
  1 percent: outplacement firms

- **Limits on length:** no limits, although most resumes are between 2–4 pages.

- **Format:** See the Web site for the format.

- No fees to person submitting resume.

- Resumes remain online six months.

- **Procedures for updating/renewing:** via Web site.

- It is not possible to limit who can see a resume.

- It is not possible to shield a resume from being viewed by a current employer, and users are not required to enter their names (a name can be shown as anonymous).

- **Assistance provided to the person submitting a resume:** Most necessary information has been provided on the Web site, so the process is fairly straight-forward.

- **Search options available to employers viewing resumes:** keywords and Push technology.

- **Technology to match jobs to resumes and e-mail resumes to clients:** Push data to clients or job seekers.

- **Average number of daily hits on resumes:** confidential.

The Irish Jobs Page

Ireland, Europe,
Australia, USA
All Career Fields
Rating: ★ ★

The Irish Jobs Page is Ireland's longest established recruitment site that deals with recruitment in Ireland. It also has separate resume banks for the United States, mainland Europe, and Australia.

- **URL:** `http://www.exp.ie`

- **Ownership/sponsorship:** Software Expressions.

- Started accepting resumes in 1996.

- **Approximate number of resumes online in April 1998:** 1,000.

- Resumes are in all career fields.

- **Total number of corporate subscribers/employers:** 70.

- **Of corporate subscribers/employers, the percentages include the following:**

  50 percent: direct-hire employers
  50 percent: staffing firms

- **Fee structure for corporate subscribers/employers:** variable.

- **Methods and rules for submitting resumes:** online form only.

- 100 percent of resumes received by Web form.

- 100 percent of resumes received from individuals.

- No limits on length.

- Format specified by submission form.
- No fees to person submitting resume.
- Resumes remain online six months.
- **Procedures for updating/renewing:** online form.
- It is not possible to limit who can see a resume.
- It is not possible to shield a resume from being viewed by a current employer.
- **Assistance provided to the person submitting a resume:** none.
- **Search options available to employers viewing resumes:** online form.
- **Technology to match jobs to resumes and e-mail resumes to clients:** none.
- **Distinguishing factors:** Ireland's longest-running employment site.

JobBank USA

USA
All Career Fields
Rating: ★ ★ ★

JobBank USA was noted as one of the largest employment Web sites on the Internet in *USA Today*, August 26, 1996, and has received many awards, including an Excellence in the Electronic Recruiting Industry (EERI) award.

- **URL:** `http://www.jobbankusa.com`
- **Ownership/sponsorship:** JobBank USA, Inc.
- Started accepting resumes in 1995.
- **Approximate number of resumes online in April 1998:** 60,000–65,000.
- Resumes are in all career fields.
- **Total number of corporate subscribers/employers:** 500–600.
- **Of corporate subscribers/employers, the percentages include the following:**

  50 percent: direct-hire employers

  40 percent: staffing firms

  10 percent: contract/consulting firms
- **The fee structure for corporate subscribers/employers is as follows:**

  $1,900/year

  $225.00/month

  $595.00/three-month trial
- **Methods and rules for submitting resumes:** online via JobBank USA's Resume Builder form.
- 100 percent of resumes received by Web form.
- 100 percent of resumes received from individuals.
- **Limits on length:** 15K or five pages.
- **Format:** JobBank USA's Resume Builder form.
- No fees to person submitting resume.
- Resumes remain online for one year.
- **Procedures for updating/renewing:** real-time editing/updating online.
- It will be possible by the end of 1998 to limit who can see a resume in the next software version.
- It will be possible by the end of 1998 to shield a resume from being viewed by a current employer in the next software version.

- **Assistance provided to the person submitting a resume:** online and e-mail support.

- **Search options available to employers viewing resumes:** The database is searchable by keyword, salary, geographical location, relocation status, citizenship status, and date of resume entry. Qualified resumes are easily found by using JobBank USA's QuickScan feature, which lists a candidate's employment background.

- **Technology to match jobs to resumes and e-mail resumes to clients:** available in the next software version at the end of 1998.

- **Average number of daily hits on resumes:** unknown.

- **Special features:** MetaSearch pages provide job seekers access to all major job databases and newspapers nationwide. MetaSearch is a convenient tool for searching various sites from one location.

JobCenter Employment Services, Inc.

USA
All Career Fields
Rating: ★ ★ ★ ★

JobCenter maintains a database of resumes from prospective employees and matches them with what an employer is looking for, based on a keyword search. When matches occur, JobCenter sends copies of the resumes electronically to the employer. JobCenter also sends the job seekers a message to inform them about who has their resumes for review. JobCenter also sends the job description so that the job seekers know exactly what the employer is looking for. Job Center can also post your job ad to appropriate Usenet newsfeed groups (ones that you choose).

- **URL:** http://www.jobcenter.com

- **Ownership/sponsorship:** privately owned.

- Started accepting resumes in 1995.

- **Approximate number of resumes online in April, 1998:** 21,000.

- Resumes are in all career fields.

- **Total number of corporate subscribers/employers:** 13,500.

- **Of corporate subscribers/employers, the percentages include the following:**

  80 percent: direct-hire employers
  10 percent: staffing firms
  10 percent: contract/consulting firms

- **Fee structure for corporate subscribers/employers:** $15.00 per week. Minimum of two weeks per ad.

- **Methods and rules for submitting resumes:** online posting directly at the JobCenter Web site, as well as e-mail submission.

- **Percentage of resumes received by sources is as follows:**

  5 percent: e-mail
  95 percent: Web form

- **Percentage of resumes received from people is as follows:**

  90 percent: individuals
  8 percent: colleges or universities
  2 percent: outplacement firms

- No limits on length.

- **Format:** open.

- **Fees to person submitting resume are as follows:**

  No charge for availability of online searches at the JobCenter Web site.

  $5.00 charge for six months of JobDirect: Resumes are matched with job ads, and the job seeker is notified via e-mail of every match. Matching and notification are done each business day. JobCast is currently included with JobDirect. JobCast publishes a resume to a job seeker's choice of Usenet newsgroups once every other week.

  $5.00 charge for proofing by a professional resume consultant.

- Resumes remain online six months.

- **Procedures for updating/renewing:** online edit form with unlimited edits.

- It is not possible to limit who can see a resume.

- It is possible to shield a resume from being viewed by a current employer by using a confidential resume.

- **Assistance provided to the person submitting a resume:** proofing, toll-free customer service.

- **Search options available to employers viewing resumes:** Free searches on the Web site at any time. Notification of matching resumes automatically sent to employers' e-mail addresses each business day.

- **Technology to match jobs to resumes and e-mail resumes to clients:** proprietary.

- **Average number of daily hits on resumes:** 50,000.

- JobCenter feels that it has created the highest quality database of online resumes on the Internet. JobCenter's special features include the following:

JobCenter automatically hyperlinks every posting made to its database. This step makes it easy for someone to contact you when your posting is seen online.

JobCenter does not automatically activate each resume that is posted; instead, the company requires the individual to call the toll-free number to activate the resume. This step provides JobCenter with the opportunity to visually verify the information.

A large percentage of JobCenter's customers opt for the fee-based service, which includes e-mailing the matching job ads to them. This service increases the quality of the resumes because only those people who are truly interested in looking for work would pay for the service.

jobEngine

USA

IT and Computer Industry Professionals

Rating: ★ ★ ★ ★

More than five million computer professionals use Ziff-Davis publications (such as *PC Magazine* and *PC Week*) and the Ziff-Davis Web site, ZDNet, which directs its visitors to the jobEngine recruitment site. I-Search provides the recruitment database service for this site, which specializes in information technology (IT) and computer-industry professionals.

- **URL:** `http://www.jobEngine.com`

- **Ownership/sponsorship:** A joint venture of I-Search Inc. and Ziff-Davis Publications.

Part II: Resume Banks

- Started accepting resumes in 1997.
- **Approximate number of resumes online in April 1998:** 100,000.
- Resumes primarily from IT and computer-industry professionals.
- **Total number of corporate subscribers/employers:** 500.
- **Methods and rules for submitting resumes:** Simply cut and paste the resume directly into a Web form online.
- 100 percent of resumes received online.
- 100 percent of resumes received from individuals.
- Length limited to 32,000 characters.
- Format not specified. jobEngine's special, patented resume-extraction technology is 95 percent accurate with most standard resume formats.
- No fees to person submitting resume.
- Resumes remain online until removed. An e-mail is sent 60 days from the last update to remind the applicant to update or remove the resume.
- **Procedures for updating/renewing:** online editing.
- It is possible to limit who can see a resume.
- It is possible to shield a resume from being viewed by a current employer.
- **Assistance provided to the person submitting a resume:** online Help.
- **Search options available to employers viewing resumes:** The most sophisticated resume database search on the market today. Employers enter criteria for the desired candidate; they are then presented with a match list that ranks the most appropriate candidates first. Using this ranked list, employers can easily review the background summary, which contains key summarized information, and the original text of the candidate's resume.
- **Technology to match jobs to resumes and e-mail resumes to clients:** The employers can contact directly those candidates who interest them by using the e-mail feature of the same Web browser they are using to review resumes.
- **Average number of daily hits on resumes:** 117,594 as of May 1998.
- **Special features:** I-Search's relational search capability is far more powerful than a simple text search. With text search, you have to work a lot harder to find the data you need, and sometimes you can't find it at all! Text-search methods produce results that exhibit two major retrieval problems: low precision and low recall:

  Low precision: Simple text search methods look for the character string you enter within any part of a document. Because the search is not limited to a specific part of the text, incorrect matches are made and too many matches are returned. This problem increases the work you have to do to look at each one.

  Low recall: Similarly, because text search finds only exact word matches, near matches are missed. Also missed are conceptual matches that happen to use different words. (For example, you may want "Oracle" to be a match when you search for "Relational Database" as a skill.)
- I-Search solves the problems of the text-search methods through the use of extensive skill (synonym) lexicons.

The JobExchange

USA
All Career Fields
Rating: ★ ★ ★

The JobExchange Network partners with several newspapers for its job announcements. These newspapers include Charleston's *Post Courier*, Hackensack's *Bergen Record*, Madison's *Wisconsin State Journal*, Milwaukee's *Journal Sentinel*, Pittsburgh's *Post-Gazette*, Tacoma's *The News Tribune*, Toledo's *Blade*, and the nationwide *CNHI*. The resume program and candidate-search program contain a list of 27,000 job occupations along with a description of these occupations so that both job seekers and employers use the same terminology.

- **URL:** http://www.jobexchange.com
- **Ownership/sponsorship:** private.
- Started accepting resumes in 1997.
- **Approximate number of resumes online in April 1998:** 45,000.
- The JobExchange has over 27,000 job titles and job descriptions on its site.
- **Total number of corporate subscribers/employers:** 11,000.
- **Of corporate subscribers/employers, the percentages include the following:**

  60 percent: direct-hire employers
  20 percent: staffing firms
  20 percent: contract/consulting firms

- **Fee structure for corporate subscribers/employers:** $22.00 per resume download online, or $21.00 prepaid to a participating newspaper.
- **Methods and rules for submitting resumes:** You can go online and enter for free; or you can send your resume to The JobExchange or to a participating newspaper to be entered for you at a cost of $15.00.

- **Percentage of resumes received by sources is as follows:**

  90 percent: Web form
  10 percent: other paper (job fairs, mailings)

- **Percentage of resumes received from people is as follows:**

  90 percent: individuals
  1 percent: colleges or universities
  3 percent: outplacement firms
  1 percent: other

- No limits on length.
- Format is specified online.
- **Fees to persons submitting resumes:** None unless they want The JobExchange to type in the resume for them. This service costs $15.00.
- **Length of time resumes remain online:** Six months, but they can be renewed indefinitely.
- **Procedures for updating/renewing:** Respond to an e-mail message, go online, and update or mail the update to The JobExchange.
- It is possible to limit who can see a resume; however, the limits are not foolproof because people can enter under different names or hire a recruiter to search on their behalf.
- It is possible to shield a resume from being viewed by a current employer; however, the limits are not foolproof because people can enter under different names or hire a recruiter to search on their behalf.

Part II: Resume Banks

- **Assistance provided to the person submitting a resume:** Online advice and references are extensive. Participating newspapers contribute editorial content for advice; an 800 number is available for people to use; and persons can mail in their resumes for assistance in typing.

- **Search options available to employers viewing resumes:** Extensive options are available. These options enable the searcher to narrow the search to very specific criteria to eliminate unqualified candidates, broaden the search to include marginal candidates, and everything in between. Searchers can see a capsule view of the resumes so that they can see how many criteria are matched before paying for a download.

- **Technology to match jobs to resumes and e-mail resumes to clients:** both available.

- **Average number of daily hits on resumes:** currently, 4,000–5,000; increases daily.

- **Special features:** Classified ads are interactive with resumes online. JobBank represents classified ads from newspapers all over the country. The cost of resumes to searchers is one of the lowest on the Internet, with no large advance purchases required. New features coming online include online classified listings (not necessarily published), professional forum rooms, employee assessments, background checks, and so on.

- **Other distinguishing factors:** The JobExchange believes it is the best because of its expertise in human resources.

Job Link USA

USA
All Career Fields
Rating: ★ ★

Job Link USA, Inc., located in Chicago, accepts resumes from college graduates as well as skilled and experienced individuals.

- **URL:** `http://www.joblink-usa.com`

- **Ownership/sponsorship:**

    Job Link USA, Inc.
    7217 W. Forest Preserve Dr.
    Suite 20
    Chicago, IL 60634

- Started accepting resumes in September 1997.

- **Approximate number of resumes online in April 1998:** 1,500.

- Resumes are accepted in all career fields.

- **Total number of corporate subscribers/employers:** 600.

- **Of corporate subscribers/employers, the percentages include the following:**

    55 percent: direct-hire employers
    5 percent: staffing firms
    45 percent: contract/consulting firms
    5 percent: other

- **Fee structure for corporate subscribers/employers is as follows:**

    For job postings:
    $30.00 per job posting

    For Resume Database:
1 week	$ 14.00
1 month	$ 48.00
3 months	$138.00
6 months	$268.00
12 months	$488.00

For Automatic Resume Notifier:
$140.00

For Company HomePage Wizard:
$40.00

- **Percentage of resumes received is as follows:**

    10 percent: e-mail
    1.5 percent: fax
    18 percent: other paper (job fairs, mailings)
    .5 percent: diskette
    80 percent: Web form

- 100 percent of resumes received from individuals.

- **Limit on length:** 7,000 characters for free online postings; 14,000 characters for subscribers.

- **Format specified:** open.

- **Fees to person submitting resume:** $10.00 for six months online.

- **Length of time resumes remain online:** three months for free resume posting; six months for subscribers.

- **Procedures for updating/renewing:** sign in with user name and password.

- It is not possible to limit who can see a resume.

- It is not possible to shield a resume from being viewed by a current employer.

- **Assistance provided to the person submitting a resume:** Please visit the following site for details:

    `http://www.joblink-usa.com/sresume.htm`

- Search options available to employers viewing resumes: By keywords, job categories, years of experience, salary, and by location.

- **Average number of daily hits on resumes:** 989.

- **Please visit the following site for details about special features:**

    `http://www.joblink-usa.com/sresume.htm`

JobLynx

USA
All Career Fields
Rating: ★ ★ ★ ½

Resume posting to the JobLynx database hands over your resume to over 9,600 registered headhunters. Confidentiality is guaranteed because only headhunters have access to your resume. The interested headhunters contact the job seeker directly.

- **URL:** `http://joblynx.com`

- **Ownership/sponsorship:** JobLynx.

- Started accepting resumes in 1994.

- **Approximate number of resumes online in April 1998:** many thousands.

- Resumes are accepted in all career fields.

- **Total number of corporate subscribers/employers:** 9,600 headhunters.

- 100 percent of corporate subscribers/employers are staffing firms.

- **Fee structure for corporate subscribers/employers:** confidential.

- **Methods and rules for submitting resumes:** online registration, e-mail, fax, postal mail.

- **Percentage of resumes received is as follows:**

    8 percent: e-mail
    2 percent: diskette
    90 percent: Web form

- 100 percent of resumes received from individuals.

- No limits on length. You also can include a cover letter.

- **Format specified:** TEXT format: .txt.

- **Fees to person submitting resume:** $39.85 for three-month registration on exclusive, confidential database searched by 9,600 headhunters with 121,938 current job openings.

- Resumes remain online 90 days and are then purged automatically.

- **Procedures for updating/renewing:** You can resubmit an updated resume at no additional cost up to two separate times during a single 90-day period.

- It is possible to limit who can see a resume. Only the 9,600-member headhunters see the resumes; they will contact the job seekers before the release of their resumes to any companies.

- It is possible to shield a resume from being viewed by a current employer because resumes are kept *completely* confidential.

- **Assistance provided to the person submitting a resume:** online instructions and a phone number for help.

- **Search options available to employers viewing resumes:** The recruiters use keyword searches of all resume contents.

- **Technology to match jobs to resumes and e-mail resumes to clients:** searchable database online for recruiter access only.

- **Average number of daily hits on resumes:** 9,000 visitors daily and climbing.

- **Special features:** JobLynx offers free 10,000 links to Web employment resources. It is currently placing a person every three minutes due to its size.

- **Other distinguishing factors:** JobLynx guarantees job-search success.

- Use JobLynx's service for two consecutive 90-day periods. If you are not presented with available employment opportunities during this time period, JobLynx will gladly refund 50 percent of your total registration fee.

JobNet

Canada
All Career Fields
Rating: ★ ★ ★

JobNet is based in Canada and uses the National Occupational Classification (NOC) to classify and describe occupations within the Canadian labor market.

- **URL:** `http://www.jobnet.org`

- **Ownership/sponsorship:** ownership.

- Started accepting resumes in 1996.

- **Approximate number of resumes online in April 1998:** 2,500.

- Resume are classified into categories based on the NOC system (National Occupational Classification) produced by the government.

- **Total number of corporate subscribers/employers:** 5,000.

- **Of corporate subscribers/employers, the percentages include the following:**

  70 percent: direct-hire employers

  10 percent: staffing firms

  20 percent: contract/consulting firms

- **Fee structure for corporate subscribers/employers:** $100.00 per job posting (multiple-posting packages available).

- **Methods and rules for submitting resumes:** Resumes must be submitted online via online forms.

- **Percentage of resumes received by sources is as follows:**

  2 percent: e-mail
  1 percents: fax
  97 percent: Web form

- **Percentage of resumes received from people is as follows:**

  40 percent: colleges or universities (JobNet has a sister site, called Alumnet, which is for university graduates.)
  60 percent: other

- No limits on length.

- **Format:** based on the form used to fill out resume submissions.

- No fees to person submitting resume.

- **Length of time resumes remain online:** forever.

- **Procedures for updating/renewing:** available.

- It is possible to limit who can see a resume.

- It is possible to shield a resume from being viewed by a current employer.

- **Assistance provided to the person submitting a resume:** telephone, e-mail, and WWW support.

- **Search options available to employers viewing resumes:** Employers can search based on a number of items, including job category, location, education, and so on.

- **Technology to match jobs to resumes and e-mail resumes to clients:** available.

- **Average number of daily hits on resumes:** 200.

- **Distinguishing factors:** JobNet is a fast-growing site that is always expanding and improving to provide better service to both individual subscribers and corporate employers.

Job Options, LLC

USA

All Career Fields

Rating: ★ ★ ★ ★

JobOptions, formerly known as E.span, pioneered online recruitment services in 1991 when most people did not even know what the Internet was. Originally known as Adnet, the company evolved into a comprehensive employment resource and information resource whose purpose is to provide comprehensive online employment services. JobOptions has received numerous awards including *Home PC's* "Best of the Web," *Net Guide's* "Best of the Web," and *USA Today's* "Hot Sites."

- **URL:** `http://www.joboptions.com`

- **Ownership/sponsorship:** JobOptions is a subsidiary of Gund Business Enterprises, Inc., a Cleveland, Ohio, organization.

Part II: Resume Banks

- Started accepting resumes in 1995.

- **Approximate number of resumes online in May 1998:** 67,000.

- JobOptions has a diverse resume database. An employer can search for candidates in all career fields.

- **Total number of corporate subscribers/employers:** 2,000.

- **Of corporate subscribers/employers, the percentages include the following:**

    85 percent: direct-hire employers
    15 percent: contract/consulting firms

- **Fee structure for corporate subscribers/employers:** JobOptions has services to meet any size company's needs. Services range from single ads that remain on the service eight weeks for $150.00 to annual packages that include unlimited ads for $3,900.

- **Methods and rules for submitting resumes:** Any job candidate can submit a resume on the site for free. Resume postings from fee-based professional recruiters are prohibited.

- 100 percent of resumes received by Web form.

- JobOptions does not currently track the source of resume postings.

- There has never been a limit on the length of the resume posted. The site's formatted resume option allows for customization, and the length is determined by the number of previous work experience fields entered.

- **Format:** Job candidates can use either the preformatted resume, or they can paste in their existing resume.

- No fees to person submitting resume.

- Resumes remain online nine months.

- **Procedures for updating/renewing:** Candidates can add, edit, and delete their resumes at any time. They can also store three formatted resumes and tailor them to a specific job.

- It is possible to limit who can see a resume because job candidates can request confidentiality.

- It is possible to shield a resume from being viewed by a current employer because job candidates can request confidentiality.

- **Assistance provided to the person submitting a resume:** A Help section is provided on the resume submission page. In addition, job candidates can call in and speak with one of the JobOptions customer service representatives.

- **Search options available to employers viewing resumes:** Employers can search by skill set, industry, location, and years of experience.

- **Technology to match jobs to resumes and e-mail resumes to clients:** JobOptions has two special services that help both the candidates and the employers:

    JobUpdate: Enables the candidates to request that those job openings that match their skills be directly mailed to them.

    ResumeUpdate: Enables employers to receive resumes that have been e-mailed to them and that meet a list of criteria that they have specified for job openings.

- **Special features:**

    A preformatted resume option creates a more professional, easier-to-read resume for the employer. This option also gives the passive or active job seeker a refined, formatted resume always on hand.

JobOptions provides a refined job search/resume search by location, industry, skill set, experience, and so on.

You can e-mail a formatted resume to an employer with the click of a button.

JobOptions provides an extensive, diverse database of jobs/employers in all MSAs.

- **Other distinguishing factors:** The resume database is completely proprietary: all the resumes are from candidates who have chosen JobOptions as their employment resource. The resumes have not been pulled from other sources on the Internet. As such, the site's resume database is an exclusive collection of resumes from qualified candidates who range from entry-level candidates to professionals with years of experience.

The Job Resource

USA
College Students and
Recent Graduates
Engineering and General
Rating: ★ ★ ★

The Job Resource describes itself as having been "started by a couple of students from Stanford University in 1996" to match employers with the most qualified college graduates and to help students obtain interviews, internships, and full-time jobs. Graduates from any school can submit resumes.

- **URL:** `http://www.thejobresource.com`
- **Ownership/sponsorship:** Roberto Angulo.
- Started accepting resumes in October 1996.
- **Approximate number of resumes online in April 1998:** 4,700 active resumes.
- Resumes are accepted from a wide variety of college graduates; however, the majority tend to be from the engineering arena.
- **Total number of corporate subscribers/employers:** approximately 650.
- **Of corporate subscribers/employers, the percentages include the following:**

  70 percent: direct-hire employers
  20 percent: staffing firms
  10 percent: other

- **Fee structure for corporate subscribers/employers:** No charge as of May 1998. Future fee structure to be determined.
- **Methods and rules for submitting resumes:** To submit a resume, simply provide your name and e-mail, and fill out a one-and-a-half page form. Your resume will be automatically formatted. Members choose a login and password to make updates, to format their resumes, and to use various other member features.
- 100 percent of resumes received by Web form.
- 100 percent of resumes received from individuals.
- **Limits on length:** Limited to three education fields (three schools) and six experience fields (employment positions).
- **Format:** Members fill out fields on a form, and the resume is stored in the

database. Members can then play with the format and rearrange fields.

- No fees to person submitting a resume. The Job Resource offers free resume posting and notification to students whose resumes have been requested by employers.

- Resumes remain online six months on average.

- **Procedures for updating/renewing:** Log in to member services by using a login and password.

- It is possible, in a way, to limit who can see a resume and to shield a resume from being viewed by a current employer. The employers see the resume, but they do not see any contact information. Therefore, unless the viewer can guess whom the resume belongs to, privacy is maintained. No contact information is given out to employers until the member/prospect/student actually replies to an employer's request.

- **Assistance provided to the person submitting a resume:** The Job Resource has an online FAQ page, which it constantly updates. The Job Resource also accepts e-mail inquiries and tries to give quick and detailed responses.

- **Search options available to employers viewing resumes:** Employers can search through resumes by using such criteria as school, major, languages spoken, computer languages, keywords, highest degree obtained, GPA, willingness to travel, full-time employment, and internship.

- **Technology to match jobs to resumes and e-mail resumes to clients:** Advanced database-query technology (cannot elaborate on details).

- **Average number of daily hits on resumes:** depends on the resume.

- **Special features include the following:**

  The Job Resource Resume Helper enables members to have access to nice-looking copies of their resumes from anywhere in the world where there is access to the Web. They can also choose from one of several designs to format their resumes instantly. Members can print their resumes directly from any Web browser, or they can choose the style they like and copy the HTML code to include in their home pages.

  Using Check Status members can see who has requested their resumes and when. They also get e-mail notification about when an employer requests their resumes.

  The Job Resource also offers career-advice articles written by resume experts and others in the industry. It also enables members to apply online to job openings posted on The Job Resource. Members can also apply at once to multiple openings that resulted from a job search (potentially to hundreds of job openings at once).

- **Other distinguishing factors:** The goal is to get companies many high-quality resumes from college students and recent graduates. (The Job Resource likes to focus on quality rather than quantity.) The Job Resource is used by students who want to post their resumes and have companies contact them. The process seems to work because one out of three students (on average) who post their resumes get contacted by at least one employer.

- The Job Resource enables a company to do a resume search. When the company gets the results, it has two options. It can send a mass personalized announcement to all students who result from a search; or it can browse through each resume and send an invitation, one by one, to a candidate. In the latter case, the student gets a personalized e-mail from an employer who has reviewed the actual resume (unlike a lot of other sites), and the announcement is more focused and applicable to the individual.

- The Job Resource enables students to keep track of the companies who have requested their resumes and when. The Job Resource is in the process of rolling out the same feature for companies so that they can see who is responding to their postings.

JobServe

UK and Global
IT Only
Rating: ★ ★ ★ ★

JobServe is the largest source of IT vacancies in the United Kingdom. JobServe is used by over 1,000 IT-recruitment agencies to advertise more than 80,000 new contract and permanent vacancies every month. JobServe is based in the United Kingdom; however, more than ten percent of the vacancies advertised are worldwide.

- **URL:** `http://jobserve.com`
- Started accepting resumes in 1994.
- **Approximate number of resumes online in April 1998:** 23,000.
- At present, JobServe accepts resumes only from IT professionals.
- **Total number of corporate subscribers/employers:** 1,200.
- All corporate subscribers/employers are staffing firms.
- **Fee structure for corporate subscribers/employers is as follows:**

  £499.00 per calendar month for approximately 1,200 curricula vitae (CVs) in either Word 6.0, WordPerfect 5.x or ASCII; and a database in DBASE III, comma-separated ASCII, or tab-separated ASCII.

  Individual CVs are purchased via e-mail for £5.00 each with immediate delivery; via fax for £9.00 each with immediate delivery; £2.99 each with overnight delivery; £1.49 each with five working days.

- **Methods and rules for submitting resumes:** Send via e-mail to `distribute@jobserve.com`.
- **Or you can send the resume by snail mail to the following postal address:**

  JobServe Ltd.
  FREEPOST CL3872
  Tiptree
  Colchester
  Essex
  CO5 0PN

- **Percentage of resumes received is as follows:**

  20 percent: e-mail
  10 percent: fax
   8 percent: other paper (job fairs, mailings)
   2 percent: diskette
  60 percent: Web form

- 100 percent of resumes received from individuals.
- No limits on length.
- **Format:** open.
- No fees to person submitting resume.

- **Length of time resumes remain online:** CVs are not available online. Each week the customers either receive all new or updated CVs, or JobServe sends them a list of IT professionals who are actively looking for work. The customers then select the CVs they require via an e-mail on-demand system.

- **Procedures for updating/renewing:** same as for registering.

- It is not possible to limit who can see a resume, but only agencies have access.

- It is possible to shield a resume from being viewed by a current employer because an agency must receive the permission of the candidate before forwarding the CV.

- **Assistance provided to the person submitting a resume:** None specific, but the staff is always helpful and will forward any comments or advice if requested.

- **Search options available to employers viewing resumes:** Most leading agency systems are able to import JobServe's data.

- **Technology to match jobs to resumes and e-mail resumes to clients:** Again, most leading agency systems are able to import JobServe's data.

- **Special features:** JobServe offers a free daily e-mail message that contains the latest vacancies, optionally "filtered" to the candidate's skills and preferences. JobServe also contacts the candidates every week until they find work.

- **Other distinguishing factors:** JobServe is distinguishable from the competition because it adds high levels of value to the CVs by attributing and typing them. JobServe is also the most widely used site by agencies and IT professionals in the United Kingdom.

Jobs Northwest

US Northwest and British Columbia, Canada
High Tech
Rating: ★ ★

Thompson & Associates' Jobs Northwest specializes in personnel with practical, on-the-job experience in high-tech industries, including software-development companies, traditional industries (such as manufacturing and banking), and consulting firms in the Pacific Northwest: Washington, Idaho, Western Montana, Oregon, and British Columbia.

- **URL:** `http://www.jobsnorthwest.com`

- **Ownership/sponsorship:** Neal Thompson, President

    Thompson & Associates, Inc.
    2448 76th Avenue SE, Suite 212
    Mercer Island, WA 98040
    Phone: (206) 236-0153
    Fax: (206) 236-2262

- Web site operational in 1995.

- Resumes are strictly high tech, including software engineers, architects, project managers, managers, program managers, programmer analysts, network engineers, and so on.

- Thompson and Associates' services are paid for by its clients, which are companies with employment needs. Thompson and Associates is not an employment agency, and it is not engaged by individuals to help them find jobs.

- **Methods and rules for submitting resumes:** e-mail.

- 100 percent of resumes that come from the Web site are received by e-mail.

- No limits on length.

- **Format:** open.

- No fees to person submitting a resume.

- **Length of time resumes remain online:** variable.

- **Procedures for updating/renewing:** resubmit.

JOBTRAK

USA
College Students and Graduates
Rating: ★ ★ ★ ★

JOBTRAK has teamed up with over 800 college and university career centers nationwide. JOBTRAK has been listing jobs since 1988. JOBTRAK describes itself as the "largest and most popular career site on the Web for college students, MBAs and alumni."

- **URL:** http://www.jobtrak.com

- **Ownership/sponsorship:** JOBTRAK Corporation

    1964 Westwood Blvd., 3rd Floor
    Los Angeles, CA 90025
    (800) 999-8725

- Started accepting resumes in 1997.

- **Approximate number of resumes online in April 1998:** 150,000.

- Resumes are in all job classifications. They are categorized by the following:

    university
    job function preferred
       (35 classifications)
    industry preferred (75 classifications)
    years of work experience
    geographic preference
    degree
    major (400 classifications)

- **Total number of corporate subscribers/employers:** Since 1988, 320,000 unique employers have posted their full-time, part-time, temporary, and internship positions on JOBTRAK.

- **Of corporate subscribers/employers, the percentages include the following:**

    96 percent: direct-hire employers
     3 percent: staffing firms
     1 percent: contract/consulting firms

- **Fee structure for corporate subscribers/employers:** Employers will pay to search resumes from students, MBAs, and alumni from their choice of campuses. Cost is on a per-campus basis and runs from $15.00 for one school to $395.00 for all universities.

- **Methods and rules for submitting resumes:** To submit their resumes, individuals must be students or alumni from one of the 800 universities participating in JOBTRAK. First go to www.jobtrak.com; then click on Students & Alumni; and then click on Submit Resume.

- 100 percent of resumes received by Web form.

- 100 percent of resumes received from individuals who are students or alumni from a college or university.

- No limits on length.

- **Format:** An open box that allows for HTML formatting. Individuals can cut and paste their Word or WordPerfect resumes directly into the system.

- No fees to the person submitting a resume.

- **Length of time resumes remain online:** Three months; at that time, individuals must indicate whether they want their resumes to remain active.

- **Procedures for updating/renewing:** on the Web site.

- It is not yet possible to limit who can see a resume.

- It is not yet possible to shield a resume from being viewed by a current employer, but the technology will be available soon.

- **Assistance provided to the person submitting a resume:** JOBTRAK has created an award-winning resume guide that is located at `www.jobtrak.com/jobmanual`. This guide provides complete instructions for creating a resume along with many samples.

- **Search options available to employers viewing resumes include the following:**

    university
    job function preferred
    industry preferred
    years of work experience
    geographic preference
    degree
    major
    keyword

- **Average number of daily hits on resumes:** JOBTRAK has 35,000 visitors per day to its Web site.

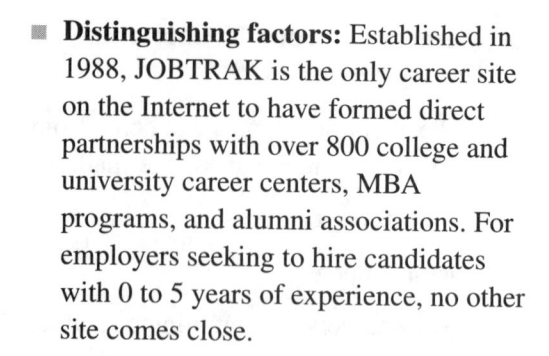

- **Distinguishing factors:** Established in 1988, JOBTRAK is the only career site on the Internet to have formed direct partnerships with over 800 college and university career centers, MBA programs, and alumni associations. For employers seeking to hire candidates with 0 to 5 years of experience, no other site comes close.

- Since 1988, over 320,000 employers have utilized JOBTRAK; and in 1997, employers posted 630,000 job openings on the system.

- According to a recent study by the company Student Monitor LLC, JOBTRAK is the most visited college-targeted site on the Internet. JOBTRAK has been featured in numerous publications and has joint ventures with the *New York Times* and *TIME* magazine. JOBTRAK was honored as the Entrepreneur of the Year by the State of California and was a semifinalist for the prestigious Global Information & Infrastructure award.

Lasting Impressions

USA
All Career Fields
Rating: ★ ★ ½

This resume data bank is offered by a resume preparation service.

- **URL:** `http://www.im-pressions.com`

- **Ownership/sponsorship:** Almeree Justice, President/Owner.

- Started accepting resumes in 1997.

- **Approximate number of resumes online in April 1998:** more than 500.

- **Resumes are grouped into the following employment categories:**

    accounting/bookkeeping
    administrative
    banking/finance
    education
    engineering
    health care
    human resources
    legal
    management
    sales/marketing
    technical
    other

- **Total number of corporate subscribers/employers:** Because Lasting Impressions does not require employers to pay a fee or sign up to view resumes, this information is not currently available. However, the company is contacted daily by employers and recruiters regarding resumes posted on its site and possible candidate placement.

- **Fee structure for corporate subscribers/employers:** free.

- **Methods and rules for submitting resumes:** To create a new resume, use The Resume Maker form and fill in the required information. You can view the resume online instantly. The following rules apply:

    All resumes created will be reviewed and are subject to approval.

    The Resume Maker can be used only to create employment resumes. Pages containing any other material, advertisements, or unsuitable language will be deleted immediately.

    Users must use a valid, working e-mail address.

    Incomplete resumes will be deleted after seven days.

    Limit one resume per person.

- 100 percent of resumes received by Web form. All resumes are created online through The Resume Maker.

- 100 percent of resumes received from individuals.

- **Format:** The Resume Maker creates a predesigned resume by using the input from the user. The result is an eye-catching, professional-looking resume Web page in chronological format. The user has the capability to add hyperlinks to previous employers' Web sites.

- Service is free for three months (effective May 1, 1998) with an option to renew for an additional six months at a cost of $20.00.

- Resumes remain online three months. Users are contacted by e-mail just prior to the end of their three-month period and given the option to renew for an additional six months.

- **Procedures for updating/renewing:** To edit a resume, use The Resume Maker form with the login name (password), e-mail address, and file name. Make changes and view changes instantly.

- It is not possible to limit who can see a resume. Because an actual Web page is created, this page can be accessed by anyone entering the site.

- It is not possible to shield a resume from being viewed by a current employer.

- **Assistance provided to the person submitting a resume:** Users can contact Lasting Impressions by e-mail if they have questions (such as forgetting their password) when creating or updating their resumes. Lasting Impressions also provides a free resume writing guide, which can be downloaded from its site.

- **Search options available to employers viewing resumes:** To complement the Resume Directory, which categorizes resumes by career field, employers can search resumes by using keywords.

- **Average number of daily hits on resumes:** 1,100.

- **Special features:** Resumes created with The Resume Maker are easy to set up and maintain. Although actual Web pages are created, no knowledge of HTML is required. Users have complete control over content, and they also have the capability to update at any time. Resumes are password protected—only the user can change the content. Each resume Web page can be submitted to search engines for maximum exposure.

- **Other distinguishing factors:** Many resume banks charge potential employers to view their resume archives. This cost reduces the number of potential job offers resulting from the site. When users create a resume by using The Resume Maker, however, their resumes are automatically added to the Resume Directory. Lasting Impressions will never charge any employer to use the Resume Directory or to view the resumes.

medsearch

USA

Health Care

Rating: ★★★★

Medsearch is a leading online service for the health-care industry from residencies to physician placement to hospital administrators and pharmaceutical researchers. Medsearch is a service of TMP Worldwide, the world's largest yellow-page advertising agency and the world's largest recruitment advertising agency, which also provides the Online Career Center (OCC).

- **URL:** `http://www.medsearch.com/`

- **Ownership/sponsorship:** TMP Worldwide.

- Started accepting resumes in 1993.

- **Approximate number of resumes online in April 1998:** 4,429.

- Resumes are in the health-care industry.

- **Total number of corporate subscribers/employers:** 159.

- **Fee structure for corporate subscribers/employers:** For employers, medsearch uses a membership model, so pricing varies depending on the size of the company. An annual membership includes unlimited access to the resume database; unlimited job postings; and a mini-home page, which includes a company logo, a profile, a link to the company's job postings, and a link to the company's Web sites.

- All resumes are placed in a central database, which employers can search by keyword.

- **Methods and rules for submitting resumes:** Job seekers can post their resumes electronically for no charge. They have the capability to manage their resumes online. Using an assigned user name and password, candidates are able to post, edit, extend, and delete resumes directly online. The real-time system enables all changes to appear on OCC/medsearch within seconds.

- Candidates can also go online to view how many times their resumes have been viewed by member companies.

- In addition, candidates have their own personalized user profiles. The profile summary includes relocation information, salary and work requirements, and educational and work status.

- After reviewing job postings on OCC/medsearch, candidates who have their resumes in the database can use the simple Apply Online feature. With a simple click of a mouse, the candidates can send their resumes directly to the company's e-mail address that is specified in the posting. There is no need to re-enter (or cut and paste) their resumes each time they want to respond to a job posting.

- If posting electronically is not an option, OCC/medsearch provides a service that will retype a hard copy of the applicant's resume and place it online for a nominal fee.

- Most of the resumes are received via the Web.

- Most of the resumes are received from individuals.

- No limits on length.

- **Format:** Each resume submitted online must contain a title line not to exceed 45 spaces (for example, *Chemical Engr/ 5 Yrs Exp/Oil Industry*). All resumes can be viewed before they appear online.

- **Fees to person submitting resume:** There are no fees unless the candidates cannot submit their resumes electronically. Then the fee is $15.00 (US) for three pages including a cover letter, and $5.00 for each additional page. Candidates can mail their resumes (cover letter optional) along with a check or money order to the following address:

   ONLINE RESUME SERVICE
   1713 Hemlock Lane
   Plainfield, IN 46168

- Resumes will be processed and entered online into the OCC/medsearch resume database.

- Resumes remain online for one year unless the candidates delete or extend them.

- **Procedures for updating/renewing:** Candidates can simply log on with their user names and passwords and manage their resumes at any time.

- It is not possible to limit who can see a resume. However, candidates can submit confidential resumes where their e-mail addresses are masked from employers. Then medsearch forwards any responses from interested employers to the candidates.

- It is not possible to shield a resume from being viewed by a current employer because an employer can recruit from someplace other than its office. For example, an employer could be recruiting from home.

- Assistance provided to the person submitting a resume: Candidates can submit questions to occ@occ.com, or they can call (800) 899-7058 for immediate assistance.

- **Search options available to employers viewing resumes:** Employers can search resumes by keyword, city, state, or region. Subset searches also enable employers to perform a "search within a search." For example, when an employer completes a keyword search, there may be far too many resumes to view individually. Instead of going back to square one to narrow the search, a second search can be performed on the list of resumes returned from the first search.

- **Technology to match jobs to resumes and e-mail resumes to clients:** Virtual agents enable recruiters and applicants to input specific criteria about an opening or an area of interest. The virtual agents perform the search for the users and "remember" it in order to accelerate future searches or to match incoming resumes or jobs to the selected criteria. Virtual agents can also e-mail search results directly to the users. The users also have the option of viewing the entire list of resumes/jobs that match their criteria or only those added since the most recent login.

- **Distinguishing factors:** OCC/medsearch currently receives over 1,000 new resumes a day. The resumes come directly from the applicants. OCC/medsearch does not download resumes from the Web. It receives over one million unique visitors per month.

• •

MedZilla™

USA
Health Care
Rating: ★ ★ ★ ★

MedZilla™ was the first on the World Wide Web to specialize in resumes from biotech, medical, pharmaceutical, and health-care professionals and scientists.

- **URL:** http://www.medzilla.com

- **Ownership/sponsorship:** MedZilla is a subsidiary of FSG Inc.

- Started accepting resumes in 1994.

- **Approximate number of resumes online in April 1998:** 2,500.

- Resumes are exclusively from professionals with expertise in biotechnology, medicine, health care, and science.

- **Total number of corporate subscribers/employers:** 50–100.

- **Of corporate subscribers/employers, the percentages include the following:**

  75 percent: direct-hire employers
  25 percent: staffing firms and contract/consulting firms

- **Fee structure for corporate subscribers/employers:** Subscription/site license based on number of recruiters and job-posting preferences.

- **Methods and rules for submitting resumes:** via interview form.

- 100 percent of resumes received by Web form.

- 100 percent of resumes received from individuals.

- No limits on length.

- **Format specified:** Resumes are free form. Additional input is requested via interview form.

- No fees to a person submitting a resume. MedZilla considers the practice of accepting fees to be highly unethical.

- **Length of time resumes remain online:** Depends on the new-resume influx rate. Generally no more than 20–25 weeks from the last update.

- **Procedures for updating/renewing:** available via MedZilla User ID.

- It is possible to limit who can see a resume. Only MedZilla subscribers can download and view resumes. Candidates are notified every time their resumes are downloaded. They know who is reading their resumes. This service is unique to MedZilla.

- It is possible to shield a resume from being viewed by a current employer provided the candidates enter their current employer's name correctly.

- **Assistance provided to the person submitting a resume:** All resumes are reviewed prior to acceptance by MedZilla. All candidates receive an e-mail confirmation when they submit their resumes, another confirmation when their resumes are accepted, and a notice every time their resumes are actually downloaded.

- Candidates are provided with extensive resources to assist in their job search, including a user-friendly resume editor to update their professional or contact information; free access to a comprehensive, interactive database of salary information; and articles about working, finding jobs, and advancing their careers.

- **Search options available to employers viewing resumes:** Any employer or recruiter can search resumes by using a simple, powerful full-text retrieval system. The system returns abstracts only, not full resumes. Abstracts are prepared by the candidates themselves via the MedZilla interview form. No contact information is allowed in resume abstracts. If the employers are licensed subscribers, they can download full resumes by using a simple form. If the employers are not subscribers, they are provided with information about obtaining a subscription.

- **Technology to match jobs to resumes and e-mail resumes to clients is as follows:**

   Voluntary by the candidates themselves. In other words, the candidates search for jobs in the resume bank and e-mail the resumes themselves.

   Via employer auto-referral profile: Every incoming resume is queried against the employer's set of keywords and phrases and forwarded to the employer if a match is found.

- **Average number of daily hits on resumes:** Approximately 90 percent of MedZilla's visitors are candidates specifically in the health-care field. The other 10 percent are employers and recruiters. MedZilla has few random visitors. Its links are carefully placed, and its search-engine terms are selected to attract only those people who are interested in the health-care field.

- Currently MedZilla hosts around 25,000 visitors each month, as calculated from unique domains. This number does not include multiple hits from different users at the same domain, and it does not include "onlookers" (people who job-surf in groups). MedZilla often receives multiple resumes from the same domain at the same time. This activity indicates that candidates tend to use Web employment services in groups of 2–5.

Minorities' Job Bank

USA

Minorities in

All Career Fields

Rating: ★ ★ ★ ½

Minorities' Job Bank is a subsidiary of Black Collegiate Services, Inc., the publisher of *The Black Collegian Magazine* and *The Black Collegian Online* (`http://www.black-collegian.com`).

The Minorities' Job Bank is dedicated to all underrepresented minorities in the workforce and features the African-American Village, the Asian-American Village, the Hispanic-American Village, the Native-American Village, and the Minorities Global Village.

- **URL:** `http://www.minorities-jb.com`

- **Ownership/sponsorship:** Black Collegiate Services, Inc.

- Started accepting resumes in 1998.

- **Approximate number of resumes online in April 1998:** 7,500.

- Resumes are accepted in all career fields.

- **Total number of corporate subscribers/employers:** 210.

- 100 percent of corporate subscribers/employers are direct-hire employers.

- **Fee structure for corporate subscribers/employers:** Employers become members of the site. Membership includes unlimited access to the resume database, unlimited posting to the jobs database, and a company profile in the directory of members/employers. Membership is $3,900 for one year. *The Black Collegian Online* has a sponsorship that also includes resume access. It does not sell resume searching as a stand-alone product.

- **Methods and rules for submitting resumes:** Applicant must have a college degree. A 3.0 GPA is preferred but not required. Applicant must set up a user account, which has name and contact information.

- **Percentage of resumes received by sources is as follows:**

  10 percent: e-mail
  20 percent: other paper (job fairs, mailings)
  5 percent: diskette from universities
  65 percent: Web form

- **Percentage of resumes received from people is as follows:**

  90 percent: individuals
  10 percent: colleges or universities

- No limits on length.

- **Format specified:** If the job seeker wants to build a resume online, information is entered into a form. Or a resume can be cut and pasted into one text field. The job seeker can also include a cover letter to the hiring manager as a separate form field.

- No fees to person submitting a resume.

- Resumes remain online for one year.

- **Procedures for updating/renewing:** Job seekers have a user name and password to access their accounts for editing, updating, and deleting their resumes. If the resume is declined because of incomplete information or if it expires, the job seekers are notified via e-mail with a message. Expiring job seekers are encouraged to return to add their resumes or to delete their accounts if they are no longer looking for employment.

- It is possible to limit who can see the resumes. Only member employers of the sites can view resumes.

- It is possible to shield a resume from being viewed by a current employer. When posting their resumes, applicants can choose to make personal information confidential.

- **Assistance provided to the person submitting a resume:** The process is very easy and trouble free. Applicants can send feedback if they have any questions. The database guides them along the process by explaining each and every step.

- **Search options available to employers viewing resumes:** Employers can search by discipline, location preference of applicant, GPA range, ethnicity, and keywords.

- **Average number of daily hits on resumes:** 9,000 visitors per day.

- **Special features:** *Computerworld* states, "This is a standout among minority job-search sites because it creates a true sense of community for African, Asian, Hispanic, and Native American professionals."

- Other distinguishing factors: *ZDNet* states, "Right now, most Internet users are young, white, and have high income. But that's starting to change, and companies like The Black Collegian, which…launched Minorities' Job Bank, a job-listing Web site aimed at minority groups, should be in prime position to take advantage of the Net's diversifying ethnic user base."

The Monster Board

USA
All Career Fields
Rating: ★ ★ ★ ★ ★

The Monster Board has been described as the Internet's largest and most successful career center. The Monster Board is a service of TMP Worldwide, the world's largest yellow-page advertising agency and the world's largest recruitment advertising agency.

- **URL:** http://www.monster.com

- **Ownership/sponsorship:** TMP Worldwide.

- Started accepting resumes in 1995.

- **Approximate number of resumes online in April 1998:** 340,000.

- Resumes are in all career fields. Resumes are categorized by the job category that job seekers select for their profiles. The Monster Board offers job seekers a selection of more than 250 job categories.

- Of corporate subscribers/employers, 100 percent are direct-hire employers.

- **Fee structure for corporate subscribers/employers includes the following:**

  $4,900   annual subscription
  $1,900   three-month introduction special

- **Methods and rules for submitting resumes:** Anyone can submit a resume to Resume City.

- 100 percent of resumes are received through The Monster Board Web site.

- The Monster Board does not track the sources of resumes.

- No limits on length.

- **Format:** The resume must be in a text file.

- No fees to person submitting a resume.

- Resumes remain in Resume City for 12 months, or until they are requested to be removed.

- **Procedures for updating/renewing:** All job seekers are given a user name and password. They can access and update their resumes at any time and as often as they want.

- Only paying Resume City subscribers can access the resume database. If job seekers are concerned about privacy, they can mark their resumes as "Private." Their name and contact information will be suppressed. Recruiters will then e-mail The Monster Board with their interest in a candidate. The Monster Board will immediately notify the job seeker of the employer's interest.

- Unfortunately, The Monster Board cannot shield a resume from being viewed by any particular individual.

- **Assistance provided to the person submitting a resume:** Extensive online Help is available; or for assistance, job seekers can contact The Monster Board at (800)-MONSTER.

- **Search options available to employers viewing resumes:** Employers can search for resumes by location, job categories selected, and keywords.

- **Technology to match jobs to resumes and e-mail resumes to clients:** The Monster Board utilizes search agents to match resumes with employers ('Cruiter) and to match job openings with job seekers (Swoop). These search-agent services browse the databases and e-mail the matches directly to your desktop. You can search the newest jobs and resumes databases without even going online.

- **Special features:** resume and job-search agents.

- **Other distinguishing factors:** A recent survey indicates that one out of every four people who submit a resume through The Monster Board receives a job offer.

National NurseSearch

USA
Nursing
Rating: ★ ★ ★

National NurseSearch specializes in the placement of experienced RNs in hospitals and home-health-care agencies nationwide.

- **URL:** http://www.nursesearch.net/

- **Ownership/sponsorship:** Kate Purcell, RN.

- Started accepting resumes in 1996.

- **Approximate number of resumes online in April 1998:** National NurseSearch is just now developing a place for resumes online. It has over 1,000 in its office.

- Resumes are accepted in all medical fields including OR techs, OR nurse managers, OB-GYN nurse managers, ER managers, ICU nurse managers, directors of nursing, nurse educators, nurse practitioners, physician assistants, department heads, clinical nurse specialists, project managers, nurse administrators, and RN staff nurses.

- **Total number of corporate subscribers/employers:** 5,000.

- **Of corporate subscribers/employers, the percentages include the following:**

  85 percent: direct-hire employers
  5 percent: staffing firms
  10 percent: contract/consulting firms

- **Fee structure for corporate subscribers/employers:** contingency contracts and retainer fees.

- **Methods and rules for submitting resumes:** Submit a professional resume with a cover letter ready to present to an employer. You can fax the resume to (405) 691-8389, e-mail with a MS Word97 attachment, or you can use postal mail to send the resume to the following address:

> National NurseSearch
> 9208 S. Villa Ave
> Oklahoma City, OK 73159-6745

- **Percentage of resumes received by sources is as follows:**

  30 percent: e-mail
  50 percent: fax
  20 percent: other paper (job fairs, mailings)

- **Percentage of resumes received from people is as follows:**

  90 percent: individuals
  10 percent: colleges or universities

- No limits on length. You can submit a resume or a curriculum vitae (CV).

- **Format:** neat and clear to read.

- No fees to person submitting resume. The employer pays the fee.

- Resumes remain online for six months if necessary.

- **Procedures for updating/renewing:** Just resubmit with a note stating that it is an updated resume or CV.

- It is possible to limit who can see a resume. National NurseSearch will keep the resume and submit it only to an employer looking for that particular candidate. Online resumes are given a file number—no names are posted.

- It is possible to shield a resume from being viewed by a current employer.

- National NurseSearch does not contact a former employer until the candidate states that it can do so for a reference.

- **Assistance provided to the person submitting a resume:** National NurseSearch helps the candidates negotiate salary, benefits, relocation fee, and real estate representation for the area they are moving to.

- **Search options available to employers viewing resumes:** Resumes are posted according to medical field: surgical OR nurses, OB-GYN nurses, OB-delivery nurses, med-surg nurses, and so on.

- **Technology to match jobs to resumes and e-mail resumes to clients:** This job is done manually. Sometimes the candidate needs help with the resume to show experience and skills.

- **Average number of daily hits on resumes:** 50.

- **Special features:** National NurseSearch networks with ten other recruiters to provide a nationwide coverage of job openings.

- **Other distinguishing factors:** National NurseSearch deals only with experienced RNs, NPs, PAs, and physicians. No new graduates or LPNs are considered.

Net-Temps

USA
All Career Fields
Rating: ★ ★ ★ ★

Net-Temps serves staffing firms and third-party recruiters to advertise job openings and retrieve resumes of qualified candidates. Net-Temps is one of the largest data banks of constantly updated resumes on the entire Internet.

- **URL:** `http://www.net-temps.com`

- **Ownership/sponsorship:** Net-Temps is a privately held company headquartered 15 miles north of Boston at the following address:

    30 Middlesex Road
    Tyngsboro, MA
    Phone: (978) 649-8575
    Fax: (978) 649-6052

- Started accepting resumes in 1996.

- **Approximate number of resumes online in April 1998:** 225,000.

- Resumes are in all job classifications but with a strong emphasis on technological jobs. Net-Temps has two resume banks. One bank is made up of hot-list candidates who come to the site, complete a form, and submit their resumes for review by Net-Temp's client-staffing firms.

- The second and larger resume bank is Spider Resumes. Net-Temp's robot agent crawls thousands of defined URLs where it knows resumes are located. For example, Yahoo and all the major search engines collect resumes. The robot agent can also find resumes at resume banks that are not password protected and from personal home pages. The spider crawls constantly, and every week a new indexed database is created for the 1,000 staffing firms that utilize the service. Any new resume posted in the past week is found; any updates to a resume are displayed; and, equally important, any resume that has been taken down (the user is no longer actively looking for a job) disappears from the database.

- **Total number of corporate subscribers/employers:** Over 1,000 staffing agencies subscribe.

- 100 percent of corporate subscribers/employers are staffing firms.

- **Fee structure for corporate subscribers/employers:** $395.00 per month for unlimited job posting to hundreds of top Web sites and unlimited searching of the resume banks. Discounts are available for multiple offices and length-of-term contracts.

- **Methods and rules for submitting resumes:** Complete the form; then cut and paste the resume.

- 100 percent of resumes received by Web form.

- 100 percent of resumes received from individuals.

- No limits on length.

- **Format:** open.

- No fees to person submitting resume.

- Resumes remain online for view by staffing firms for 30 days and then will autodelete.

- **Procedures for updating/renewing:** available.

- It is possible to limit who can see a resume. Only third-party staffing agencies that subscribe to Net-Temps can see the resumes.

- It is possible to shield a resume from being viewed by a current employer.

- **Assistance provided to the person submitting a resume:** Help FAQs.

- **Search options available to employers viewing resumes:** Simple and advanced searching is available to all subscribers.

- **Technology to match jobs to resumes and e-mail resumes to clients:** open text, livelink suite, document management software.

- **Average number of daily hits on resumes:** 150,000 per day.
- **Special features:** Net-Temps posts all jobs every night to Yahoo, Search.com, Infospace, and the Classifieds2000 Network of over 150 sites including Excite, Infoseek, Lycos, and so on.

Online Career Center (OCC)

Global
All Career Fields
Rating: ★ ★ ★ ★

Online Career Center (OCC) has been described as the Internet's earliest career site. OCC is a service of TMP Worldwide, the world's largest yellow-page advertising agency and the world's largest recruitment advertising agency.

The United States OCC site includes international job opportunities and resumes from Africa, Asia/South Pacific, Australia, Canada, Central America, Europe, Mexico, Middle East, Scandinavia, and South America. Mexico has its own version of OCC at **http://www.occ.com.mx** as does Scandinavia at **http://occ.riksmedia.se/**.

- **URL: http://www.occ.com/**
- **Ownership/sponsorship:** TMP Worldwide.
- Started accepting resumes in 1992.
- **Approximate number of resumes online in April 1998:** 95,192.
- All resumes are placed in a central database that employers can search by keyword.
- **Total number of corporate subscribers/employers:** 7,625.
- **Fee structure for corporate subscribers/employers:** For employers, OCC uses a membership model, and pricing varies depending on the size of the company. An annual membership includes unlimited access to the resume database; unlimited job postings; and a mini-home page, which includes a company logo, a profile, a link to the company's job postings, and a link to the company's Web sites.
- **Methods and rules for submitting resumes:** Job seekers can post their resumes electronically for no charge whatsoever. They have the capability to manage their resumes online. Using an assigned user name and password, candidates are able to post, edit, extend, and delete resumes directly online. OCC's real-time system enables all changes to appear on OCC within seconds. Candidates can also go online to view how many times their resumes have been viewed by member companies.
- In addition, candidates have their own personalized user profiles. The profile summary includes relocation information, salary and work requirements, and educational and work status.
- After reviewing job postings on OCC, candidates who have their resumes in the database can use OCC's simple Apply Online feature. With the simple click of a mouse, the candidates can send their resumes directly to the company's e-mail address specified in the posting. The candidates have no need to reenter (or cut and paste) their resumes each time they want to respond to a job posting.

Part II: Resume Banks

- If posting electronically is not an option, OCC provides a service that will retype a hard copy of the applicant's resume and place it online for a nominal fee.

- Most of the resumes are received via the Web.

- Most of the resumes are received from individuals.

- There are no limits to the resume length.

- **Format:** Each resume submitted online must contain a title line not to exceed 45 spaces, as in this example: *Chemical Engr/5 Yrs Exp/Oil Industry*. All resumes can be viewed before they appear online.

- **Fees to person submitting resume:** There are no fees unless the candidates cannot submit their resumes electronically. Candidates can mail their resumes (cover letter optional) along with a check or money order for $15.00 (US currency, for three pages including cover letter; $5.00 for each additional page) to the following address:

    ONLINE RESUME SERVICE
    1713 Hemlock Lane
    Plainfield, IN 46168

- Resumes will be processed and entered online into the OCC resume database.

- Resumes remain online for one year unless the candidates delete or extend them.

- **Procedures for updating/renewing:** Candidates can simply log on with their user names and passwords and manage their resumes at any time.

- It is not possible to limit who can see a resume. However, candidates can submit confidential resumes, where OCC masks their e-mail addresses from employers. Then OCC forwards any responses from interested employers to the candidates.

- It is not possible to shield a resume from being viewed by a current employer because employers can recruit from someplace other than their offices. For example, an employer can be recruiting at home.

- **Assistance provided to the person submitting a resume:** Candidates can submit questions to occ@occ.com, or they can call the toll-free number at (800) 899-7058 for immediate assistance.

- Search options are available to employers viewing resumes: Employers can search resumes by keyword, city, state, or region. Subset searches also enable employers to perform a "search within a search." For example, when an employer completes a keyword search, there may be far too many resumes to view individually. Instead of going back to square one to narrow the search, a second search can be performed pertaining only to the list of resumes returned from the first search.

- **Technology to match jobs to resumes and e-mail resumes to clients:** Virtual agents enable recruiters and applicants to input specific criteria about an opening or an area of interest. The virtual agents perform the search for the users and "remember" it to accelerate future searches or to match incoming resumes or jobs to the selected criteria. Virtual agents can also e-mail search results directly to the users. The users also have the option of viewing the entire list of resumes/jobs that match their criteria or only those added since the most recent login.

- **Distinguishing factors:** OCC currently receives over 1,000 new resumes per day. The resumes come directly from the applicants. OCC does not download resumes from the Web.
- OCC receives over 1 million unique visitors per month.

Online Opportunities

Philadelphia Area
All Career Fields
Rating: ★ ★ ★ ★

Online Opportunities started as a local, DOS-based bulletin board system in July 1992. Today it is the Philadelphia area's leading online recruitment service.

- **URL:** http://www.JobNET.com
- **Ownership/sponsorship:** Ward Christman, Executive Director (sole proprietor).
- Started accepting resumes in 1992.
- **Approximate number of resumes online in April 1998:** 32,000.
- Resumes are accepted in all career fields.
- **Total number of corporate subscribers/employers:** approximately 150.
- **Of corporate subscribers/employers, the percentages include the following:**

    33 percent: direct-hire employers
    33 percent: staffing firms
    33 percent: contract/consulting firms

- **Fee structure for corporate subscribers/employers:** Quarterly or annual subscription rate, which includes unlimited access to the resume databases in that time period.
- **Methods and rules for submitting resumes:** Preferred method of submission is the resume submission form featured on www.JobNET.com. Online Opportunities also accepts resumes via e-mail at resumes@jobnet.com. Faxed resumes are not accepted.
- **Approximate percentage of resumes received by sources is as follows:**

    1 percent: e-mail
    50 percent: other paper (job fairs, mailings)
    1 percent: diskette
    48 percent: Web form

- **Approximate percentage of resumes received from people is as follows:**

    94 percent: individuals
    2 percent: colleges and universities
    2 percent: outplacement firms
    2 percent: other

- No limits on length. Online Opportunities encourages job seekers to emphasize content and keywords that describe their qualifications rather than to create a lengthy, nondescriptive resume.
- **Format:** Job seekers copy and paste the body of their resumes into the Web-based resume submission form and then give additional information—such as salary preference, geographic preference, willingness to travel/relocate, current employment status, and personal information (name, e-mail, home phone). They can preview the resumes and make changes before the resumes are added to the database.
- No fees to person submitting a resume. Posting resumes is free through the Web site and e-mail. Paper resumes are

accepted only with a $5.00 fee for scanning. This fee (which is waived at job fairs) is payable to Online Opportunities.

- Resumes remain online indefinitely or until the job seeker requests removal of the resume.

- **Procedures for updating/renewing:** Before actually submitting their resumes, job seekers choose a user name and password that enable them to edit/update their resumes in the future.

- Every six months, Online Opportunities sends out e-mails and postcards requesting an updated resume from those who haven't updated or posted in the past six months. Online Opportunities includes their user names and passwords on the postcards and encourages job seekers to visit the Web site to edit the resumes. After a resume has been updated, Online Opportunities gives the resume an updated date for employers to realize the resume has been changed. Online Opportunities also puts the edited resumes back on top of the resume pile for searching employers.

- Currently it is not possible to limit who can see a resume. Any paying member employer/staffing firm can see all the resumes.

- It is not possible to shield a resume from being viewed by a current employer. Some job seekers choose to alter their resumes so that their current employer's name does not show.

- **Assistance provided to the person submitting a resume:** When posting the resume, the submission form fields will guide a job seeker to include all important information that an employer needs to see. Other than provide this form, Online Opportunities does not help a job seeker write the resume.

- **Search options available to employers viewing resumes:** Keyword search is available for employers. They can use any combination of keywords, or they can search by such strings as [Visual Basic], zip codes, area codes, and so on. Explanatory examples of searching are provided on the resume search page.

- **Technology to match jobs to resumes and e-mail resumes:** none at this time.

- **Average number of daily hits on resumes:** Online Opportunities doesn't track this information.

- **Special features:** For $49.95, Online Opportunities can post a job seeker's resume to over 1,400 sites/databases to give the resume national exposure. A list of distribution points is included on Jobnet.com for job seekers to view. Payment for the service can be made by credit card or check (see the Web site).

- **Other distinguishing factors:** The resumes are 90 percent from the Philadelphia region (NJ, DE, and PA) and beat out the national sites on this level because even the largest sites don't have 32,000 resumes in this area.

Online Sports Career Center

USA

Sports and Recreation

Rating: ★ ★ ★

The Online Sports Career Center is a resource of sports-related career opportunities and a resume bank for potential employers within the many segments of the sports and recreation industries.

- **URL:** `http://onlinesports.com/pages/CareerCenter.html`
- **Ownership/sponsorship:** Online Sports (`www.onlinesports.com`).
- Started accepting resumes in 1995.
- Only sports and recreation jobs are listed at the site. Resumes are not required to be listed in any other classification.
- **Of corporate subscribers/employers, the percentages include the following:**

   80 percent: direct-hire employers
   20 percent: staffing firms

- **Fee structure for corporate subscribers/employers:** free.
- **Methods and rules for submitting resumes:** Post your resume (ASCII text format) by sending e-mail to `resumes@onlinesports.com`.
- 100 percent of resumes received by e-mail.
- 100 percent of resumes received from individuals.
- No limits on length.
- **Format:** Text by e-mail only.
- No fees to person submitting a resume.
- Resumes remain online six months.
- **Procedures for updating/renewing:** Resubmit by e-mail.
- It is possible to limit who can see a resume.
- It is possible to shield a resume from being viewed by a current employer.
- **Assistance provided to the person submitting a resume:** E-mail questions will be answered only by e-mail.
- Search options available to employers viewing resumes: online review.
- **Average number of daily hits on resumes:** 5,000.
- **Special features:** The Online Sports Career Center lists career opportunities only within the sports and recreation industries and posts resumes only of individuals pursuing careers within these industries.
- **Other distinguishing factors:** The Online Sports Career Center is a resource of sports-related career opportunities and a resume bank for potential employers. The Career Center focuses exclusively on the many segments of the sports and recreation industries.

ORASEARCH

USA
Oracle Professionals
Rating: ★ ★ ★

ORASEARCH is a service that matches Oracle professionals with companies who need them.

- **URL:** `http://www.orasearch.com`
- **Ownership/sponsorship:** Advanced Data, Inc.
- Started accepting resumes in 1997.
- **Approximate number of resumes online in April 1998:** 700.
- Resumes are limited only to ORACLE jobs.
- **Total number of corporate subscribers/employers:** 80.

- **Of corporate subscribers/employers, the percentages include the following:**

  50 percent: direct-hire employers
  40 percent: staffing firms
  10 percent: contract/consulting firms

- **Fee structure for corporate subscribers/employers:** $950.00 for a six-month membership.

- **Methods and rules for submitting resumes:** Must have one year of paid experience in Oracle.

- No limits on length.

- **Format:** open.

- No fees to person submitting a resume.

- Resumes remain online one year.

- **Procedures for updating/renewing:** online.

- It is possible to limit who can see a resume.

- It is not possible to shield a resume from being viewed by a current employer.

- **Search options available to employers viewing resumes:** ORACLE software products.

- **Average number of daily hits on resumes:** 10,000.

- **Distinguishing factor:** ORASEARCH is a dedicated ORACLE resume and job site.

PassportAccess

USA
Technical
Rating: ★ ★ ★

The National Employment Weekly placed PassportAccess in the Top Five for sites offering the best job-search support for candidates. Its assessment was based on the site's being free for job seekers as well as being well suited for professionals because of quality of jobs posted, quality of resumes posted, navigability, interactively, and visual appeal.

- **URL:** `http://www.passportaccess.com`

- **Ownership/sponsorship:** privately held corporation.

- Started accepting resumes in June 1995.

- **Approximate number of resumes online in April 1998:** 151,989.

- PassportAccess's focus is on technical resumes. Technical resumes include IT, IS, programming, engineering, software, hardware, technical support, even sales and marketing if the candidate has a background in the technical industry. Each resume is read by one of PassportAccess's staff to ensure applicability to its database.

- **Of corporate subscribers/employers, the percentages include the following:**

  50 percent: direct-hire employers
  35 percent: staffing firms
  15 percent: contract/consulting firms

- **Fee structure for corporate subscribers/employers:** $800.00 per workstation license for one year of unlimited access to the database.

- **Methods and rules for submitting resumes:** A resume can be cut and pasted into the online form located on the Web site. There are no long forms to fill out.

- **Percentage of resumes received by sources is as follows:**

40 percent: e-mail
10 percent: other paper (job fairs, mailings)
10 percent: newsgroups
40 percent: Web form

- **Percentage of resumes received from people is as follows:**

    70 percent: individuals
    5 percent: colleges or universities
    15 percent: outplacement firms
    10 percent: other

- No limits on length; however PassportAccess will not upload summaries.

- **Format:** must be full-text resume.

- No fees to person submitting resume.

- **Length of time resumes remain online:** Because a recruiter can search by date, PassportAccess does not purge.

- **Procedures for updating/renewing:** Contact Webmaster through Web site.

- Is it possible to limit who can see a resume? Job seekers can limit some information on their resumes, but to be accepted, their resumes must have some sort of contact information.

- It is not possible to shield a resume from being viewed by a current employer.

- **Assistance provided to the person submitting a resume:** A candidate can contact the Webmaster through e-mail or telephone.

- **Search options available to employers viewing resumes:** PassportAccess's Internet-based software eliminates the waiting that occurs on the World Wide Web. Users have direct TCP/IP remote connection into the server. This access enables them to launch searches unheard of on any other resume Web-based search site. A subscriber can save searches and can use as many as 20 keywords on one search to locate the exact candidate.

- **Technology to match jobs to resumes and e-mail resumes to clients:** When users bundle eQuest software with their PassportAccess resume search license, they are able to completely automate their searches while they are offline.

- Anytime new resumes are added to the PassportAccess database, their eQuest search or searches will automatically be launched. Any matching full-text resumes will be forwarded to whatever e-mail address they designate. They can even designate more than one e-mail address.

- Each individual eQuest requisition can be edited at any time. Employers can set the exact length of time the requisition is to run, and they can still launch highly designated search strings to return only the exact candidates they need.

- **Average number of daily hits on resumes:** hundreds of subscribers access the database each day and perform searches.

- **Other distinguishing factors:** PassportAccess is a full-service resume collection company. It is not owned by a large advertising firm looking to entice its subscribers into paying for additional ad revenue. It proactively seeks out technical candidates. PassportAccess is adding thousands of technical candidates each week. Its average upload of resumes ranges from as few as 3,000 to as many as 5,000 resumes per week.

Part II: Resume Banks

PeopleBank The Employment Network

Global
All Career Fields
Rating: ★ ★ ★

PeopleBank is a London-based resume bank.

- **URL:** `http://www.peoplebank.com`
- **Ownership/sponsorship:** Owned by the management of the company.
- Started accepting resumes in 1995.
- **Approximate number of resumes online in April 1998:** 92,000.
- Resumes are accepted in all career fields.
- **Total number of corporate subscribers/employers:** 750.
- **Of corporate subscribers/employers, the percentages include the following:**

  50 percent: direct-hire employers
  45 percent: staffing firms
  5 percent: contract/consulting firms

- **Fee structure for corporate subscribers/employers:**

  Introduction Fee Contract: The employer pays for the contact details of the PeopleBank candidates whom the employer wants to interview. The fee is payable only if the candidates agree to release their details. No other fee is payable when a PeopleBank candidate is hired. The employer pays a fee based on the following schedule:

Starting Salary	Fee
Up to £19,999	£100 + Value Added Tax (VAT)
£20,000–£39,999	£200 + VAT
£40,000 and above	£300 + VAT

  Placement Fee Contract: The employers pay a fee when a candidate is hired via PeopleBank. For clients who want to pay upon success only, the following fees are payable on placement of a PeopleBank candidate:

Starting Salary	Fee
Up to £19,999	£1,500 + VAT
£20,000–£39,999	£2,250 + VAT
£40,000 and above	£3,000 + VAT

  Candidate Personality Profile: Reports cost £20 + VAT per report.

- **Methods and rules for submitting resumes:** Candidates complete the PeopleBank structured curriculum vitae (CV). The CV form ensures that all the relevant information is captured and enables the CV to be searched in a very sophisticated way by the clients.
- **Percentage of resumes received is as follows:**

  40 percent: other paper (job fairs, mailings)
  60 percent: Web form

- 100 percent of resumes received from individuals.
- **Limits on length:** must conform to PeopleBank standards.
- **Format:** A detailed Web form is completed by the candidate.
- No fees to person submitting a resume.
- Resumes remain online until removed by candidate or cleansed by PeopleBank

(every six months). Candidates can remain on PeopleBank (and are encouraged to do so) for the span of their working careers. Remaining on PeopleBank is more like headhunting for the masses than a service used only at the moment that the candidate is specifically looking for a new job.

- **Procedures for updating/renewing:** All done via the Web site. Candidates can access their resumes and update them at any time. Resumes are password protected to ensure that only the rightful owner can edit a resume.

- It is possible to limit who can see a resume and to shield a resume from being viewed by a current employer. The resume is made anonymous, which means that employers cannot view the personal contact details (name, address, and so on) of the candidate until the candidate allows them to do so. The employer views the resume (without personal details) and informs PeopleBank that it wants to contact the candidate. PeopleBank then contacts the candidate and describes the position and the employer. If the candidate authorizes PeopleBank to do so, it releases the candidate's personal details to the employer.

- **Assistance provided to the person submitting a resume:** Detailed Help section describing how to get the best out of a PeopleBank resume.

- **Search options available to employers viewing resumes:** Very detailed. Employers can search by one or a combination of the following criteria:

Salary

Type of job (permanent or contract)

Age of CV (For example, an employer may want to see only CVs that have been posted in the last seven days.)

Desired occupation (Candidates specify what occupations they are interested in.)

Previous occupations and length of time in previous occupations

Industry experience (This category is different from the occupation category. Consider, for example, a salesman in publishing. *Salesman* is the occupation; *publishing* is the industry.)

Age

Education level

Location of job (This category finds candidates who want to work only in the location of the job.)

Key skills

Psychometric matching

- **Technology to match jobs to resumes and e-mail resumes to clients:** Employers run searches by using the criteria mentioned in the preceding point. They then can see resumes of matching candidates.

- **Special features:** Psychometric matching of candidates to jobs. This feature enables employers to incorporate subjective as well as objective criteria into their searches.

- **Other distinguishing factors:** Candidates do not have to have access to the Web. They can complete a PeopleBank registration form, which enables them to have their details processed on the database.

PursuitNet Online

USA and Canada
Higher-Level Positions in
Professions and Sales
Rating: ★ ★ ★ ½

PursuitNet specializes in professional, technical, sales, and management-level individuals qualified to seek jobs in the $30,000–$200,000 range. PursuitNet matches your skills and desires with compatible jobs anywhere in the United States or Canada.

- **URL:** http://www.pursuit.com/jobs

- **Ownership/sponsorship:** corporate.

- Started accepting resumes in 1995.

- **Approximate number of resumes online in April 1998:** More than 5,000 now but expected to grow to more than 100,000 within a few months.

- Resumes are mostly in professional, technical, managerial, and sales areas with qualifications in the range of $30,000–$300,000 for annual salary.

- **Total number of corporate subscribers/employers:** Most of PursuitNet's efforts are in satisfaction of requirements submitted into the PursuitNet Online system by other recruiting agencies throughout the United States and Canada.

- **Of corporate subscribers/employers, the percentages include the following:**

    10 percent: direct-hire employers
    75 percent: staffing firms
    15 percent: contract/consulting firms

- **Fee structure for corporate subscribers/employers:** 20 percent–30 percent of annual salary.

- **Methods and rules for submitting resumes:** Free through the Web site form at http://www.pursuit.com/jobs, where all instructions are provided.

- 100 percent of resumes are received by Web form, the only manner in which the service operates.

- **Percentage of resumes received is as follows:**

    50 percent: individuals
    5 percent: colleges or universities
    5 percent: outplacement firms
    40 percent: other (recruiters/associates)

- Maximum resume length is equivalent to three pages.

- **Format:** specified through the Web form.

- No fees to person submitting a resume.

- Resumes remain online permanently as long as the resume is updated each month by an individual actively seeking a job and annually by someone potentially interested in advancements.

- **Procedures for updating/renewing:** online (password for access).

- **It is possible to limit who can see a resume:** The only time a resume is seen by any outside party is when a potential match with an actual job takes place.

- **It is possible to shield a resume from being viewed by a current employer:** In the designated place on the resume form, simply indicate any employer that you don't want to receive the resume.

- **Assistance provided to the person submitting a resume:** Online guidelines are provided to assist the individual, and automatic editing is accomplished as a part of the submission process.

- Search options available to employers viewing resumes: None. Employers are not provided such an option. All they need to do is submit the job opening, and PursuitNet does the rest of the matching process. The employers are presented online with only the best matches, which are ranked by a complex algorithm.

- **Technology to match jobs to resumes and e-mail resumes to clients:** The entire system is online to match the best of the candidates to the jobs presented. Many factors are considered, and only those candidates who remain are ranked and presented online for the client to consider.

- **Special features:** PursuitNet Online is the only known service that provides a career-long service interacting with a large number of recruiters throughout the United States and Canada to effect placements with their clients. Both direct-hire and contract placements are accommodated by this fully online system.

- **Other distinguishing factors:** According to PursuitNet Online, it is the most advanced system on the Web. It is into its fourth year with the current online system and expects to have an entirely revised system operational in about a month or two, after more than a year in development. PursuitNet is in the testing mode now, and the new system is a joy to behold!

Regional Re-Careerment Center

Indiana
White-Collar Professionals
Rating: ★ ★

This site was created by a grant to assist white-collar individuals in Indiana who have been displaced from previous employment through no fault of their own.

- **URL:** `http://web.iquest.net/reg-recar`

- **Ownership/sponsorship:** Funding provided by the Indiana Department of Workforce Development. The grant is administered by Interlocal Association in Greenfield, Indiana.

- Started accepting resumes in October 1995.

- **Approximate number of resumes online in April 1998:** 150.

- **Resumes are categorized as follows:**

  general management, administrative, executive
  accounting, banking, finance
  manufacturing
  engineering, construction
  computer systems, networking
  advertising, communications
  human resources
  sales and marketing

- **Total number of corporate subscribers/employers:** The site receives 2,000 hits per day and has placed over 1,500 clients in white-collar, professional jobs in the last three years.

- **Fee structure for corporate subscribers/employers:** never a fee.

- **Methods and rules for submitting resumes:** Put your resume on a floppy disk in Word for Windows or a text file. Submit the disk with your name, address, telephone number, e-mail address (if you have one), two categories to be listed under, and a brief description of what you do. Send the disk to the following address:

Part II: Resume Banks

Jeff Skinner (RRC North)
6801 Lake Plaza Drive, Suite C-302
Indianapolis, IN 46220

- **Percentage of resumes received is as follows:**

  10 percent: e-mail
  10 percent: fax
  75 percent: diskette
  5 percent: Web form

- 100 percent of resumes received from individuals.

- No limits on length.

- **Format:** Word or a text file on a floppy disk.

- **Fees to person submitting a resume:** If you are a white-collar professional and an Indiana resident who has been displaced from previous employment through no fault of your own, there is no charge. White-collar professionals who are not Indiana residents have a fee of $15.00 (checks made payable to Interlocal Association).

- Resumes remain online until the job seekers request that they be removed or until RRC no longer has a home page.

- **Procedures for updating/renewing:** Word or text file on a floppy disk.

- It is not possible to limit who can see a resume.

- It is not possible to shield a resume from being viewed by a current employer.

- **Assistance provided to the person submitting a resume:** If an Indiana resident, the job seeker will receive whatever job-related help is needed. If the person is not an Indiana resident, then no help is available.

- **Search options available to employers viewing resumes:** Resumes are organized by categories. From employer feedback, the site has been advised to keep the site simple.

- **Technology to match jobs to resumes and e-mail resumes to clients:** The site promotes all new clients to companies, Human Resource people, and recruiters through an e-mail marketing database of over 3,000 addresses.

- **Average number of daily hits on resumes:** 2,000.

- **Special features:** its simplicity.

- **Other distinguishing factors:** Regional Re-Careerment Center has been featured on local newscasts in the Indianapolis market on stations WRTV and WISH, in *The Indianapolis Star* newspaper, in the *National Business and Employment Weekly* publication, and in *Employment Weekly,* a local Indianapolis publication. In December 1997, the center was the sponsor of a statewide conference called "Professionals Need Your Help, Too…Providers' Prescription for a New Job Search," which was attended by over 200 employment and training professionals.

- For people looking for employment, Regional Re-Careerment Center offers training—in computers, printers, fax machines, copy machines, and telephone banks—to upgrade their job search skills. It also provides resources, such as individual career counseling, to put these job skills to work.

Resume Blaster!

USA
All Career Fields
Rating: ★ ★ ★

Resume Blaster! can e-mail your resume to over 1,000 recruiters nationwide. If the recruiters are interested in you for any of their positions, they will contact you directly.

- **URL:** http://www.resumeblaster.com

- **Ownership/sponsorship:**
  PC Pros, Inc.
  (877) GO-BLAST

- Started accepting resumes in 1997.

- **Approximate number of resumes online in April 1998:** Resume Blaster! sends the resumes directly to the recruiters' e-mail inbox, so this information does not apply.

- Resume Blaster! has a General Blast, which goes to recruiters who accept resumes from all job classifications. And it has a Disciplined Blast, which goes not only to the recruiters who accept all resumes, but also to the recruiters who have selected the same job classifications as those the candidate selects.

- **Total number of corporate subscribers/employers:** more than 1,500 recruiters and executive search firms.

- **Of corporate subscribers/employers, the percentages include the following:**

  90–95 percent: staffing firms
  5–10 percent: contract/consulting firms

- **Fee structure for corporate subscribers/employers:** free for recruiters to receive resumes.

- **Methods and rules for submitting resumes:** Fill in the online sign-up form, which includes the type of work you do, what you're looking for, your location requirements, your salary requirements, and many other pieces of information recruiters require for matching you up with open job positions.

- **Percentage of resumes received by:**

  5 percent: fax
  95 percent Web form

- 100 percent of resumes received from individuals.

- No limits on length.

- **Format:** Format is in plain text so that all recruiters can read the resumes regardless of which word processing platform they are using.

- **Fees to person submitting resume:** $49.00–$89.00 depending on service selected.

- Resumes remain online indefinitely.

- **Procedures for updating/renewing:** You are able to modify the resume on the Web site with e-mail and password.

- It is possible to limit who can see a resume to some degree. You can limit the resume from going to certain firms that are in certain job classifications.

- It is possible to shield a resume from being viewed by a current employer. Resume Blaster! puts only recruiters on the list, not employers.

- **Assistance provided to the person submitting a resume:** You can use online Help, or you can send an e-mail message for help. If you prefer to order over the phone, you can use the toll-free number, (877) GO-BLAST.

- **Search options available to employers viewing resumes:** None. Resumes go directly to the e-mail inbox of recruiters who are subscribed to the list.

- **Technology to match jobs to resumes and e-mail resumes to clients:** Resume Blaster! is a resume distribution service, so it doesn't do job matching, which is up to the recruiters and the candidates.

- **Special features:** As stated earlier, Resume Blaster! is unlike resume database sites where you can post your resume and it sits there in a database, passively waiting for someone to find it in a keyword search. Instead, Resume Blaster! distributes a resume to recruiters who have specifically subscribed with the site.

Resume-Net

California's Silicon Valley Computer Professionals
Rating: ★ ★ ½

Resume-Net went online with 240 resumes in September 1995. Resume-Net is focused on the computer industry in the Silicon Valley area of California, which it serves from its location in San Jose.

- **URL:** `http://www.resume-net.com/`

- **Ownership/sponsorship:** privately held company

    Resume-Net
    PO Box 2053
    San Jose, CA 95109

- Started accepting resumes in 1995.

- **Approximate number of resumes online in April 1998:** 400.

- Resumes are accepted in various job classifications for the Silicon Valley computer industry.

- **Fee structure for corporate subscribers/employers:** no fees for employers.

- Methods and rules for submitting resumes: e-mail resumes to `resumes@resume-net.com`.

- 100 percent of resumes received by e-mail.

- **Percentage of resumes received is as follows:**

    90 percent: individuals
    10 percent: placement firms

- No limit on length.

- **Format:** Resume-Net supports Word, WordPerfect, PostScript, PDF, HTML, and text.

- **Fees to person submitting resume:** monthly fee is $10.00.

- Resumes remain online until monthly fee is not paid.

- **Procedures for updating/renewing:** Updates are submitted via e-mail.

- It is not possible to limit who can see a resume.

- It is not possible to shield a resume from being viewed by a current employer.

- **Assistance provided to the person submitting a resume:** Silicon Valley Computer Industry Employers list (see the special features comments that follow).

- **Search options available to employers viewing resumes:** Keyword and full-text search; search by classification and location. Search is by case-insensitive substring search to allow the maximum number of resume matches.

- **Technology to match jobs to resumes and e-mail resumes to clients:** Search engine for use by employers to find employees. Search results are presented in HTML format to allow easy linking to matching resumes.

- **Average number of daily hits on resumes:** 3,000.

- **Special features:** Resume-Net has an extensive listing of Silicon Valley computer companies, complete with HTML links to their home pages.

ResumeXPRESS!

USA

All Career Fields

Rating: ★ ★ ★

ResumeXPRESS! is a service of Online Solutions, Inc., developed and managed by Wayne M. Gonyea, co-author of *Electronic Resumes* (McGraw-Hill, 1996). ResumeXPRESS! distributes resumes electronically to thousands of employers, employment recruiters, and online resume database services nationwide who have requested to receive resumes from job seekers. ResumeXPRESS! also maintains a resume database.

- **URL:** `http://resumexpress.com`

- **Ownership/sponsorship:** Wayne M. Gonyea

OnLine Solutions, Inc.
1584 Rt. 22B
Morrisonville, NY 12962
(518) 643-2873

- Started accepting resumes in 1994.

- **Approximate number of resumes online in April 1998:** 4,000.

- Resumes are accepted in all career fields.

- **Total number of corporate subscribers/employers:** 1,000 (increasing rapidly).

- **Of corporate subscribers/employers, the percentages include the following:**

  20 percent: direct-hire employers
  75 percent: staffing firms
   5 percent: online databases

- **Fee structure for corporate subscribers/employers:** no cost.

- **Methods and rules for submitting resumes:** Accepted by e-mail, by Web site, on disk, or by USPS from job seekers and/or third parties (resume writers, career counselors, and so on).

- **Percentage of resumes received by sources is as follows:**

  95 percent: e-mail
   2 percent: other paper (job fairs, mailings)
   1 percent: diskette
   2 percent: Web form

- **Percentage of resumes received from people is as follows:**

  40 percent: individuals
   5 percent: outplacement firms
  55 percent: other (career counselors, resume writers)

- No limits on length.

- **Format:** prefers ASCII.

- **Fees to person submitting resume:** $89.95 retail, which includes a one-year posting in the ResumeXPRESS! database.

- Resumes remain online one year.

- **Procedures for updating/renewing:** Contact ResumeXPRESS!

- It is not possible to limit who can see a resume.

- It is possible to shield a resume from being viewed by a current employer by posting the resume as confidential.

- **Assistance provided to the person submitting a resume:** Phone consultation and review of resume.

- **Search options available to employers viewing resumes:** Resumes are always fully searchable by keywords at all times—no restrictions, no cost.

- **Technology to match jobs to resumes and e-mail resumes to clients:** Registered employers establish the characteristics of the resumes they are seeking by using keywords. Queries can be modified, added, or deleted at any time by entering the password-protected registration area. Search criteria remain "live" on the database. This live criteria enable every resume that matches the search criteria to be selected and sent out automatically via e-mail.

- **Average number of daily hits on resumes:** 200–300.

- **Special feature:** Sorted resume response, as previously described.

- **Other distinguishing factors:** Also contains options for ExecutiveXPRESS! to send executive resumes to a selected list of executive/retained recruiters and venture capitalists.

Saludos Career Web

USA
All Career Fields
Rating: ★ ★ ½

Saludos Career Web, supported by *Saludos Hispanos* magazine, is devoted exclusively to promoting Hispanic careers and education. Saludos Career Web has been awarded the four-star rating from the *McKinley Guide*.

- **URL:** http://www.saludos.com/respost.html

- **Ownership/sponsorship:** *Saludos Hispanos* magazine.

- Started accepting resumes in 1996.

- **Approximate number of resumes online in April 1998:** 75.

- Resumes are in all career fields including academic, administration, advertising, computing and technology, engineering, finance/accounting/insurance, health care, human resources, marketing, media, sales, science, and telecommunications.

- **Total number of corporate subscribers/employers:** Saludos Career Web doesn't have subscribers. Employers are free to view all posted resumes without charge or subscription fee.

- **Fee structure for corporate subscribers/employers:** No subscription fee at this time.

- **Methods and rules for submitting resumes:** Be bilingual in English and Spanish and be enrolled in a four-year college or university with expected graduation within one year of posting your resume or have completed a two-year or four-year college program.

- **Approximate percentage of resumes received by sources is as follows:**

  20 percent: e-mail
  5 percent: fax
  50 percent: other paper (job fairs, mailings)
  25 percent: Web form

- **Approximate percentage of resumes received from people is as follows:**

  75 percent: individuals
  25 percent: colleges or universities

- **Limits on length:** one page in length.

- **Format:** Headings include Objective, Experience, Education, Skills, Honors and Accomplishments, Training and Courses.

- No fees to person submitting a resume.

- Resumes remain online 60 days.

- **Procedures for updating/renewing:** must resubmit updated resume.

- It is not possible at this time to limit who can see a resume.

- It is not possible to shield a resume from being viewed by a current employer.

- **Assistance provided to the person submitting a resume:** Online directions and Web-based form to fill in. Or candidates can e-mail their resumes in plain-text format.

- **Search options available to employers viewing resumes:** search by job category.

- **Technology to match jobs to resumes and e-mail resumes to clients:** The employer can view resumes by job category online. No matching and mailing services are offered at this time.

- **Average number of daily hits on resumes:** 20–25 hits per day.

- **Distinguishing factors:** In order to post a resume on the Saludos Career Web, candidates must be bilingual (English and Spanish).

Science Professional Network

USA
Sciences
Rating: ★ ★ ★

The Science Career Fair Resume Bank is offered in conjunction with *Science*-sponsored career fairs. Candidates who plan to attend one or more of the *Science*-sponsored career fairs can post their resumes for the exhibiting employers.

- **URL:** `http://www.sciencemag.org`

- Ownership/sponsorship: American Association of the Advancement of Science (AAAS), Science Business Publications Inc.

- Started accepting resumes in January 1998.

- **Approximate number of resumes online in April 1998:** 250–300.

- Resumes are in the life sciences (agriculture, anatomy/physiology, biochemistry, biology, botany/plant science, cell biology, clinical research, developmental biology, environmental science, genetics, immunology, marine science, medicine, microbiology, molecular biology, neuroscience, nutrition/health care, oncology, pathology, pharmacology, structural Biology, toxicology, veterinary medicine, and virology) and the sciences (astronomy, atmospheric science, chemistry, computer science, engineering, geoscience, informatics, materials science, mathematics, and physics).

- **Total number of corporate subscribers/employers:** Science Professional Network collects resumes from scientists who plan on attending the career fairs. Only the exhibitors to these fairs are allowed to access the resume database. Science Professional Network averages 15 exhibitors per career fair. The site is now considering whether to open the database to all scientists who want to include their resumes in the database and to all potential customers who would like to access the database.

- **Of corporate subscribers/employers, the percentages include the following:**

  90 percent: direct-hire employers
  5 percent: staffing firms
  5 percent: other

- **Fee structure for corporate subscribers/employers:** They must advertise in certain issues and exhibit at the career fairs to have access to the data bank of resumes. The rates vary depending on the size of the ad they run.

- **Methods and rules for submitting resumes:** All resumes are submitted through an electronic form on the Web site. Scientists can also submit hard copies of their resumes at the career fairs.

- **Percentage of resumes received is as follows:**

  50 percent: other paper (job fairs, mailings)
  50 percent: Web form

- 100 percent of resumes received from individuals.

- No limits on length.

- **Format:** A form is provided for general information; then the job seeker attaches a resume to the form.

- No fees to person submitting resume.

- **Length of time resumes remain online:** seven weeks.

- **Procedures for updating/renewing:** Job seekers can update their resumes by submitting a new copy of the resume online.

- It is possible to limit who can see a resume. Only employers who have a password can access the database. Science Professional Network monitors those who are coming into the site to make sure that resumes aren't passed on to others.

- It is not possible to shield a resume from being viewed by a current employer.

SEEK

Australia
All Career Fields
Rating: ★ ★ ★ ★

Seek Communications is an Australian owned-and-operated online jobs-database and career-development site that is focused on the Australian marketplace.

- **URL:** http://www.seek.com.au

- **Ownership/sponsorship:** private ownership.

- Started accepting resumes in March 1998.

- **Approximate number of resumes online in April 1998:** 1,000.

- Resumes are spread broadly across all industry/occupation categories (13 industries, more than 100 occupations).

- **Total number of corporate subscribers/employers:** more than 200.

- **Of corporate subscribers/employers, the percentages include the following:**

    5 percent: direct-hire employers
    95 percent: staffing firms and contract/consulting firms

- **Fee structure for corporate subscribers/employers:** Corporations/employers pay to place advertisements on the site. Access to resume database is given to advertisers over a specified threshold.

- **Methods and rules for submitting resumes:** Resumes are submitted online by the user through a browser interface. Users can submit multiple resumes. Users can also select whether their resume is to be private (for the convenience of using their resumes when applying for positions) or accessible by advertisers.

- **Percentage of resumes received by sources is as follows:**

    5 percent: e-mail
    95 percent: Web form

- **Percentage of resumes received from people is as follows:**

    95 percent: individuals
    5 percent: outplacement firms

- **Limits on length:** Approximately 10,000 characters is the maximum size.

- **Format:** Format is according to a specified template. Applicants enter free text into a number of areas (with most areas being optional) that include work experience, profile, education, personal interests, and so on. Users also specify which type of work they are looking for (location, industry, occupation, and work type) to enable searching by employers.

- No fees to persons. All services to job seekers are free.

- Resumes can remain in the database for one year, but they remain accessible to advertisers for only three months. In either case, job seekers receive two expiry notices, which permit them to extend their resumes for a further period.

- **Procedures for updating/renewing:** Users can update their resumes at any time via a browser interface. To renew, users simply click on the hypertext link in the expiry notices and select the option of extending their resumes.

- It is possible to limit who can see a resume. Resumes can be seen only by advertisers (employers) who meet specified advertising thresholds. The advertisers can search the database to find those matches for actual vacant positions.

- Currently it is not possible to shield a resume from being viewed by a current employer, although SEEK is considering a move down this path. At present, users can see who the site advertisers are (and therefore who can potentially see their resumes).

- **Assistance provided to the person submitting a resume:** Instructions on the site are clear, and an example resume is provided. Users are also informed that they can contact the customer service staff by phone or e-mail if they have any problems. All queries are promptly attended to.

- **Search options available to employers viewing resumes:** Employers can search for relevant potential employees by using any or all of the following: location, industry, occupation, work type, and keyword.

- **Technology to match jobs to resumes and e-mail resumes to clients:** Employers can access resumes that match their searches directly through browser interface.

- **Average number of daily hits on resumes:** Resumes appear in a list at the rate of approximately 800 per day.

- **Special features:** The site provides users with a free service that enables them to create a resume online and to lodge their resume for the purpose of attracting potential employers. Within two months of going live, a significant number of placements have been made through this process (with the first placement within three days of going live).

- **Other distinguishing factors:** In the editorial areas of the site, there are substantial resources assisting job seekers in all aspects of the job search process.

SelectJOBS

USA

Computer Professionals

Rating: ★ ★ ★

Founded in 1996, the SelectJOBS Web site was designed specifically for computer professionals. By advertising in computer magazines and trade journals, SelectJOBS directs job seekers and employers to its Web site. Its resume database features daily matching between employers and job seekers.

- **URL:** http://www.selectjobs.com

- **Ownership/sponsorship:** http://www.selectjobs.com Incorporated.

- Started accepting resumes in 1996.

- **Approximate number of resumes online in April 1998:** Over 28,000 resumes currently on database. SelectJOBS receives new submissions every day.

- SelectJOBS is mainly a site for computer professionals, but it does have resumes and job listings for skills outside of that profession.

- **Total number of corporate subscribers/employers:** Over 300 active clients as of June 1998.

- The site doesn't track the percentages of corporate subscribers/employers, but it has a fair combination of all.

- **Fee structure for corporate subscribers/employers:** All fee structures include resume database search, job propagation to six other sites, posting of all jobs, link to subscriber's Web site, and subscriber's color logo on job listings on the SelectJOBS Web site. The fees are as follows:

  $ 50.00 for one job listing for 30 days
  $ 50.00 for resume search only for 30 days (does not include items listed in preceding paragraph)
  $360.00 for unlimited postings for 30 days
  $300.00 for unlimited postings for a six-month commitment

- **Methods and rules for submitting resumes:** Candidates either can visit the Web site to post their own resumes, or they can send their resume via e-mail for SelectJOBS to post. The site does not accept faxed resumes.

- SelectJOBS doesn't track where the resumes are submitted from, but it receives them via e-mail, from its listings that candidates have seen on newsgroups or other sites, and from job seekers searching the Web.

- The main bulk of resumes comes from individuals, then from colleges and universities, and some from third parties.

- **Length:** 2,000 characters maximum, which includes spaces.

- **Format:** Job seekers can submit their resumes via e-mail in either a Word or ASCII plain-text attachment, or they can visit the Web site and post the resume themselves.

- There is no charge to post resumes.

- **Length of time resumes remain online:** Resumes stay in the bank until the job seekers tell SelectJOBS to delete their resumes from the database. People searching the resume database can specify the time frame they want to view (for example, past 90 days, past 45 days, past 3 years).

- **Procedures for updating/renewing:** Job seekers can go online and modify their resumes whenever they want, or they can send their updated resumes to SelectJOBS, and it will repost them.

- It is not possible to limit who can see a resume. The only way to limit who views a resume is not to have the resume viewable to any employer. It is an everyone-or-no-one situation.

- It is not possible to shield a resume from being viewed by a current employer.

- **Assistance provided to the person submitting a resume:** Job seekers can contact the site via phone, e-mail, or in the suggestion box to receive assistance in posting their resumes.

- **Employers can search the database in the following ways:**

    By the location where candidates reside or where candidates are willing to relocate to

    By the skills the job seekers possess (those skills they have entered into the system)

    By the education the job seekers possess

    By time frame (for example, resumes that have been entered or modified within the last 45 days, 90 days, 365 days, and so on)

    By keywords

- SelectJOBS has developed its own matching algorithm that matches the skills requested by the client's job description to the skills possessed by the job seeker. The database runs this algorithm on a daily basis (after the close of the business day). The resume run is reviewed by the staff and then sent via e-mail or fax to the clients each day (provided that there are new matches for a particular job).

- **Average number of daily hits on resumes:** SelectJOBS doesn't track this one figure, but overall it has a combined total of over 20 million hits per month.

- **Special features include the following:**

    Offering daily resume matching.

    Posting client's jobs to six other sites (HeadHunter.Net, Classifieds2000, America's Job Bank, Career City, Yahoo!, and regional newsgroups). SelectJOBS is always looking for new sites to add to its service.

Offering links from its Web site to its clients' Web sites.

Offering clients their color logos on their job listings.

Offering banner ads.

Offering the option of contracting with the site to set up a button/link on their Web sites. With this link, they can have all their job listings on our site appear on theirs.

Redoing the User Group portion of the Web site that will offer user groups the chance to list their groups, contact information, and events.

Showbizjobs

USA
Entertainment
Rating: ★ ★ ★

Showbizjobs is a niche recruiting site for the entertainment industry.

- **URL:** `http://www.showbizjobs.com`
- **Ownership/sponsorship:** owned by Paul Buss

    Entertainment Recruiting Network
    7095 Hollywood Blvd. Suite 711
    Hollywood, CA 90028
    `Info@showbizjobs.com`
    Fax (213) 851-6442

- Started accepting resumes in 1997.
- **Approximate number of resumes online in April 1998:** 600.
- Resumes are in show production, editing, TV/film production, film librarian, graphic artists, 3-D animators, animators, ride-and-show engineering, audio technician, and traditional classifications.
- **Total number of corporate subscribers/employers:** 25.
- 100 percent of corporate subscribers/employers are direct-hire employers.
- **Fee structure for corporate subscribers/employers:** Corporate clients are registered as members of the network. They pay a $250.00 annual fee and $100.00 per job posting for a 30-day run. Access to the database is free to the recruiters (via passcodes) for the duration of their postings/membership.
- Resume candidates are charged $35.00 per six-month posting to the database.
- **Methods and rules for submitting resumes:** Candidates must use the online form and limit the length to one page; e-mail and HTTP references are hot-linked automatically in the resume display.
- 100 percent of resumes received by e-mail.
- **Percentage of resumes received is as follows:**

    95 percent: individuals
    5 percent: other

- **Limit on length:** one-and-one-half pages.
- **Format:** Form fields define zones; however, the form within the zones is unlimited. Not all word processing commands transfer to HTML format; therefore, Showbizjobs does not guarantee perfect matches with the primary document.
- **Fees to person submitting a resume:** $35.00. Candidates using credit cards

get immediate submission to the database. With payment by check, however, resumes go live on the date that payment is received.

- Resumes remain online six months.

- **Procedures for updating/renewing:** Automatic e-mail is sent to resume clients one month prior to expiration with a prompt to renew. Renewal fee is $35.00 for six months.

- Only client-company recruiters can view the resumes. Resume clients can view/edit/delete their own resumes at any time.

- It is not possible to shield a resume from being viewed by a current employer if the current employer is a client company.

- **Assistance provided to the person submitting a resume:** online Help pages, tips, and e-mail to Webmaster.

- **Search options available to employers viewing resumes:** Extensive search features include searches by name, city, job category, ID number, and words (which are highlighted within the body of the resume on the search results along with the percentage accuracy of the search results).

- **Technology to match jobs to resumes and e-mail resumes to clients:** When resume clients check their resume sections, the system automatically searches their criteria against the job database and displays a match list with links directly to those job listings.

- **Average number of daily hits on resumes:** 500 individual references.

- **Distinguishing factors:** According to Showbizjobs.com, there are no other sites on the Web that provide such a legitimate service with a list of clients as reputable as its own.

SIRC: Shawn's Internet Resume Center

USA
Executives
Rating: ★ ★ ★

SIRC bills itself as the "executive's resume center." InPursuit's Employment Network, anchored by SIRC, won a 1997 Excellence in the Electronic Recruiting Industry (EERI) award.

- **URL:** http://www.inpursuit.com/sirc/

- **Ownership/sponsorship:** owned by InPursuit of Warrenton, VA.

- Started accepting resumes in 1995.

- **Approximate number of resumes online in April 1998:** 500. To maintain the executive-level quality of its resumes, SIRC requires that job seekers must meet its criteria to be included. This policy makes it possible for SIRC to be a niche service that targets experienced executives.

- Resumes are in all job classifications; however, the service targets experienced executives.

- **Total number of corporate subscribers/employers:** Unknown. Searching resumes and contacting candidates is free, so SIRC does not have a means for accurately counting corporate users.

- **Of corporate subscribers/employers, the percentages include the following:**

    60 percent: direct-hire employers
    30 percent: staffing firms
    10 percent: contract/consulting firms

- **Fee structure for corporate subscribers/employers:** Searching is free. New fee-based corporate subscriber/employer services will include corporate profiles, unlimited job posting, and the capability for seekers to apply for jobs online.

- **Methods and rules for submitting resumes:** online submission.

- **Percentage of resumes received is as follows:**

  99 percent: e-mail
  1 percent: diskette

- 100 percent of resumes received from individuals.

- No limits on length.

- **Format:** The format has not been specified. However, a new automated system will format the resumes automatically. The job seekers can format their work experience and education sections as desired.

- No fees to person submitting a resume.

- **Length of time resumes remain online:** As long as SIRC is in business, or until seeker requests removal.

- **Procedures for updating/renewing:** New automated system will allow job seekers to log on and update their resumes online.

- It is not possible at this time to limit who can see a resume.

- It is not possible at this time to shield a resume from being viewed by a current employer.

- **Assistance is provided to the person submitting a resume:** Submission form is self-explanatory. SIRC provides access to an online resume tutorial.

- **Search options available to employers viewing resumes:** Employers can search on more than just a keyword (state, years' experience, and job category).

- **Technology to match jobs to resumes and e-mail resumes to clients:** None at this time; however, the system will allow for this technology in the future.

- **Average number of daily hits on resumes:** 1,000.

- Special features include the following:

  For employers:
  SIRC Executive Bookstore
  Posting jobs
  Sponsorship packages
  List of employers using SIRC

  For job seekers:
  Resume Clinic
  SIRC Executive Bookstore
  Articles on resume writing
  SIRC Job Board

- **Distinguishing factors:** SIRC is getting ready to launch a major set of improvements. Job seekers will have more control of their resumes and will have more information to help them in their searches. Employers will be able to subscribe for additional services, such as unlimited job postings and corporate profiles.

Skill Scan for Computer Professionals

USA
All Computer Professionals
Rating: ★ ★ ★ ★

Skill Scan is a CD-ROM database of resumes from computer professionals seeking contract and/or permanent employment. Produced weekly by Online Resource Group (ORG), Skill Scan is distributed to the nation's top consulting firms, agencies, and corporations.

- **URL:** `http://www.skillscan.com`

- **Ownership/sponsorship:** privately owned

    Online Resource Group, Inc.
    3100 Meridian Park Drive, Suite N
    Greenwood, IN 46142
    voice: (800) 262-9915
    fax: (800) 369-4067

- Started accepting resumes in 1994.

- **Approximate number of resumes online in April 1998:** more than 12,000.

- Accepts resumes from all computer professionals. Accepts no entry level or international resumes. Resumes are screened.

- **Total number of corporate subscribers/employers:** more than 200.

- **Of corporate subscribers/employers, the percentages include the following:**

    5 percent: direct-hire employers
    45 percent: staffing firms
    45 percent: contract/consulting firms
    5 percent: other

- **Fee structure for corporate subscribers/employers:** $395.00 monthly or $3,500 yearly.

- **Methods and rules for submitting resumes:** Any format is accepted, but ASCII is preferred.

- **Percentage of resumes received is as follows:**

    50 percent: e-mail
    50 percent: fax

- 100 percent of resumes received from individuals.

- No limits on length.

- **Format:** ASCII preferred.

- No fees to person submitting a resume.

- Resumes remain online up to nine months.

- **Procedures for updating/renewing:** via home page or resubmission.

- It is not possible to limit who can see a resume.

- It is not possible to shield a resume from being viewed by a current employer.

- **Assistance provided to the person submitting a resume:** E-mail questions are encouraged and replied to immediately.

- **Search options available to employers viewing resumes:** Skill Scan's database can be searched by several predefined job titles, over 500 predefined skills, state, zip code, contract or permanent employment, last name, and date of resume. Skill Scan's built-in "smart" search engine for full-text search is designed, for example, to know that Visual Basic can be VB or VisBasic or VisualBasic.

- **Technology to match jobs to resumes and e-mail resumes to clients:** Client performs searches.

- **Special features:** Produced weekly on CD-ROM and distributed directly to decision makers via overnight delivery.

- Other distinguishing factors: 100 percent satisfaction guaranteed (98 percent customer retention without contract). Free demonstration by visiting `http://www.skillscan.com/info`.

SkillSearch

USA
All Career Fields
Rating: ★ ★ ★

SkillSearch, established in 1990, is a fee-based service. Its resume database is not online and is available only to SkillSearch staff.

- **URL:** `http://www.skillsearch.com/`

- **Ownership/sponsorship:** SkillSearch Corporation.

- Started accepting resumes in 1990.

- **Approximate number of resumes online in April 1998:** none available online, confidential service.

- Resumes are accepted in all classifications, but they are heavy in professional, experienced fields, such as management, finance, engineering, manufacturing, and so on.

- **Total number of corporate subscribers/employers:** approximately 1,000.

- **Of corporate subscribers/employers, the percentages include the following:**

  60 percent: direct-hire employers
  20 percent: staffing firms
  20 percent: contract/consulting firms

- **Fee structure for corporate subscribers/employers:** Ranges from 3 searches of the database up to 40 searches, and from $1,700 to $9,995. Custom packages are also available. Searches include a posting of the job online on the SkillSearch site available to the public.

- **Methods and rules for submitting resumes:** You can fill out a paper profile, or you can use SkillSearch's software program on diskette.

- **Percentage of resumes received is as follows:**

  70 percent: diskette
  30 percent: paper (job fairs, mailings)

- No resumes are scanned or pulled from the Internet. You must be a SkillSearch member to participate.

- 100 percent of resumes received from individuals.

- **Limits on length:** SkillSearch has its own format, but length can vary depending on experience.

- **Format:** SkillSearch uses over 150 variables to create an applicant profile/resume. Format is based on a survey of Human Resource professionals.

- **Fees to person submitting resume:** Amount depends on whether the person is affiliated with one of SkillSearch's affinity partners (more than 130 alumni associations, some banks). Suggested standard cost is $99.00 initial sign-up fee and $29.00 annual renewal.

- **Length of time resumes remain online:** Resumes are not online. Resumes remain in the system for as long as the account is active or until the job seekers cancel their involvement.

- **Procedures for updating/renewing:** Contact information can be updated online; more extensive changes can be faxed or e-mailed. Members can update at any time.

- Renewals are processed on an annual basis. With some credit cards, annual renewal is automatically debited to their accounts.

- Only SkillSearch employees have access to entire database. When an employer runs a search, matching profiles/resumes are sent to the employer.

- It is possible to shield a resume from being viewed by a current employer as well as any other companies the SkillSearch member doesn't want to see the resume.

- **Assistance provided to the person submitting a resume:** The SkillSearch profile is extensive, so members can get help from SkillSearch support staff to fine-tune their resumes for the best response. When a profile matches the needs of a SkillSearch client, the resume is sent out, and the member is contacted by the employer if the employer is interested. In addition, proactive SkillSearch members can view recent searches online and request that their resumes be sent to those jobs that interest them (if their resumes have not been sent already).

- **Search options available to employers viewing resumes:** Searches are performed by professional SkillSearch staff, but employers can match based on general parameters (education, location, experience) as well as on such items as desired salary, own or rent home, open to relocation, previous employers, current employers, and so on.

- **Technology to match jobs to resumes and e-mail resumes to clients:** proprietary SkillSearch system.

- **Distinguishing factors:** The SkillSearch resume database is designed for the experienced, degreed professional who is currently employed. Although not actively seeking employment, this professional is open to better opportunities. SkillSearch enables this professional to passively keep an eye on the job market without going through the hassle of a job search or jeopardizing current employment.

Transition Assistance Online

Global
Separating US Military,
Spouses, and Dependents
Rating: ★ ★ ★ ★

Transition Assistance Online (TAO) aids separating US military service members and veterans in finding employment in the civilian sector and federal government, and aids companies in finding and hiring these individuals. The site includes a resume database, job postings, company profiles, job hunting and resume writing advice, and so on.

- **URL:** `http://www.taonline.com`

- **Ownership/sponsorship:** DI-USA, Inc. and Army Times Publishing Company (Gannett).

- Started accepting resumes in late 1996.

- Approximate number of resumes online in April 1998: more than 15,000–25,000.

- Resumes are from separating US military service members, veterans, spouses, and dependents. The resumes are spread out into many categories that include technical and engineering fields, health care, security, communications, transportation, warehousing, purchasing, and so on.

- **Total number of corporate subscribers/employers:** more than 350–500.

- **Of corporate subscribers/employers, the percentages include the following:**

    95 percent: direct-hire employers
    2 percent: staffing firms
    2 percent: contract/consulting firms
    1 percent: other

- **Fee structure for corporate subscribers/employers:** Complex fee structure that depends on which services the employers want (resume searching, advertising, job posting); the position of the advertisement; and the length of posting, advertisement, and/or search. Current advertising fees are posted at the following address:

    `http://www.taonline.com/advertise.html`

- Methods and rules for submitting resumes: See `http://www.taonline.com/submitres.html` for the entire list. Basically, resume submissions can come in by e-mail, e-form (`http://www.taonline.com/submitresfor.html`), or postal mail (scanned in); or resumes can be uploaded via Transition Assistance Software, which can be found in all base exchanges worldwide.

- **Percentage of resumes received is as follows:**

    30 percent: e-mail
    40 percent: other paper (job fairs, mailings)
    30 percent: Web form

- 100 percent of resumes received from individuals.

- **Limits on length:** three pages or fewer —with no cover letters, attachments, and so on.

- **Format:** ASCII-text scannable resume format, left justified. See `http://www.taonline.com/submitres.html` for details.

- **Fees:** Resume submission is free to all US military service members, veterans, spouses, and dependents.

- Resumes remain online three–five months.

- **Procedures for updating/renewing:** Just resubmit a resume after 90 days by using the same methods (e-mail, e-form, or postal mail). Resumes in the three-through-five-month range are archived to other searchable directories.

- Is it possible to limit who can see a resume? Only reputable employers who have paid a fee and who have been authorized can view the resumes by using a login and password.

- It is not possible to shield a resume from being viewed by a current employer if the current employer is a paying corporate customer.

- **Assistance provided to the person submitting a resume:** Extensive job-hunting and resume-writing resources are available on the online site in the Transition Information Center at `http://www.taonline.com/ticindex.html`.

- **Search options available to employers viewing resumes:** Employers can search resumes by using two search engines (Excite and in-house) with keywords, concepts, and so on. Resume submitters can search job postings free of charge by using an in-house search engine with keywords, occupations, and/or regions. (TAO will soon expand its search capabilities to include state and country.)

- **Technology to match jobs to resumes and e-mail resumes to clients:** TAO has developed a system to provide employers with the most current resumes that best fit their needs on a timely basis. Using an "offline" process, TAO automatically searches its resume bank for the employer's keyword specifications. When TAO finds resumes that match the employer's requirements, it e-mails the employer daily, weekly, or on whatever schedule it wants. Employers can also search the resume databases themselves.

- **Average number of daily hits on resumes:** Total hits on the site are over 600,000 per month and increasing by 25,000 per month.

- **Special features include the following:**

  Military personnel are able to send their resumes electronically to TAO via e-mail or by using Transition Assistance Software (TAS), which TAO publishes. TAS is available at every DoD installation around the world and is, in fact, the best-selling military resume-writing/job-search-organizer software.

  DI-USA has established a relationship with one of the world's largest military-affiliated associations, which is sending TAO separating service members' resumes from its monthly job fairs, which are held across the country.

  Additionally, TAO has implemented a program that automatically receives the most recent and qualified Defense Outplacement Referral System (DORS) resumes electronically on a regular basis.

- **Distinguishing factors:** Since its introduction in January of 1997, TAO—a joint venture between The Army Times Publishing Company and DI-USA, Inc.—has become the fastest growing and most popular employment search site for transitioning military personnel on the Web. TAO resume bank has more current military resumes than any other online service.

Tripod Resume Builder

USA
All Career Fields
Rating: ★ ★ ★ ★

Tripod is the hip, homegrown Web community for individuals who embrace the innovative and pioneering spirit of the Web. Membership in Tripod is free and confidential; in other words, the service is not sold to direct marketers. With your membership, you get a free Web site. Tripod's Resume Builder is a key feature of the site and has been helping job seekers find jobs online since 1995.

- **URL:** `http://www.tripod.com/jobs_career/resume/`

- **Ownership/sponsorship:** Part of Tripod.com—Tripod, Inc. is a wholly owned subsidiary of Lycos, Inc. (NASDAQ: LCOS).

- Started accepting resumes in 1995.

- **Approximate number of resumes online in April 1998:** thousands.

- Resumes are in all career fields.

- **Total number of corporate subscribers/employers:** Tripod doesn't work in this way; it is a completely free service.

- 100 percent of resumes received by Web form.

- 100 percent of resumes received from individuals.

- No limits on length.

- **Format:** The Resume Builder template form is offered for ease of use. With Tripod's Homepage Builder, however, users can create any type/style/format resume they choose.

- No fees to person submitting a resume.

- Resumes remain online indefinitely—until the creators remove them.

- **Procedures for updating/renewing:** Return to the online form and update the resume as you like. You can find a form developed especially for editing the resume at the following address:

    `http://www.tripod.com/service/resume/Editor`

- **Search options available to employers viewing resumes:** Keywords, names, geography (city, state, country).

- **Technology to match jobs to resumes and e-mail resumes to clients:** Tripod is not this type of service; it is more a free-to-search and free-to-post service.

- **Average number of daily hits on resumes:** in the thousands, sometimes hundreds of thousands.

- **Special features:** Only Tripod's "new and improved" Resume Builder will automatically generate the best choice from six different resume formats based upon your personal job history and search criteria. The Resume Builder then enables you to circulate your resume easily to other online resume sites.

- Other distinguishing factors: A Resume FAQ, which answers such questions as "Do I really need a resume? When do I need it? What kind should I build?"

- In addition, Tripod offers reviews of 22 other sites that will post your resume for free.

Virtual Job Fair

USA

High Tech

Rating: ★ ★ ★

Westech ExpoCorp provides both *High Technology Careers* magazine and Virtual Job Fair—both specifically geared toward technical professionals.

- **URL:** `http://www.VJF.com`

- **Ownership/sponsorship:** Westech ExpoCorp.

- Started accepting resumes in 1994.

- **Approximate number of resumes online in April 1998:** 100,000.

- Virtual Job Fair is 100 percent high tech, and its resume database is driven by skill keywords, such as Oracle, not by classifications.

- **Total number of corporate subscribers/employers:** 800.

- **Of corporate subscribers/employers, the percentages include the following:**

    94 percent: direct-hire employers
    2 percent: staffing firms
    4 percent: contract/consulting firms

- **Fee structure for corporate subscribers/employers:** $25.00 per listing plus $300.00 per month. Virtual Job Fair also has the following flat-rate packages: less than 100 positions for $1,800 per month; unlimited number of positions for $2,300 per month.

- **Methods and rules for submitting resumes:** The Virtual Job Fair Resume Center is a very easy and powerful candidate/employer matching service. Virtual Job Fair asks candidates to paste their resumes and answer a few multiple-choice questions in the following categories: Job Goals, Contact Information, Enrollment Options, Experience, and Education.

- 100 percent of resumes received by Web form.

- 100 percent of resumes received from individuals.

- No limits on length.

- **Format:** The site asks candidates to copy their resumes from text files on their computers and then to paste the files into the text block provided.

- No fees to person submitting a resume.

- **Length of time resumes remains online:** Candidates are notified after 60 days that they must update their resumes within 30 days or their resumes will become inactive.

- **Procedures for updating/renewing:** The Virtual Job Fair Resume Center gives candidates the option of changing or removing their resumes at any time. All they need to do is enter their user names and passwords in order to access their resumes. By following very simple instructions, they can quickly delete or update their resumes.

- It is possible to limit who can see a resume and to shield a resume from being viewed by a current employer. The Virtual Job Fair Resume Center is the only service that allows you to choose—absolutely free—to post your resume privately. If you choose this feature, your resume can be searched by employers, but they are not provided with your personal information. The employers are provided with an e-mail box (not your e-mail address) to contact you. You choose which employers to respond to.

- **Assistance provided to the person submitting a resume:** The site has an FAQ page, which viewers can refer to if they have any questions. For further assistance, candidates can refer to the Questions/Comments page to direct their questions and comments.

- **Search options available to employers viewing resumes:** Employers use a powerful query tool to find the best fit among the candidates for their positions. This advanced search mechanism enables employers to enter specific job criteria way beyond simple text search. Furthermore, employers can contact applicants through pop-up e-mail, and they can print and review selected resumes.

- **Average number of daily hits on resumes:** 5,500.

- **Special features:** Westech Virtual Job Fair also has an advanced job search option that enables candidates to enter not only an exact or best-match keyword search, but also the name of the company and location where they are seeking employment.

- **Other distinguishing factors:** Virtual Job Fair is the only major jobs site that is 100 percent high tech, with over 25,000 high-tech jobs. The site also includes career articles and Westech Career Expo dates and locations. All jobs are identified by the hiring company (company links beside each job title) rather than by giant piles of clustered jobs without any description or reference to the company.

Virtuallyhired

Chicago Area
High Technology
Rating: ★ ★ ★

Nu_Way's founder, Steve Riess, has been placing I/S professionals in the Chicago marketplace for over 20 years. Virtuallyhired is not a resume bank; however, its employees personally review every resume that they receive. If there are job opportunities that appear to offer a good match, the staff will contact the job seeker directly by telephone.

- **URL:** `http://www.virtuallyhired.com`
- **Ownership/sponsorship:** Nu_Way Search, Inc.
- Started accepting resumes in 1996.
- **Approximate number of resumes online in April 1998:** Virtuallyhired is not a resume database in the traditional sense. After submitting your resume when you visit the site, you are asked to indicate which jobs are of interest to you. Your resume is kept on file, and when you return to the site in the future, you can effortlessly flag any jobs that catch your interest.
- Resumes are accepted in the area of information systems (I/S).
- **Total number of corporate subscribers/employers:** None. This is a private site.
- **Methods and rules for submitting resumes:** form, e-mail attachment, and fax.
- **Percentage of resumes received is as follows:**

   95 percent: e-mail
   1 percent: fax
   4 percent: Web form

- 100 percent of resumes received from individuals.
- No limits on length.
- **Format:** Any is okay, but Microsoft Word is preferred.
- No fees to person submitting resume.
- **Technology to match jobs to resumes and e-mail resumes to clients:** The finest available—the human brain.
- **Special features:** Pools of Inspiration (job search information).
- **Other distinguishing factors:** fun site.
- Virtuallyhired.com is a unique site serving the Chicago market with a jungle theme, which enables candidates to make specific selections in various criteria from the hundreds of positions available. The search criteria enable the candidates to cut through the "jungle" and pursue jobs that are appropriate.
- This format will soon be extended to other major markets in cities around the United States.

VirtualResume

USA
All Career Fields
Rating: ★ ★ ★

VirtualResume is devoted exclusively to resumes. Its sister Web site—CAREERspan—is an employment opportunities online service that is free for both job seekers and employers.

- **URL:** http://www.virtualresume.com

- Ownership/sponsorship:

    VirtualSight Communications
    11 Sterling Place
    Suite 4F
    Brooklyn, NY 11217

- Started accepting resumes in 1996.

- **Approximate number of resumes online in April 1998:** 10,000.

- Resumes are accepted in all career fields. Resumes are clustered into job categories.

- **Fee structure for corporate subscribers/employers is as follows:**

    VirtualResume $ 89.00 per month/
                          $700.00 per year
    VirtualResume PLUS $119.00 per month/
                          $1,000 per year

- **Methods and rules for submitting resumes:** All resumes must be submitted through the Web site. Only individuals seeking employment can post resumes; agencies cannot post candidates.

- 100 percent of resumes received by Web form.

- 100 percent of resumes received from individuals.

- No limits on length.

- **Format:** ASCII, HTML.

- **Fees to person submitting resume:** No fee for basic resume posting or guest access to the resume database.

- Resumes remain online six months.

- **Procedures for updating/renewing:** All resume posters can update, renew, or delete their resumes anytime they like by logging in to their accounts.

- Is it possible to limit who can see a resume? Anyone can search the full database. Only VirtualResume members can view contact information. Confidential resumes are posted without name or contact information.

- Is shielding a resume from being viewed by a current employer possible? Confidential resumes are posted blind. Recruiters can contact candidates only via a form.

- **Assistance provided to the person submitting a resume:** Customer service is always willing to assist.

- **Search options available to employers viewing resumes:** job category, location, and/or keyword.

- **Technology to match jobs to resumes and e-mail resumes to clients:** VirtualResume Resumes can be e-mailed directly to employers; resume posters can choose to receive e-mailed jobs.

- **Special features:** Resume posters can choose to be posted by VirtualResume to Usenet resume newsgroups. The postings appear under the candidate's own name and e-mail address.

Western New York Resumes

Western New York State
All Career Fields
Rating: ★ ★ 1/2

Western New York Resumes is done in conjunction with the employment paper, *Western New York JOBS Weekly*. Both sites are actively promoted to local hiring managers as a source for finding applicants for their available positions in Western New York.

- **URL:** `http://www.wnyjobs.com/resumes.html`

- **Ownership/sponsorship:** JOBS Weekly.

- Started accepting resumes in 1997.

- **Approximate number of resumes online in April 1998:** 100.

- Resumes are accepted in all career fields. New classifications appear as needed.

- **Total number of corporate subscribers/employers:** unlimited; unrestricted viewership.

- **Fee structure for corporate subscribers/employers:** free.

- **Methods and rules for submitting resumes:** E-mail in text format to `resumes@wnyjobs.com` (no attachments will be accepted); fax to (716) 648-5658; or mail to the following address:

    Resumes Dept.
    C/O JOBS Weekly
    31 Buffalo St.
    Hamburg, NY 14075

- **Percentage of resumes received is as follows:**

    25 percent: e-mail
    5 percent: fax
    70 percent: other paper (job fairs, mailings)

- 100 percent of resumes received from individuals.

- **Limits on length:** last three employers for work history.

- **Format:** order specified on Web site.

- **Fees to person submitting resume:**

    $10.00/one month
    $15.00/two months
    $20.00/three months

- **Length of time resumes remain online:** up to three months or longer if renewing.

- **Procedures for updating/renewing:** by e-mail, postal mail, or telephone.

- It is not possible to limit who can see a resume. A confidential service is offered: Your name and contact information will *not* appear online. At the employer's request, a representative from Western New York Resumes will forward the contact information to you to act upon.

- It is not possible to shield a resume from being viewed by a current employer.

- **Assistance provided to the person submitting a resume:** Western New York Resumes will rewrite the resume to meet the format order.

- **Search options available to employers viewing resumes:** Resumes grouped by category.

- No technology to match jobs to resumes and e-mail resumes to clients.

- **Average number of daily hits on resumes:** 50.

- **Special features:** Western New York Resumes targets regional employers (greater Buffalo and Rochester, New York), who are promoted by its popular employment site Western New York JOBS at `www.wnyjobs.com` and by the weekly employment paper *JOBS Weekly*.

- **Other distinguishing factors:** Resume site is free for employers to view. Targets the Western New York State area.

Worldwide Resume/Talent Bank

Global
All Career Fields
Rating: ★ ★ ★ ½

In 1989, Gonyea & Associates created the first career guidance agency to operate 100 percent online. The Worldwide Resume/Talent Bank is its online resume posting service. Gonyea & Associates hosts the Gonyea Online Career Center on America Online, which also offers its other popular service Help Wanted-USA, an online employment advertising service. Both services are available at Gonyea & Associates' two online sites: The Gonyea Online Career Center on AOL (keyword: *gonyea*) and the Internet Career Connection Web site. All resumes entered into the Worldwide Resume Bank appear at both online locations.

- **URL:** http://www.iccweb.com
- **Ownership/sponsorship:** Gonyea & Associates, Inc.

    1151 Maravista Drive
    New Port Richey, FL 34655
    Voice mail: (813) 372-1333

- Started accepting resumes in 1989.
- **Approximate number of resumes online in April 1998:** more than 5,000.
- Resumes are accepted in all job classifications.
- **Total number of corporate subscribers/employers:** Unknown. The site receives about one million hits per month.
- **Fee structure for corporate subscribers/employers:** no fee.
- **Methods and rules for submitting resumes:** Visit the site; enter online.
- No limits on length.
- **Format:** enter online.
- **Fees to person submitting resume:** $25.00 for a six-month posting.
- Resumes remain online six months unless extended.
- **Procedures for updating/renewing:** Visit site, enter password and ID, and edit yourself.
- It is not possible to limit who can see a resume.
- It is not possible to shield a resume from being viewed by a current employer.
- **Assistance provided to the person submitting a resume:** whatever assistance is needed.
- **Search options available to employers viewing resumes:** keyword search.
- **Technology to match jobs to resumes and e-mail resumes to clients:** soon to be implemented.
- **Average number of daily hits on resumes:** Unknown. The two online locations receive more than 1,000,000 visitors each month.
- **Special features:** Users can post their own resumes, edit them any time they want, renew them anytime, and/or delete them themselves.

Your Resume Online

USA
All Career Fields
Rating: ★ ★ ½

Part II: Resume Banks

Your Resume Online is a service of Southern Cross Associates, a company that provides Web page design, Web page hosting, and Web page promotion. Southern Cross Associates places your resume online and provides you with your own address on the Internet.

- **URL:** `http://www.southerncross.net/rz/rz12.htm`

- **Ownership/sponsorship:** Southern Cross Associates.

- Started accepting resumes in 1997.

- **Approximate number of resumes online in April 1998:** 50.

- Resumes are accepted in all career fields.

- **Total number of corporate subscribers/employers:** individuals only.

- **Fee structure for corporate subscribers/employers:** one standard price for the service.

- **Methods and rules for submitting resumes:** e-mail, fax, floppy disk, postal mail.

- **Percentage of resumes received is as follows:**

    70 percent: e-mail
     5 percent: fax
    15 percent: other paper (job fairs, mailings)
    10 percent: diskette

- 100 percent of resumes received from individuals.

- No limits on length.

- **Format:** The site will fit the resume to suit its unique layout.

- **Fees to person submitting resume:** one standard price for the service.

- **Length of time resumes remain online:** Price is for one full year.

- **Procedures for updating/renewing:** The site allows reasonable updating for free.

- It is possible to limit who can see a resume and to shield a resume from being viewed by a current employer. The resume owners dictate to whom they distribute the unique URL that the site allocates to them.

- **Assistance provided to the person submitting a resume:** spelling, parsing, and general critiquing.

- **Search options available to employers viewing resumes:** individual choice.

- **Special features:** The site provides a service whereby job seekers can have their resumes available in a very presentable format as an Internet site. Southern Cross Associates prepares the site and hosts it for one year for a very affordable price.

- **Other distinguishing factors:** Southern Cross Associates makes the resume fit to standard browser pages so that a printout can be made whenever required. The site also prepares much more comprehensive resumes with graphics and links to other sites. Again, this service is extremely affordable.

- Sample sites:

    Standard:
      `http://www.southerncross.net/rz/rz11.htm`

    Vanity:
      `http://sc.honolulu.hi.us/vj/v101.htm`

Part II: Resume Banks

> **Note:** The following entry was added as we were going to press.

TRAINING Magazine's TrainingSuperSite

USA and Global
Training and Human Resource Fields
Rating: ★ ★ ★

TrainingSuperSite is the leading Web site resource for the training and HR industries.

- **URL:** http://www.trainingsupersite.com

- **Ownership/sponsorship:** Lakewood Publications and TRAINING Magazine

  Lakewood Publications/
  TrainingSuperSite
  50 South 9th Street
  Minneapolis, MN 55402

- Started accepting resumes in 1996.

- **Approximate number of resumes online April 1998:** 2,800 (all within a six-month recency)—25-30 percent of these are international.

- The TrainingSuperSite Resume Database focuses on the training, training development, training management, and human resource fields.

- **Total number of corporate subscribers/employers:** Over 100 subscriptions have been processed.

- **Fee structure for corporate subscribers/employers:** Subscriptions are available for $200/month. Package pricing and discounts are available.

- **Methods and rules for submitting resumes:** Applicants are required to fill out an online form. Upon submission, they are given a username and password. They are required to update their resumes within six months, otherwise their resume is purged from the system.

- 100 percent of resumes received by Web form.

- **Percentage of resumes received from:**

  individual: 70 percent
  college or university: 10 percent
  outplacement firm: 10 percent
  other: 10 percent

- No limits on length.

- **Format:** It is a database-driven system that accepts only text entries.

- No fees to person submitting resume.

- Resumes remain online six months from last edit.

- **Procedures for updating/renewing:** Users can update their information using their username and password for access.

- It is not yet possible to limit who can see resume. This will be a feature in 1999.

- It is not yet possible to shield resume from viewing by current employer possible. This will be a feature in 1999.

- **Assistance provided to the person submitting a resume:** Links to books, software, and other reference material.

- **Search options available to employers viewing resumes:** Location, Employment Preferences, Employment Types, Employment Levels, Preferred HR Specialty, Willingness to Relocate and by keyword (full-text search).

- **Technology to match jobs to resumes and e-mail resumes to clients:** Resume distribution service is provided ($50 charge to employee, free to employers). E-mail notification of newly posted jobs sent free to employees (upon request only).

- **Average number of daily hits on resumes:** Up to 500 database searches and 900 resume accesses daily.

- **Special features:**

    Free resume submission and ability to update.

    Free job notification service (e-mail notification of newly posted job opportunities).

    Affordable pricing and volume discounts.

Appendix A

Resumix ResumeBuilder™

The Resumix Resume Builder™ is an online resume template. Companies make this template available to job seekers at their own Web site or at other online posting sites. Job seekers may fill in the blanks or cut and paste an ASCII resume into a resume template, as discussed on page 70.

Resumix ResumeBuilder™

Form Instructions Sample Resume

Personal Information

Name (as you'd like it to appear on the resume):

Address 1: [Home ▼]

City: ____ State: ____ Zip: ____

Address 2: [Work ▼]

City: ____ State: ____ Zip: ____

Phone Numbers

[Home ▼] _____ (optional)

[Work ▼] _____ (optional)

[Fax ▼] _____ (optional)

E-Mail Address: _____ (optional)

Objective

Give a brief one or two sentence description of the type of employment or position you desire.

(Please use carriage returns.)

Education

Please fill in your educational background. List at least one school you attended.

School: ⬚ Major: ⬚
Degree: ⬚ Year of Graduation: ⬚ GPA: ⬚

School: ⬚ Major: ⬚
Degree: ⬚ Year of Graduation: ⬚ GPA: ⬚

School: ⬚ Major: ⬚
Degree: ⬚ Year of Graduation: ⬚ GPA: ⬚

School: ⬚ Major: ⬚
Degree: ⬚ Year of Graduation: ⬚ GPA: ⬚

Employment History

Please fill in the name of the employer, your job title, the dates you work (MM/YY format), and a brief description of your job responsibilities. Fill in at least one.

Employer: ⬚
Job Title: ⬚
From: ⬚ To: ⬚
Description of Duties: (please use carriage returns)

Cyberspace Resume Kit ....

[scrollable text box]

Employer: [____]
Job Title: [____]
From: [____] To: [____]
Description of Duties: (please use carriage returns)

[scrollable text box]

Employer: [____]
Job Title: [____]
From: [____] To: [____]
Description of Duties: (please use carriage returns)

[scrollable text box]

Employer: [____]
Job Title: [____]
From: [____] To: [____]
Description of Duties: (please use carriage returns)

[scrollable text box]

Employer: [____]
Job Title: [____]

From: [ ] To: [ ]
Description of Duties: (please use carriage returns)

[text area]

Employer: [ ]
Job Title: [ ]
From: [ ] To: [ ]
Description of Duties: (please use carriage returns)

[text area]

Additional Information

Use this area to write any additional information you may wish to include on your resume (e.g. - additional skills, strengths, abilities, etc.). (Please use carriage returns.)

[text area]

Requisition Number: [ ]

To format your resume, press the Format button. Your formatted resume is displayed in an HTML format that you may save for your files.

[Format]

To Submit your resume, press the Submit button. **This will submit your resume to Resumix to be considered for Resumix job opportunities. Resumix is not an Employment Agency.** Once submitted, an HTML version of your resume is displayed that you may save for your files.

Cyberspace Resume Kit

[Submit]

To clear this form, press the Clear Form button.

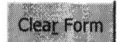

[Clear Form]

Appendix B

HRSC Online Resume Writer

The HRSC Online Resume Writer is the Web site resume template used to apply for federal jobs online, as discussed on page 118.

Human Resource Services Center

National Capital Region
Servicing OSD, Defense Agencies & DoD Field Activities

[HRSC | Opportunities]

Online Resume Writer

Enter your information in the areas provided below. Be sure to fill out all of the requested information.

If you would like to see a demo of the online resume builder, please click [Here].

NEW OR UPDATED RESUME?

Is this submission an update which will replace your resume currently on file? ○ Yes ○ No
Please see the HRSC Job Kit for information on when updated resumes are processed.

YOUR NAME:

First: [ ] MI: [ ] Last: [ ]

SOCIAL SECURITY NUMBER:

SSN: [ ] - [ ] - [ ]

MAILING ADDRESS:

Street: [ ] Apt No: [ ]
City: [ ] State: [ ]
Zip Code: [ ]
Home Phone Number: [ ] - [ ] - [ ]
Work Phone Number: [ ] - [ ] - [ ]
E-mail Address: [ ]
Vacancy Announcement Number: [ ]

If you are currently a federal employee, do you wish to be considered under both merit promotion and competitive procedures? ○ Yes ○ No

NOTE: THIS SHOULD ONLY BE FILLED OUT IF YOUR ARE CURRENTLY A FEDERAL EMPLOYEE AND THE AREA OF CONSIDERATION FOR THE VACANCY YOU ARE APPLYING FOR IS ALL SOURCES.

SUMMARY OF SKILLS

Include in this portion of your resume a summary of the skills you possess. Describe these skills in one or two words. It is not necessary to list all of your skills. Be sure to emphasize those skills in occupations where you are most interested in employment and those that are relevant to your career.

EXPERIENCE

(When Describing Duties Be Sure To Include):
Start and end dates (month and year).
Hours worked per week.
Position Title.
Pay Plan, Series, Grade (if Federal civilian position). List highest grade held and number of months held at that grade level. If experience describes Federal civilian positions at different grade levels, include month and year promoted to each grade.
Employer's name (agency or company name) and mailing address.
Supervisor's name and telephone number.
All major tasks. Be sure to include any systems which you have worked on; software programs or special tools and equipment you have used; and any special programs you have managed.
Any other job related information you wish to include, e.g., licenses/certificates (including date(s) certified and state), awards, language proficiencies, professional associations, etc.

There is space to include up to six (6) different positions/employers.

Employed From:	To:
Hours Worked per Week:	
Position Title:	
Pay Plan, Series, Grade (Salary if you are currently a non-government employee):	
Agency or Company Name:	
Mailing Address:	
Supervisor:	
Supervisor Phone:	

Work Experience:

Employed From: [ ] **To:** [ ]
Hours Worked per Week: [ ]
Position Title: [ ]
Pay Plan, Series, Grade (Salary if you are currently a non-government employee): [ ]
Agency or Company Name: [ ]
Mailing Address: [ ]
Supervisor: [ ]
Supervisor Phone: [ ]

Work Experience:
[ ]

Employed From: [ ] **To:** [ ]
Hours Worked per Week: [ ]
Position Title: [ ]
Pay Plan, Series, Grade (Salary if you are currently a non-government employee): [ ]
Agency or Company Name: [ ]
Mailing Address: [ ]
Supervisor: [ ]
Supervisor Phone: [ ]

Work Experience:
[ ]

Employed From: [ ] **To:** [ ]
Hours Worked per Week: [ ]
Position Title: [ ]
Pay Plan, Series, Grade (Salary if you are currently a non-government employee): [ ]
Agency or Company Name: [ ]
Mailing Address: [ ]
Supervisor: [ ]
Supervisor Phone: [ ]

Work Experience:
[ ]

Employed From: [ ] **To:** [ ]
Hours Worked per Week: [ ]
Position Title: [ ]
Pay Plan, Series, Grade (Salary if you are currently a non-government employee): [ ]
Agency or Company Name: [ ]
Mailing Address: [ ]
Supervisor: [ ]
Supervisor Phone: [ ]

Work Experience:
[ ]

Employed From:	☐ To: ☐
Hours Worked per Week:	☐
Position Title:	☐
Pay Plan, Series, Grade (Salary if you are currently a non-government employee):	☐
Agency or Company Name:	☐
Mailing Address:	☐
Supervisor:	☐
Supervisor Phone:	☐

Work Experience:
☐

TRAINING/EDUCATION

Give your highest level of education. If degree completed (e.g., AA, BA, MA), list your major field of study, name of college or university, and year degree awarded. If your highest level of education was high school, list either the highest grade you completed; year you graduated; or the date you were awarded your GED. List specialized training pertinent to your career goals below.

Degree:	☐
Major:	☐
University:	☐
Year of Graduation:	☐

Degree:	☐
Major:	☐
University:	☐
Year of Graduation:	☐

Degree:
Major:
University:
Year of Graduation:

Degree:
Major:
University:
Year of Graduation:

Degree:
Major:
University:
Year of Graduation:

Degree:
Major:
University:
Year of Graduation:

SPECIALIZED TRAINING

List any other specialized training pertinent to your career goals.

Supplemental Information

Repeat your Name and Social Security Number (for identification purposes).

NAME: First: [ ]   MI: [ ]   Last: [ ]
Social Security Number: [ ] - [ ] - [ ]

1. **LOWEST ACCEPTABLE GRADE:**
   [ ]

2. **CURRENT/FORMER FEDERAL CIVILIAN EMPLOYEES:**
   - List highest grade held and number of months held at that grade level.
     Highest Grade: [ ]
     Number of Months: [ ]
   - Provide employment status: [– Choose One –]

3. **MILITARY SERVICE AND VETERANS PREFERENCE:**
   (When notified you will be required to provide photocopies of DD-214(s) (Member-4 Copy). In addition, if claiming a compensable disability or other 10 point veteran's preference you must provide an "Application for 10 point Veterans' Preference (SF-15)" and supporting documentation listed on the reverse of the SF-15.)
   - Discharged from the military service under honorable conditions: ○ N/A ○ No ○ Yes (List dates and branch for all active duty military service.)
     [   ]
   - If all your active military duty was after October 14, 1976, list the full names and dates of all campaign badges or expeditionary medals you received or were entitled to receive.
     [   ]
   - Retired Military: ○ No ○ Yes,
     Rank at which Retired [   ],
     Date of Retirement [   ]
   - If claiming Veterans' Preference, indicate eligibility: [– Choose One –]

   You will be required to provide documentation to verify eligibility/status.

For applicants submitting their resume via E-mail or through use of Resume Writer, please mail all documents required by the particular vacancy announcement under separate cover referencing the vacancy announcement number.

If you would like to see your resume formatted for printing, please click on the **Format** button to display your resume within your browser. You may then use your browser's print command to print it out.	If you would like to submit your resume to the HRSC now, please click on the **Submit** button. A copy of your resume will be displayed after it is submitted to the HRSC.	To reset/clear this form, press the **Clear** button.	To cancel and go back to the Job Opportunities page, please click on the **Cancel** button.
[Format]	[Submit]	[Clear]	[Cancel]

If you experience any difficulties, (or if you aren't using a forms-capable browser) you may email your response to this form to: resume@hrsc.osd.mil.

Please report problems with this page, links, etc. to webmaster@hrsc.osd.mil.

Appendix C

HRSC Civilian Job Kit

The HRSC Civilian Job Kit is a set of instructions for applying for federal jobs online, as discussed on page 118. The HRSC Civilian Job Kit also contains do's and don'ts and general rules for applying for federal jobs.

HUMAN RESOURCE SERVICES CENTER
NATIONAL CAPITAL REGION
Servicing OSD, Defense Agencies & DoD Field Activities

CIVILIAN JOB KIT

IT IS IMPORTANT TO READ THESE INSTRUCTIONS COMPLETELY

BACKGROUND:

The National Capital Region (NCR) Human Resource Services Center (HRSC) is now using an automated system to fill vacancies. The patented artificial intelligence software reads information in your resume and extracts your skills and other significant information. **Why is this important to YOU?** With one properly prepared resume, the HRSC will consider all your skills for many jobs. You no longer have to submit a separate application for each vacancy! Once you are notified your resume is in our database, you self nominate yourself for vacancies for which you wish to be considered (see page 5). One-stop job shopping has never been easier. This automated system will accept applications through the HRSC web site. Resumes may also be submitted through the regular mail or E-mail. Preparing a resume is easy. Remember to focus on format and content. This job kit contains all the information you need to successfully complete your resume and apply for employment. **Only resumes will be accepted. The SF-171 and OF612 will no longer be accepted.**

HOW THE AUTOMATED SYSTEM WORKS:

The computer "reads" your resume and identifies information such as your name, address, education, and unique skills. Summarize your most important skills **first.** You might list specific skills. For example, if you have office clerical experience, you might list skills such as proofing, word processing, secretarial, shorthand, mail, filing, typing, etc. Below the summary of skills, describe your work experience. (Refer to the sample resumes following these instructions.) List only the skills that you feel are relevant to your career.

WHO MAY APPLY:

- Resumes are being accepted for all vacancies filled by the NCR HRSC. Please refer to individual vacancy announcements for specific information on the area of consideration.

- NOTE: Current or former displaced employees who are eligible for consideration under the Interagency Career Transition Assistance Plan (ICTAP) will be provided priority consideration for those vacancies for which they are well-qualified within their commuting area. Candidates must submit proof of eligibility (as identified in 5 CFR 330.707 (2)) with their resume to receive this priority consideration. Contact your servicing agency for more information about the ICTAP program.

RESUME PREPARATION INSTRUCTIONS:

- The best method is to visit our web site at: littp://www.hrsc.osd.mil/. Applicants will find our Resume Writer - a resume preparation program that will assist them in preparing their resume. The web site also allows applicants to submit their resume directly on line.
- If you do not have access to a browser, prepare the resume according to the fortnat and sample in this job kit.

DO

- Follow all instructions carefully and completely (resumes will be scanned so this is important).
- Limit your resume to three pages. **Resumes that are longer will only have the first 3 pages scanned.**
- **TYPE** your resume, ensuring it is clear and legible. Typewriters or word processors may be used. Handwritten resumes will NOT be accepted. A typewritten original or a high quality photocopy is acceptable.
- Provide a laser printed original if possible. **Avoid** dot matrix printers, bubble jet printers. and low quality copies.
- Type with black ink on 8.5" x 11" white bond paper printed on one-side only.
- **E-mail** your resume to: **resume@hrsc.osd.mil** (Note: the word **"resume"** must be in the subject line of your E-mail message; include a string of 10 "@" symbols immediately before the start of your text; type your resume in the body of the E-mail message, do **not** send as an attachment) and remember to use hard returns at the end of each line; **or, Mail** your resume and all other documentation as required by the vacancy announcement unfolded in an envelope 9.5" x 12" or larger.
- Use a minimum margin of one (1) inch on all sides of your printed resume.
- Use standard business type fonts such as courier (10 to 12 point); or, times new roman, etc., in 12 point. A smaller or larger point will result in poor scanning and extraction.
- Use boldface and/or all capital letters for section headings as long as the letters do not touch each other.
- Include a summary of your job-related skills at the beginning of your resume after your name, address, and phone number. In the experience portion of your resume, describe in detail how these skills are/were used. Remember to type your name and social security number in the top left comer of each page of your resume.
- Proofread for any errors. Pay particular attention to spelling.

- Be specific when naming the computer software or types of equipment, etc., with which you have experience. (e.g., Microsoft Word, Lotus 1-2-3, Excel, computer-assisted design equipment, etc.)
- Describe your experience with specific words rather than vague descriptions.
- Be truthful! Falsification of your resume could result in termination of, or withdrawal of, an offer of Federal employment, and may be punishable by fine or imprisonment. **If selected, you will be required to sign a statement that all application materials are true, correct, complete, and made in good faith.**

DON'T

- Staple, fold, bind or punch holes in your resume.
- Use vertical or horizontal lines, graphics, or boxes.
- Use two-column format or resumes that look like newspapers.
- Use fancy treatments such as italics, underlining, shadows, or bullets.
- Use acronyms or abbreviations. Only use acronyms that are well established and commonly understood.
- Submit your resume on colored paper.
- Submit your resume as an attachment to an E-mail.
- Submit any documentation not specifically requested.
- Expect your resume or any documents submitted to be returned.

WHAT TO SUBMIT WHEN APPLYING:

- A properly prepared resume (samples included with this job kit).
- Any other documentation specifically required by the vacancy announcement.

HOW TO SUBMIT YOUR RESUME:

Use any one of the following methods to submit your resume:

1. Upload your resume on our web site at: http://www.hrsc.osd.mil/

2. E-mail to: resume@hrsc.osd.mil (Note: "resume" must be in the subject line; include a string of 10 "@" symbols immediately before the start of your text; type your resume in the body of your mail message, DO NOT send as an attachment.)

3.

Or mail to:

Resume
Washington Headquarters Services
NCR Human Resource Services Center
5001 Eisenhower Avenue, Room 2E22
Alexandria, VA 22333-0001

NOTE: DO NOT FAX YOUR RESUME

HOW YOU WILL KNOW YOUR RESUME IS ACTIVE:

You will be notified within two weeks of receipt and disposition of your resume package. **You will not be considered for employment unless all information requested in this job kit is received and processed. RESUMES THAT ARE UNSCANNABLE AND/OR HANDWRITTEN WILL BE DESTROYED. Please note the 2 week resume processing period and the connection to the closing date of vacancies - get your resume in early.**

WHEN TO SUBMIT A NEW RESUME:

New resumes will be accepted at any time, however, updated resumes will only be processed on the first workday of each month. Hence, if your updated resume is received after the first workday, it will be updated only on the first workday of the succeeding month. This does not mean postmarked before the first workday of the month - the updated resume must be in the HRSC by COB prior to the first workday of the month. Revised resumes must be accompanied by a cover letter indicating the desire to replace the resume on file in the database. If you fail to provide the cover letter, the resume will be destroyed and you will be notified that you already have a resume on file. For updating resumes electronically submitted, this can be accomplished by providing this cover memo before the 10 "@" symbols.

GENERAL INFORMATION AND HELPFUL HINTS:

For ideas on where you might obtain INTERNET access, resume preparation assistance, or typing services, contact your state employment service, local schools, colleges, universities, public libraries, or look in the telephone book under Data Processing Services, Typing Services, etc. Newspapers often list these services in the classified section. You should bring a copy of this job kit with you. **The sender assumes all costs of submission.**

PRIVACY ACT INFORMATION

The Office of Personnel Management is authorized to rate applicants for Federal jobs under Sections 1302, 3301, and 3304 of Title 5 of the U.S. Code. Section 1104 of Title 5 allows the Office of Personnel Management to authorize other federal agencies to rate applicants for Federal jobs. We need the information you put on your resume and associated application forms to see how well your education and work skills qualify you for a Federal job. We also need information on matters such as citizenship and military service to see whether you are affected by laws we must follow in deciding who may be employed by the Federal Government.

We must have your Social Security Number (SSN) to keep your records straight because other people may have the same name and birthdate. The SSN has been used to keep records since 1943, when Executive Order 9397 asked agencies to do so. Giving us your SSN or any other information is voluntary. However, we cannot process your application if you do not give us the information we request.

ALL QUALIFIED RESUMES WILL RECEIVE CONSIDERATION FOR POSITION VACANCIES WITHOUT REGARD TO POLITICAL, RELIGIOUS, LABOR ORGANIZATION AFFILIATION OR NON-AFFILIATION, MARITAL STATUS, RACE, COLOR, SEX, NATIONAL ORIGIN, NON-DISQUALIFYING PHYSICAL HANDICAP, OR AGE. SELECTION SHALL BE BASED SOLELY ON JOB RELATED CRITERIA.

****

THE WASHINGTON HEADQUARTERS SERVICES NCR HRSC IS AN EQUAL OPPORTUNITY EMPLOYER

Index

A

AJB (America's Job Bank), 4–5
American Standard Code for Information Interchange. *See* ASCII (American Standard Code for Information Interchange)
America's Employers resume bank, 194
America's Job Bank (AJB), 4–5
America's Talent Bank, 5
America's TV JobNetwork resume bank, 195
A+ On-line Resumes resume bank, 193–94
applicant tracking services, 43
Army Times Publishing Company, 130–31, 132
artificial intelligence, 45
ASCII (American Standard Code for Information Interchange)
    conversion by OCR software, 44
    saving newsgroup resumes in, 152
    saving scannable resumes in, 59–60, 68
Australian Resume Server resume bank, 196–97
automated staffing, 43

B

Bonds, Scott, 142
BridgePath
    BridgePath Direct, 145
    BridgePath Hunter, 145
    BridgePath Slate, 145
    BridgePath Weekly, 145
    charges for services, 145, 146
    focus on recent graduates and passive job seekers, 142–43
    history of, 142
    operating methods, 143–45
    Resume Path, 146
    Resume Review, 146
    search criteria for employers, 144
    services to employers, 145
    signing up for services, 144
BridgePath resume bank, 197–99
Bussey, Craig, 76

C

Caere Corporation, 44
Canadian Resume Centre resume bank, 199–200
Career Avenue resume bank, 201–2
CareerCast resume bank, 202–3
CareerCity resume bank, 203–4
Careerfile resume bank, 204–6
CareerMagazine resume bank, 206–7
CareerMart resume bank, 207–8
CareerMosaic resume bank, 208–9
CareerPath resume bank, 209–11
Career Shop resume bank, 211–12
CareerSite resume bank, 213–14
CareerWeb resume bank, 215–17
chronological/functional combination resumes
    preparing, 20
    samples, 21–22, 23–24
    See also chronological resumes; functional resumes; resume preparation
chronological resumes
    preparing, 13–14
    sample, 15–16
    See also chronological/functional combination resumes; functional resumes; resume preparation
Civilian Job Kit, 118
college students/alumni resumes. *See* BridgePath
Colorado Online Job Connection resume bank, 217–18
Computer People resume bank, 218–19
Contract Employment Weekly resume bank, 219–20
Contract Engineering resume bank, 220–21
Costello, Paul, 55
curriculum vitae (CV, vita), 25–26
CV (curriculum vitae, vita), 25–26

D

Defense Outplacement Referral System (DORS), 133
Department of Defense job applicants. *See* STAIRS (Standard Automated Inventory and Referral System)
Department of Labor job bank, 4–5
DICE High Tech Jobs Online resume bank, 221–22
Dictionary of Occupational Titles, 132
DI-USA, 130
DiversiLink resume bank, 222–23
DORS (Defense Outplacement Referral System), 133

E

EasyResume™ resume bank, 224–25
Employment Service offices, state
 assistance to veterans, 132
 job bank, 4–5
Engineering Jobs.Com resume bank, 225–26
Entry Level Job Seeker Assistant resume bank, 226–27
extraction engines, 50–52

F

federal civilian jobs, 118
federal government job applicants. *See* STAIRS (Standard Automated Inventory and Referral System)
FormReader™, 114
functional resumes
 preparing, 17
 sample, 18–19
 See also chronological/functional combination resumes; chronological resumes; resume preparation
Future Access Employment Guide resume bank, 227–28

G

Gillette, Chris, 130–31, 133
Gillette, G. Roderick, 130

H

Harris, Al, 132
HeadHunter.NET resume bank, 228–29
HealthCareerWeb resume bank, 229–31
Hire for Intranet, 56
Hoffman, Auren, 142
Hospitality Net Virtual Job Exchange resume bank, 231–33
HRSC (Human Resource Services Center), 115–18
HRSC (Human Resource Services Center)
 resume samples, 121–22, 123–24, 125–26, 127–28
HTML (Hypertext Markup Language) resumes
 benefits of, 75
 creating a test resume, 92
 establishing URL addresses, 93
 importance of counters, 77
 including photographs, 76
 overusing links, 76–77
 recommended links, 78–79
 resume samples, 94–95, 96–97, 98–100, 101–4, 105, 106, 107–9, 110–11
 selecting colors and graphics, 77
 software for creating, 92
 submitting to resume banks, 93
 uploading to a server, 92
 using forms to create resumes
  ResumeBuilder™ resume sample, 85–86
  ResumeBuilder™ resume sample with HTML coding, 87
  ResumeBuilder™ sample form, 80–84
  World Wide Web sources for, 79, 88
 using HTML code to create resumes
  graphic images, 91–92
  links, 91
  tags, 88–92
 World Wide Web sources for help, 92
 See also newsgroup resumes; scannable resumes
HTML (Hypertext Markup Language) tags
 anchor, 91
 color, 89
 document beginning/ending, 88
 head and body, 88–89
 horizontal lines, 90
 in-line images, 91–92
 line breaks, 90
 ordered lists, 90
 paragraphs, 90
 section headings, 89
 style, 90
 unordered lists, 90
Human Resource Services Center (HRSC), 115–18
Human Resource Services Center (HRSC)
 resume samples, 121–22, 123–24, 125–26, 127–28
Hypertext Markup Language resumes. *See* HTML (Hypertext Markup Language) resumes

I

InstaMatch Resume Database resume bank, 233–34
Insurance Career Center resume bank, 234–35
Internet Job Locator resume bank, 235–36
Irish Jobs Page resume bank, 236–37

J

JobBank USA resume bank, 237–38
JobCenter Employment Services, Inc. resume bank, 238–39
jobEngine resume bank, 239–40
JobExchange resume bank, 241–42
Job Link USA resume bank, 242–43
JobLynx resume bank, 243–44
JobNet resume bank, 244–45
Job Options, LLC resume bank, 245–47
Job Resource resume bank, 247–49
JobServe resume bank, 249–50
Jobs Northwest resume bank, 250–51
JOBTRAK resume bank, 251–52

K

Kameda, Lori, 53, 73
keyword summaries, 71–72
knowledge base, extraction engine, 50

L

Lasting Impressions resume bank, 252–54
Lindsey, Bob, 130, 131
Local Veteran's Employment Representatives (LVER), 132

M

Manager's Workbench, 53
Mancusi-Ungaro, Greg, 56–57
medsearch resume bank, 254–56
MedZilla™ resume bank, 256–57
military resumes. *See* TAOnline (Transition Assistance Online)
Minorities' Job Bank resume bank, 257–59
Monster Board resume bank, 259–60
MOS/Military Skills Translator, 132

N

National NurseSearch resume bank, 260–61
Net-Temps resume bank, 261–63

newsgroup resumes
    advantages *vs.* disadvantages, 155–56
    creating a subject line, 151–52
    privacy risks, 155
    reposting, 155
    resume newsgroups, 153–54
    resume samples, 157–58, 159–60, 161–62, 163–65, 166–67, 168–69, 170–71, 172–73, 174–77
    saving in ASCII format, 152
    submitting newsgroup resumes through resume banks, 154–55
    tips for writing, 152
    updating, 156
    See also HTML (Hypertext Markup Language) resumes; scannable resumes
newsgroups, Usenet
    access to, 150
    for beginners, 151
    definition of, 149
    operation of, 150
Noyce, Robert, 44

O

Ochoa, Mel, 142–43, 146
OCR. *See* optical character recognition (OCR)
Omnifont technology, 46, 48–49
Online Career Center resume bank, 263–65
Online Opportunities resume bank, 265–66
Online Resume Writer, 118
Online Sports Career Center resume bank, 266–67
optical character recognition (OCR)
    and artificial intelligence, 45
    and fax machines, 69–70
    function of, 44–45
    history of, 46–48
    importance of document condition, 45–46
    maximizing character recognition, 72
    Omnifont technology, 46, 48–49
    trainable font capability, 47
ORASEARCH resume bank, 267–68

P

PartnerPool, 57
PassportAccess resume bank, 268–69
People Bank The Employment Network resume bank, 270–71
Perkins, Lars, 55
pixels, 44
PostMaster submission service, 93
PursuitNet Online resume bank, 272–73

R

Recruiting Workbench, 57
Regional Re-Careerment Center resume bank, 273–74
ResLink, 54
Restrac
    Hire for Intranet, 56
    history of, 55
    PartnerPool, 57
    Recruiting Workbench, 57
    services provided, 55–57
    WebHire, 55–56
resume banks
    criteria for evaluating, 183–84
        availability of help, 190
        corporate sponsorship, 185
        database size and currency, 187
        fees, 188–89
        geographical coverage, 186
        renewal requirements, 189
        resumes/daily page hits ratio, 188
        resumes/subscribers ratio, 187–88
        special features, 190
        stability, 184–85
        types of resumes accepted, 186–87
    duplicate postings, 181
    interactive services, 180–81
    keeping resumes current, 181
    mailing services, 183
    passive data banks, 180
    privacy risks, 181–82
    submitting resumes, 179–80
    See also under specific name of resume bank
Resume Blaster! resume bank, 275–76
ResumeBuilder™
    HTML coding for resume sample, 87
    resume sample, 85–86
    sample form, 80–84
    template, 70
    Web site, 79
Resume-Net resume bank, 276–77
Resume Path, 146
resume preparation
    accomplishment-focused resume sample, 9–11
    arranging information, 27–29
    career objective statements, 33
    choosing a resume format, 13–14, 17, 20, 25–26
    chronological/functional combination resumes, 20
    chronological/functional combination resume samples, 21–22, 23–24
    chronological resumes, 13–14
    chronological resume sample, 15–16
    curriculum vitae (CV, vita), 25–26
    educational qualifications
        college degrees, 36–37
        listing coursework, 37–39, 147
        placement in resumes, 34–35
        vocational certificates, 35–36
    examining accomplishments, 8, 146
    functional resumes, 17
    functional resume sample, 18–19
    "how to contact" information, 28–29
    identifying strengths and weaknesses, 8
    layout considerations, 26–29
    print *vs.* white space, 27
    resume length, 26, 146
    reviewing work-related knowledge, 7–8
    self-evaluation, 7–8
    sentences *vs.* sentence fragments, 27–28, 147
    summary statements, 33–34
    targeting potential employers, 12–13
    using bullets, 27–28
    work histories
        format and styles for, 40
        importance of job-relevancy, 39, 146
        ten years rule, 39
    writing job descriptions, 40–42
Resume Review, 146
resumes, scannable. *See* scannable resumes
resume samples
    accomplishment-focused, 9–11
    animated, 30–32
    chronological, 15–16
    chronological/functional combination, 21–22, 23–24
    functional, 18–19
    HTML, 94–95, 96–97, 98–100, 101–4, 105, 106, 107–9, 110–11
    newsgroup, 157–58, 159–60, 161–62, 163–65, 166–67, 168–69, 170–71, 172–73, 174–77
    ResumeBuilder™, 85–86
    STAIRS/HRSC, 121–22, 123–24, 125–26, 127–28
    standard form *vs.* ASCII format, 61–62, 63–64, 65–67
    TAS (Transition Assistance Software), 134–35, 136, 137–38, 139, 140, 141
resume tracking process
    converting resumes to ASCII format, 44
    editing converted resumes, 50
    scanning resumes, 44, 50
    skill extraction systems, 50–52
    using artificial intelligence for interpretation, 45
resume tracking services, 43
ResumeXPRESS! resume bank, 277–78

Resumix™
    history of, 52
    Manager's Workbench, 53
    ResLink, 54
    services provided, 53–54
Resumix Federal™, 113
Richards, Carla, 53–54
Rodriguez, Richard Scott, 130
Roos, Hans, 44–46, 69
rules, extraction engine knowledge base, 50

S

Saludos Career Web resume bank, 278–79
sample resumes. *See* resume samples
scannable resumes
    conversion to ASCII format, 44
    faxing resumes, 69–70
    getting more hits, 54–55
    importance of document condition, 45–46, 69
    mailing resumes, 68–69
    sending both traditional and scannable resumes, 71–73
    sending dual-purpose resumes, 72
    submitting by e-mail
        avoiding optical character recognition, 59
        e-mail messages *vs.* e-mail attachments, 68
        saving in ASCII format, 59–60, 68
        standard form *vs.* ASCII format resume samples, 61–62, 63–64, 65–67
    tips for preparing, 57–58
    using keywords, 54–55, 71–72
    using resume templates, 70
    using special fonts and formatting, 45–46
    vs. paper resumes, 43
    See also HTML (Hypertext Markup Language) resumes; newsgroup resumes
scanners, 44
Science Professional Network resume bank, 279–80
SEEK resume bank, 280–82
SelectJOBS resume bank, 282–84
Showbizjobs resume bank, 284–85
SIRC: Shawn's Internet Resume Center resume bank, 285–86
Skill Scan for Computer Professionals resume bank, 286–87
SkillSearch resume bank, 288–89
STAIRS (Standard Automated Inventory and Referral System)
    administered by HRSC (Human Resource Services Center), 115
    attaching folders, 115
    Civilian Job Kit, 118
    entering work experience, 116
    faxing resumes, 118
    federal civilian jobs, 118
    federal government *vs.* private sector resumes, 118
    filing for multiple positions, 115
    including social security numbers, 117
    integration of Resumix Federal™, 113
    job filing methods, 114, 117–18
    listing skills, 116
    Online Resume Writer, 118
    preparing resumes for, 114
    resume length, 116
    resume samples, 121–22, 123–24, 125–26, 127–28
    suggested resume format, 119–20
    supplemental sheet requirements, 117
    updating resumes, 116
    use of FormReader™ to extract skills, 114
    using nouns and verbs, 116
Standard Automated Inventory and Referral System. *See* STAIRS (Standard Automated Inventory and Referral System)

T

TAOnline (Transition Assistance Online)
    challenges faced by former military personnel, 129
    charges for services, 133
    employer search process, 133
    history of, 130–31
    services offered, 130–31, 133
    submitting resumes, 133
    TAS (Transition Assistance Software), 131–32
    TAS (Transition Assistance Software) resume samples, 134–35, 136, 137–38, 139, 140, 141
TAP (Transition Assistance Program), 131
TAS (Transition Assistance Software)
    description of, 131
    MOS/Military Skills Translator, 132
    printing federal application forms, 131
    resume samples, 134–35, 136, 137–38, 139, 140, 141
    where to purchase, 131, 132
TRAINING Magazine's TrainingSuperSite, 299-300
Transition Assistance Online resume bank, 289–91
Transition Assistance Program (TAP), 131
Transition Assistance Software. *See* TAS (Transition Assistance Software)
Tripod Resume Builder resume bank, 291–92

U

Usenet newsgroups. *See* newsgroups, Usenet

V

veterans, military. *See* TAOnline (Transition Assistance Online)
Virtual Job Fair resume bank, 292–93
Virtuallyhired resume bank, 294
VirtualResume resume bank, 294–95
vita (curriculum vitae, CV), 25–26

W

WebHire, 55–56
Western New York Resumes resume bank, 295–96
Whitten, Glenn, 46, 60, 69, 72–73
Worldwide Resume/Talent Bank resume bank, 297

Y

Your Resume Online resume bank, 297–98

Index

Resume Banks Organized by Career Field

All Career Fields

America's Employers, 194
America's TV JobNetwork, 195
A+ On-line Resumes, 193–94
Australian Resume Server, 196–97
Canadian Resume Centre, 199–200
Career Avenue, 201–2
CareerCast, 202–3
CareerCity, 203–4
Careerfile, 204–6
CareerMart, 207–8
CareerMosaic, 208–9
CareerPath, 209–11
CareerSite, 213–14
HeadHunter.NET, 228–29
InstaMatch Resume Database, 233–34
Internet Job Locator, 235–36
Irish Jobs Page, 236–37
JobBank USA, 237–38
JobCenter Employment Services, Inc., 238–39
JobExchange, 241–42
Job Link USA, 242–43
JobLynx, 243–44
JobNet, 244–45
Job Options, LLC, 245–47
Lasting Impressions, 252–54
Monster Board, 259–60
Net-Temps, 261–63
Online Career Center, 263–65
Online Opportunities, 265–66
PeopleBank The Employment Network, 270–71
Resume Blaster!, 275–76
ResumeXPRESS!, 277–78
Saludos Career Web, 278–79
SEEK, 280–82

SkillSearch, 288–89
Tripod Resume Builder, 291–92
VirtualResume, 294–95
Western New York Resumes, 295–96
Worldwide Resume/Talent Bank, 297
Your Resume Online, 297–98

All Career Fields (College Students and Recent Graduates)

BridgePath, 197–99
Job Resource, 247–49

All Career Fields (College Students/ Graduates)

JOBTRAK, 251–52

All Career Fields (Entry Level Only)

Entry Level Job Seeker Assistant, 226–27

Biotech

Future Access Employment Guide, 227–28

Business

CareerWeb, 215–17

Computer Industry

CareerMagazine, 206–7
jobEngine, 239–40
Resume-Net, 276–77
SelectJOBS, 282–84
Skill Scan for Computer Professionals, 286–87

Engineering

CareerMagazine, 206–7
CareerWeb, 215–17
Contract Engineering, 220–21
DiversiLink, 222–23
EngineeringJobs.Com, 225–26

Engineering (College Students and Recent Graduates)

Job Resource, 247–49

Entertainment

Showbizjobs, 284–85

Executives

SIRC: Shawn's Internet Resume Center, 285–86

Finance

CareerMagazine, 206–7
Career Shop, 211–12

Health Care

HealthCareerWeb, 229–31
medsearch, 254–56
MedZilla™, 256–57

High Technology

DICE High Tech Jobs Online, 221–22
Jobs Northwest, 250–51
Virtual Job Fair, 292–93
Virtuallyhired, 294

Hispanic Engineers

DiversiLink, 222–23

Hospitality

Hospitality Net Virtual Job Exchange, 231–33

Human Resources

TRAINING Magazine's TrainingSuperSite, 299-300

Information Technology

CareerWeb, 215–17
Computer People, 218–19
DICE High Tech Jobs Online, 221–22
EngineeringJobs.Com, 225–26
Future Access Employment Guide, 227–28
jobEngine, 239–40
JobServe, 249–50

Insurance

Insurance Career Center, 234–35

Management

Career Shop, 211–12

Manufacturing

CareerMagazine, 206–7

Marketing

Future Access Employment Guide, 227–28

Military

Transition Assistance Online, 289–91

Minorities

Minorities' Job Bank, 257–59

Nursing

National NurseSearch, 260–61

Oracle Professionals

ORASEARCH, 267–68

Professionals (White-Collar)

Regional Re-Careerment Center, 273–74

Professions (Higher-Level Positions)

PursuitNet Online, 272–73

Retail

CareerMagazine, 206–7

Sales

CareerMagazine, 206–7
Career Shop, 211–12
Future Access Employment Guide, 227–28

Sales (Higher-Level Positions)

PursuitNet Online, 272–73

Sciences

Science Professional Network, 279–80

Software Development

Colorado Online Job Connection, 217–18

Software Engineering

EasyResume™, 224–25

Sports and Recreation

Online Sports Career Center, 266–67

Technical

Contract Employment Weekly, 219–20
PassportAccess, 268–69

Technology

Career Shop, 211–12

Training

TRAINING Magazine's TrainingSuperSite, 299-300

Index

Resume Banks Organized by Geographic Area

Australia

Australian Resume Server, 196–97
Computer People, 218–19
Irish Jobs Page, 236–37
SEEK, 280–82

British Columbia, Canada

Jobs Northwest, 250–51

California (Silicon Valley)

Resume-Net, 276–77

Canada

Canadian Resume Centre, 199–200
EasyResume™, 224–25
JobNet, 244–45
PursuitNet Online, 272–73

Chicago Area

Virtuallyhired, 294

Colorado

Colorado Online Job Connection, 217–18

Delaware (Northern)

America's TV JobNetwork, 195

Europe

Irish Jobs Page, 236–37

Global

CareerMosaic, 208–9
Hospitality Net Virtual Job Exchange, 231–33
JobServe, 249–50
Online Career Center, 263–65
PeopleBank The Employment Network, 270–71
TRAINING Magazine's TrainingSuperSite, 299-300
Transition Assistance Online, 289–91
Worldwide Resume/Talent Bank, 297

Indiana

Regional Re-Careerment Center, 273–74

Ireland

Irish Jobs Page, 236–37

New Jersey (Southwestern)

America's TV JobNetwork, 195

New York (Western)

Western New York Resumes, 295–96

Pennsylvania (Eastern)

America's TV JobNetwork, 195

Philadelphia Area

Online Opportunities, 265–66

United Kingdom

JobServe, 249–50

United States

America's Employers, 194
A+ On-line Resumes, 193–94
BridgePath, 197–99
Career Avenue, 201–2
CareerCast, 202–3
CareerCity, 203–4
Careerfile, 204–6
CareerMagazine, 206–7
CareerMart, 207–8
CareerPath, 209–11
Career Shop, 211–12
CareerSite, 213–14
CareerWeb, 215–17
Contract Employment Weekly, 219–20
Contract Engineering, 220–21
DICE High Tech Jobs Online, 221–22
DiversiLink, 222–23
EasyResume™, 224–25
EngineeringJobs.Com, 225–26
Entry Level Job Seeker Assistant, 226–27
Future Access Employment Guide, 227–28
HeadHunter.NET, 228–29
HealthCareerWeb, 229–31
InstaMatch Resume Database, 233–34
Insurance Career Center, 234–35
Internet Job Locator, 235–36
Irish Jobs Page, 236–37
JobBank USA, 237–38
JobCenter Employment Services, Inc., 238–39
jobEngine, 239–40
JobExchange, 241–42
Job Link USA, 242–43
JobLynx, 243–44
Job Options, LLC, 245–47
Job Resource, 247–49
JOBTRAK, 251–52
Lasting Impressions, 252–54
medsearch, 254–56
MedZilla™, 256–57
Minorities' Job Bank, 257–59
Monster Board, 259–60
National NurseSearch, 260–61
Net-Temps, 261–63
Online Sports Career Center, 266–67
ORASEARCH, 267–68
PassportAccess, 268–69
PursuitNet Online, 272–73
Resume Blaster!, 275–76
ResumeXPRESS!, 277–78
Saludos Career Web, 278–79
Science Professional Network, 279–80
SelectJOBS, 282–84
Showbizjobs, 284–85
SIRC: Shawn's Internet Resume Center, 285–86
Skill Scan for Computer Professionals, 286–87
SkillSearch, 288–89
TRAINING Magazine's TrainingSuperSite, 299-300
Tripod Resume Builder, 291–92
Virtual Job Fair, 292–93
VirtualResume, 294–95
Your Resume Online, 297–98

United States (Northwest)

Jobs Northwest, 250–51

Using the Internet and the World Wide Web in Your Job Search
The Complete Guide to Online Job Seeking and Career Information
By Fred E. Jandt and Mary B. Nemnich

Dozens of screen captures, hundreds of Web addresses, and clear explanations show job seekers how to find thousands of job opportunities online, with expert advice on everything from getting connected to getting the job. This is the best book available on using the World Wide Web as a job search tool because it lists specific Web sites for job seekers and potential employers; includes updated advice on electronic resume preparation; explains how to include photographs and voice with a resume; provides real-life examples of online job search success; covers all major online services, Internet job databases, and the World Wide Web; PLUS it has a glossary of Internet terms!

ISBN: 1-56370-292-4

308 pp.
$16.95
Order Code: J2924

The Customer is Usually WRONG!
Contrary to What You've Been Told... What You Know to Be True!
By Fred E. Jandt

This book starts with the truth... after all, it *is* used in customer service training by the Cadillac Division of the General Motors Corporation! Jandt presents a model whose customer service skills are based on negotiation skills taken from his famous, best-selling "win-win" negotiating model. Unlike other customer service books that exclude government and nonprofit organizations, this book has specific information for people in the public and not-for-profit sectors who deal with the general public daily.

ISBN: 1-57112-067-X
211 pp.
$12.95
Order Code: CUW

Résumé Magic
Trade Secrets of a Professional Resume Writer
By Susan Britton Whitcomb

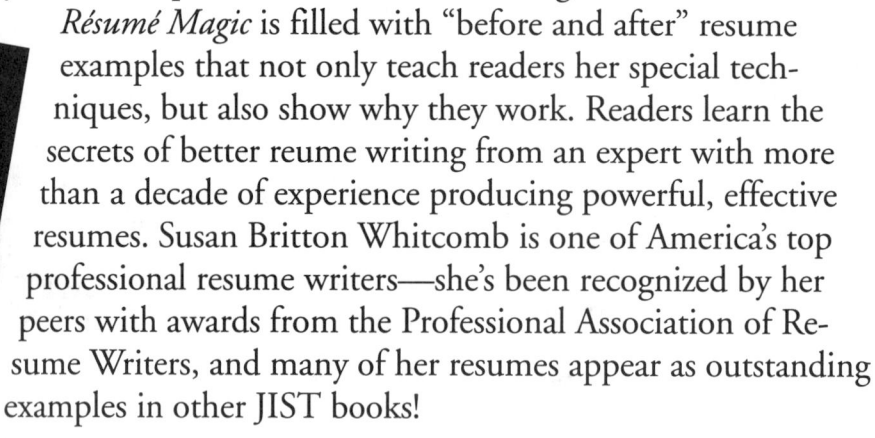

Anyone can improve their resume following Whitcomb's advice! *Résumé Magic* is filled with "before and after" resume examples that not only teach readers her special techniques, but also show why they work. Readers learn the secrets of better reume writing from an expert with more than a decade of experience producing powerful, effective resumes. Susan Britton Whitcomb is one of America's top professional resume writers—she's been recognized by her peers with awards from the Professional Association of Resume Writers, and many of her resumes appear as outstanding examples in other JIST books!

ISBN: 1-56370-522-2
350 pp.
$18.95
Order Code: J5222

Networking for Everyone!
Connecting with People for Career and Job Success
By L. Michelle Tullier, Ph.D.

Trend analysts predict that nearly half of all working Americans—some 60 million of us by the year 2000—will be part of the contingency workforce, working as freelancers, consultants, temporary employees, or entrepreneurs. This means a life of constant self-promotion to survive and thrive! The Publishers Marketing Association has awarded this book as one of three of the best career books for 1998!

Partial Table of Contents:
- Planning Your Networking Strategy
- Developing Your Network
- Fact-Finding Mission
- Places to Network

ISBN: 1-56370-440-4
393 pp.
$16.95
Order Code: J4404

The Quick Interview and Salary Negotiation Book
Dramatically Improve Your Interviewing Skills in Just a Few Hours!
By J. Michael Farr

Research shows that most job seekers do not present themselves effectively in job interviews. Yet the decision to hire or not to hire—and how much to pay—is made during those critical minutes! Just knowing how to handle the first 30 seconds of a discussion on pay may be worth, literally, thousands of dollars.

Partial Table of Contents:

- All the Information and Techniques That Most People Need to Do Well in Interviews
- Job Seeking Skills
- How to Answer Tough Interview Questions and Handle Unusual Interview Situations
- Salary Negotiations—How to Make a Few Thousand Dollars a Minute

ISBN: 1-56370-162-6
379 pp.
$12.95
Order Code: J1626

The Best Jobs for the 21st Century
Expert Reference on the Jobs of Tomorrow
By J. Michael Farr and LaVerne Ludden, Ed.D.

The "best" jobs depend on *your* perspective. Suppose that you asked ten people to list the best jobs for the next century, and suppose that each person had to work independently. Would the lists be identical? Of course not! And that's the premise of this new and different reference book. Split into three sections, the book presents facts on the best jobs with the highest pay, the fastest growth, and the most openings; contains information for youth, older workers, part-time, and the self-employed; and has lists for 12 major interest areas. These jobs were selected because they meet one or more of three criteria: the number of job openings by the year 2006, the average annual earning equal to or greater than $40,000, and the occupation that has 100,000 or more job openings each year.
A very informative, user-friendly, somewhat light-hearted reference book!

ISBN: 1-56370-486-2
616 pp.
$16.95
Order Code: J4862

Gallery of Best Resumes
A Collection of Quality Resumes by Professional Resume Writers
By David F. Noble, Ph.D.

This is the best collection of resumes and cover letters you'll ever find! It contains an enormous array of the best resumes submitted by members of the Professional Association of Résumé Writers, and includes more than 200 great resumes with a wide range of styles, formats, designs, occupations, and situations—all arranged in easy-to-find groups.

Partial List of Resume Categories

- ❖ Accounting/Finance
- ❖ Communications
- ❖ Consultant
- ❖ Education/Training
- ❖ Graduating/Graduate Students
- ❖ Maintenance/Manufacturing
- ❖ Sales/Marketing
- ❖ Technology/Engineering/Science

ISBN:1-56370-144-8
400 pp.
$16.95
Order Code: GBR

Professional Resumes for Executives, Managers, and Other Administrators
A New Gallery of Best Resumes by Professional Resume Writers
By David F. Noble, Ph.D.

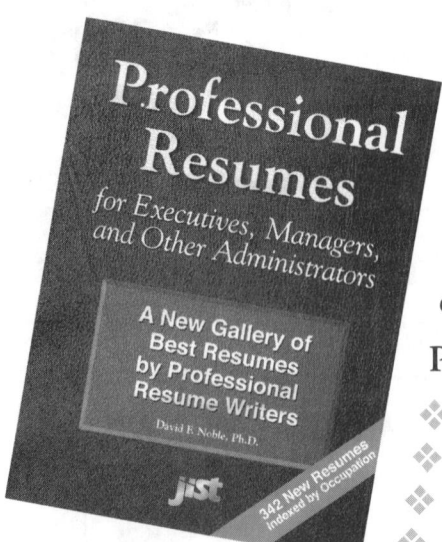

A superior collection of 342 *new* professionally designed and written resumes, submitted by members of the Professional Association of Résumé Writers and the National Résumé Writers Association. This collection targets top management and those seeking upper-management positions. There is professional analysis of each sample that explains when and how to use a specific format.

Partial Table of Contents:

- ❖ Best Resume Design and Layout Tips
- ❖ Best Resume Writing Style Tips
- ❖ Professional Resumes
- ❖ Best Cover Letter Tips

ISBN: 1-56370-483-8
624 pp.
$19.95
Order Code: J4838

JIST Ordering Information

JIST specializes in publishing the very best results-oriented career and self-directed job search material. Since 1981 we have been a leading publisher in career assessment devices, books, videos, and software. We continue to strive to make our materials the best there are so that people can stay abreast of what's happening in the labor market, and so they can clarify and articulate their skills and experiences for themselves as well as for prospective employers. **Our products are widely available through your local bookstores, wholesalers, and distributors.**

The World Wide Web

For more occupational or book information, get online and see our Web site at **www.jist.com**. Advance information about new products, services, and training events is continually updated.

Quantity Discounts Available!

Quantity discounts are available for businesses, schools, and other organizations.

The JIST Guarantee

We want you to be happy with everything you buy from JIST. If you aren't satisfied with a product, return it to us within 30 days of purchase along with the reason for the return. Please include a copy of the packing list or invoice to guarantee quick credit to your order.

How to Order

For your convenience, the last page of this book contains an order form.

24-Hour Consumer Order Line:
Call toll free 1-800-JIST-USA
Please have your credit card (VISA, MC, or AMEX) information ready!

Mail: Mail your order to:

JIST Works, Inc.
720 North Park Avenue
Indianapolis, IN 46202-3490
Fax: Toll-free 1-800-JIST-FAX

JIST Order Form

Please copy this form if you need more lines for your order.

Purchase Order #: _____

Billing Information
Organization Name: _____
Accounting Contact: _____
Street Address: _____
_____
_____
City, State, Zip: _____
Phone Number: ( ) _____

Phone: 1-800-JIST-USA
Fax: 1-800-JIST-FAX

Shipping Information (if different from above)
Organization Name: _____
Contact: _____
Street Address: (we *cannot* ship to P.O. boxes) _____
_____
City, State, Zip: _____
Phone Number: ( ) _____

Credit Card Purchases: VISA____ MC____ AMEX____
Card Number: _____
Exp. date: _____
Name as on card: _____
Signature: _____

Quantity	Order Code	Product Title	Unit Price	Total

Subtotal	
+Sales Tax *Indiana Residents add 5% sales tax.*	
+Shipping / Handling *Add $3.00 for the first item and an additional $.50 for each item thereafter.*	
TOTAL	

JIST Works, Inc.
720 North Park Avenue
Indianapolis, IN 46202

JIST thanks you for your order!